New Testament Studies V.

CROWN THEOLOGICAL LIBRARY

Crown Theological Library

WORKS ALREADY PUBLISHED

Descriptive Prospectus on Application.

New Testament Studies

V

BIBLE READING IN THE EARLY CHURCH

BY

ADOLF HARNACK

PROFESSOR OF CHURCH HISTORY IN THE UNIVERSITY OF BERLIN

TRANSLATED BY

THE REV. J. R. WILKINSON, M.A.

LATE SCHOLAR OF WORCESTER COLLEGE, OXFORD;
AND RECTOR OF WINFORD

WILLIAMS & NORGATE

14 HENRIETTA STREET, COVENT GARDEN, LONDON

NEW YORK: G. P. PUTNAM'S SONS

1912

PREFACE

ALL that need be said of the interest and importance of the question of the use of the Holy Scriptures in the Early Church has been set forth in the Introduction.

The "History of the New Testament" includes not only the history of its versions in various languages, but also the history of its use.   Again, the history of the use is also, in its first stages at least, included in the subject of "Introduction to the New Testament," because the question *in what sense* the collection of writings known as the New Testament was regarded as a *Canon* of religion is not decided by saying that it was regarded as canonical, but can only be answered by finding out what use was actually made of this collection.   No objection, therefore, can be raised against our including the following investigation in our *New Testament Studies*, which deal principally with the subject of "Introduction to the New Testament."   The public use of the New Testament in the ancient Church is, as a matter of course, included in every considerable work on the History of the Canon of Scripture—*cf.* Glaue's *Die Vorlesung heiliger Schriften im Gottesdienste* (1907)—and it is simply an oversight that the private use has not also been taken into consideration. The knowledge of the latter use is quite indispensable

v

if we would know what the New Testament signified
as the Canon of the Early Church.   It is true that in
this investigation the Old Testament should not be
separated from the New; but in the Church the Old
Testament has stood in the shadow of the New ever
since the New Testament came into being.

In the following pages will be found a series of
interesting references of which little notice has hitherto
been taken in works on Church history, though they
throw peculiar light upon the character and life of the
Early Church.   Though I have aimed at comprehensive-
ness, it is certain not only that much has escaped my notice,
but also that I have only lightly touched upon some
questions although they are closely connected with the
main problem, such as the character and distribution of
religious and theological literature other than Scripture,
the relation between public lection and private reading,
the use of verses of Scripture as amulets, and so forth.
I have also endeavoured to be as concise as possible,
and have left the reader to draw complete inferences
from many instances which I have quoted.   My chief
object, as will be seen from the work itself, has been
to bring to light, in connection with the use of sacred
writings, the peculiar characteristics of the Christian
religion, even in its ancient Catholic form, as compared
with the mystery-religions.   In this sense I might have
described my book as belonging to the comparative
study of religions.   Again, though I did not definitely
intend this, it serves to confirm the view that the

Reformation, by placing the Bible in the hands of every Christian layman, has only returned to the simple confidence of the Early Church. It is therefore with peculiar pleasure that I submit my investigations to the man whom, on the occasion of his jubilee, we greet with thankful acclaim as *vindex reformationis et reformatorum.*[1]

A. HARNACK.

BERLIN, 30*th March* 1912.

---

[1] The German edition is dedicated by Professor Harnack to Theodor Brieger.

CONTENTS

x

BIBLE READING IN THE EARLY CHURCH

INTRODUCTION

THE question of the private use of Holy Scripture in the Early Church is from many aspects of peculiar interest. In the first place, it has formed, since the time of the Reformation, a subject of controversy between Catholic and Protestant. In the second place, it made its appearance in the famous controversy between Lessing and Goeze, and received enhanced importance through the intervention of Walch, but was not brought to a fruitful issue, seeing that the two antagonists, Lessing and Walch, were removed from the field by death. In the third place, the question is worthy of special consideration in connection with the modern comparative study of religions; for we must investigate and decide whether in the Christian religion the sacred writings played the same part as in other religions—whether, that is, these writings were not meant for the private use of individuals, but were reserved altogether,

1

or in the first place, for priests and for the purposes of public-religious service. If in the case of Christianity this question is to be answered in the negative, it then follows that in an important point there is a very considerable difference between Christianity and many other religions.

I

The controversy between Catholics and Protestants is often incorrectly conceived by both parties, especially by Protestants. The former say that Protestantism is mere Biblicism, and that Protestants assert that it is a divine command, and necessary for salvation, that every believer should read the Holy Scriptures;[1] the Protestants assert that Catholicism forbids laymen to read the Bible, the use of which it reserves for priests (and monks). These assertions are not, however, true to the facts. Although isolated instances in support of both theses can be deduced from history, the true attitude of the respective Churches cannot be by any means thus described: Protestantism does not assert that private Bible reading is necessary for salvation, nor can it be proved that Catholicism as a matter of universal principle forbids the layman to read the Bible. On the contrary, *Catholicism also has at all times undoubtedly regarded Bible reading as useful and salutary for every man in the abstract,* and is *still of the same opinion;*

---

[1] Compare, *e.g.*, O. Schmid in the second edition of Wetzer and Weltes' *Kirchenlexicon* (ed. Kaulen), Bd. ii. col. 684 ff.

while Protestantism acknowledges that there are true Christians who do not read the Bible.[1]

Wherein, then, lies the controversy between the two Churches, if we leave out of consideration on either side prohibitions and regulations of special scope and determined by temporary circumstances, if we further leave out of consideration that Catholicism has for centuries forbidden the use of translations which it regards as false or doubtful, if we moreover neglect the fact that Protestantism disseminates books of extracts from the Bible, school Bibles and the like, for use in place of the Bible itself? The difference between the two Churches on this point may be expressed in two propositions:—(1) According to the Protestant view the Bible is a free gift to the community and to the individual, without restriction or reserve; while according to the Catholic view the Bible is in the possession of the organised Church, which is bound to administer her property, as also the means of grace, for the good of the individual, according to her own judgment and in the spirit of strict and yet loving parental care. (2) According to the Protestant view the Holy Scriptures, and these only, are the ultimate source and norm of all Christian knowledge; while according to the

---

[1] O. Ritschl has dealt exhaustively with the question of Biblicism and Traditionalism in early Protestant theology in the first volume of his *Dogmengeschichte des Protestantismus* (1908), which is dedicated exclusively to this question. He has not, however, according to my recollection, ever touched upon private Bible reading in the sense of a religious duty, because Protestantism has never set up such a duty.

Catholic view, tradition, together with the living word of the infallible Church, stands side by side with the Bible as equal, indeed in many aspects as superior, to it in authority.[1]

From these points of difference the difference in the attitude of the two Churches towards the Holy Scriptures may be explained in all its aspects.[2] Their formulation is dogmatic in character; we have here no occasion to deal with them as such.[3]

The Catholic Church, however, asserts that her judgment to-day and during the last centuries concerning the Holy Scriptures is the same as it has ever been. This is a *quaestio facti* which is subject to the control of history. It is true that the Roman Catholic theologians admit that during the first thousand years of

---

[1] " It is impossible that the most intimate and authoritative rule of faith should be the dead (!) letter of Scripture" (O. Schmid, *loc. cit.*, col. 683).

[2] We may mention another point. The Roman Church is very suspicious and critical in her attitude towards all translations of the Bible into the vulgar tongue, while she sets *one* translation, the Latin (in Jerome's version), on a level with the authentic text. She believes that on this condition alone she can preserve her hierarchic and homogeneous character and can exercise her controlling influence. It does not trouble her in the least that she thus sets herself in opposition to facts of history ; for she is accustomed to this. Of course she decrees that no such opposition exists.

[3] The first of the Protestant theses shows itself dogmatic if it is based upon the idea of the general priesthood ; apart from this idea it is unassailable, because it only declares that the Bible, like any other book, is in principle addressed to everyone, and that the reading, though it can indeed under certain circumstances be discouraged, can yet never be forbidden. The second Protestant thesis is purely dogmatic, and even as such is subject to serious doubt.

our era no instance of the prohibition of Bible reading can be discovered; [1] but they contend that during that period the Church had not had any conclusive experience of the danger of Bible reading.[2] This is an extra-

[1] They *now* admit this (*vide* O. Schmid, *loc. cit.*, col. 679). "During the whole of the first thousand years of the Christian era no instance is known either of prohibition or of restriction of Bible reading on the part of the Church." In times gone by attempts have not been lacking to prove instances of restriction. They are based upon St Jerome, ep. liii. 7, and other passages. But the attempts which originated with Bellarmine are, so far as I know, now given up. Instances of counsel not to read such-and-such a book too soon, and in general of careful supervision of Bible reading, belong of course to quite another sphere. One can regard unrestricted Bible reading as useless and dangerous and yet still contend for full liberty in Bible reading, because one regards every prohibition as the greater evil, and accounts it unfit that grown men should be restricted by prohibitions.

[2] It is asserted that the Waldenses and the Albigenses were the first sects who by their use of the Bible made the prohibition of Bible reading appropriate and necessary. It is true that decrees against Bible reading first began to appear at this time. But this was not because these Bible-reading sects were more dangerous than the Bible-reading Valentinians and Arians, but because the Church in the period of Innocent III. had gained a greater sense of power. Moreover, all prohibitive decrees before the sixteenth century still refer partly only to particular cases and are partly conditional. Even the Tridentine decrees are still silent; but the question is treated as a matter of principle in the third and fourth rules of the constitution "Dominici gregis custodiae" of Pius IV. in the year 1564, whereby the Index Librorum Prohibitorum was published for which the Tridentine decrees had made preparation. Still, even these rules only refer to the translations into vulgar tongues. These only are also almost exclusively referred to in the following decrees which partly accentuate, partly attenuate, the ordinance of Pius IV., though they indeed increase the power of the Pope in these matters. As with all other important dogmas and decrees, there reigns even among Catholic theologians a controversy, which discloses absolute disagreement, as to the present rule concerning the Bible reading of the laity in the vulgar tongue (*vide* Reusch, *Der Index der verbotenen Bücher* [1885], II. i. S. 861 f.).

ordinary assertion, for I do not know any time when such experiences were more vivid and various than in the days of the Gnostics, the Montanists, the Monarchians, the Arians, and so forth.   An attempt is made to escape from the difficulty by such futile and obscure statements as that "there were of course during this

Fessler and others declare that according to the decree of Benedict XIV. there does not really exist for Catholics any decree against Bible reading, seeing that translations into the vulgar tongue which are approved by the Apostolic See or are supplied with notes from the Fathers or from other Catholic scholars are subject to no prohibition, so that their use must be regarded as allowed.   Others, however, are of the contrary opinion.   In the case of Germany there is besides the question of the legal validity of the constitution of 1564. Now we come to the question whether the Bible in the Latin Vulgate version has also been withdrawn from the laity.   Here the condemnation of several pertinent propositions of the Jansenists in the bull "Unigenitus" of the year 1713 comes into consideration.   In this bull the following propositions are condemned : " Utile et necessarium est omni tempore, omni loco et omni personarum generi studere et cognoscere spiritum, pietatem, et mysteria sacrae scripturae " (79) ; " Lectio sacrae scripturae est pro omnibus " (80) ; "Obscuritas sancti verbi Dei non est laicis ratio dispensandi se ipsos ab eius lectione " (81) ; "Dies dominicus a Christianis debet sanctificari lectionibus pietatis et super omnia sanctarum scripturarum ; damnosus est, velle Christianum ab hac lectione retrahere" (82) ; "Abripere e Christianorum manibus Novum Testamentum . . . est illis Christi os obturare " (84) ; "Interdicere Christianis lectionem sacrae scripturae, praesertim evangelii, est interdicere usum luminis filiis lucis et facere, ut patiantur speciem quandam excommunicationis " (85).   Can we then say that this bull is only directed against the use of the Bible in the vulgar tongue ?   It is surely concerned with the principle whether the laity should be allowed any unrestricted use of the Bible at all.   Though in actual practice this view may be laxly enforced in some Roman Catholic countries, in others it is only the more strictly enforced ; and even where the laxer practice prevails, it is always under the principle that the Church has the right to regulate the use of the Bible by the laity—that is, to limit and to forbid it.

period many heretical sects that appealed to Holy Scripture in support of their systems of doctrine; but the appeal was made only to particular passages, and no assertion was made as to the principle of Bible reading such as could have summoned the Church to a clear and definite statement on this question."[1] "*Only particular passages*": When has the Bible ever been made use of in another way? "*No assertion as to the principle of Bible reading*": Is it then the Catholic view that the danger in the use of the Bible is only dependent upon the assertion as to the principle of Bible reading? No —the simple fact that until late in the Middle Ages no decree was published against Bible reading does not indeed prove, yet makes it at least highly probable, *that the Catholic Church at that time held quite other views concerning its own relation to the Holy Scripture, that is, concerning its right to supervise the laity in their reading of the Bible, than at later times.* In order to weigh the value of this probability, to elevate it even to the rank of historical certainty, it is necessary to study the history of the private use of the Holy Scriptures in the Early Church. If the result of our investigation be that no decree was at that time ever issued against Bible reading, but rather that all without exception were exhorted to read the Bible, that the Bible was in the hands of multitudes of laymen, that the interpretation of the Bible was left even to laymen, that in fine, though the dangers of Bible reading did not escape

---

[1] O. Schmid, *loc. cit.*, col. 679 f.

observation, yet still nothing was done to meet them by means of restrictions upon reading—then we can no longer suppose that the Catholic Church held indeed at that time the same views concerning the Holy Scriptures as it does to-day, but that, oblivious of its duty, it did not put them into force. We must rather conclude that during that long period of many centuries the Church was convinced that every individual Christian had a right to the Bible, and that it did not belong to the Church to restrict this right.

II

Lessing, by his controversy with Goeze, has earned the immortal glory of having broken the spell of the dogma of the Bible.   Under this dogma Protestantism suffered in yet higher degree than Catholicism.   We can to-day scarcely imagine with what crushing weight this dogma pressed upon religion, upon the spheres of historical investigation and all other realms of culture, while its spell still prevailed unbroken; indeed, even those theologians who imagine that they still hold fast to this dogma have no suspicion how the bells sounded before they were cracked! In their looser theological arguments they in some places make play with the doctrines of the inspiration, infallibility, clearness, and sufficiency of Holy Scripture; in a hundred other places they know nothing of these formidable things, and they make use of the freedom which, since Lessing, has pressed forward in irresistible progress.   In earlier times theologians were much more logical than their orthodox successors; they knew what it meant to possess an inspired book, and what demands such a possession implied.

It is true that even they were not fully conscious of this; even they allowed themselves to make deductions; otherwise sense and reason would have broken down.[1]

---

[1] They attenuated and in a hundred instances did not draw the conclusions which resulted from the nature of a divine book. In a hundred instances they treated it as an ordinary book because it was simply impossible to draw all the conclusions implied by the divine character of a book. Is, for example, such a book translatable? The Alexandrian Jews at least were logical enough to see that it was impossible, and indeed blasphemous, for men to do this. They therefore made a virtue of necessity and straightway claimed that their translation also was inspired. The Roman Church could not be so bold; but the ambiguous and timid decree of the Council of Trent that the Vulgate should be held *pro authentica*, and that no one should dare or claim to reject it, runs along the same lines. Also in the repugnance which large circles of Lutherans have always felt to any improvement of Luther's translation there lies a grain of that correct logic according to which the authorised version of the sacred volume must have stood under a *providentia Dei specialissima*, if it was to reproduce correctly the wording of the sacred original. Moreover, an inspired document is not only untranslatable without the same divine assistance that created it, but it is also uninterpretable. Catholicism is therefore absolutely in the right in its claim that the power of interpreting Holy Scripture lies only in the Church, which alone has the promise to be led by the Holy Spirit into all truth. Inspiration and a sacred court of interpretation necessarily hang together. If Protestantism substitutes the endowment of each individual Christian with the Holy Spirit, this expedient is unsatisfactory for the very reason that no provision is made for the case, which again and again recurs with each passage of Scripture, that the interpretations are divergent. Of course the sacred tribunal of interpretation is also an impossibility if its decisions must admit the control of philology and grammar. The doctrine of inspiration has at all times been taken seriously only as a question of dogmatics and upon paper, and as such has gained simply a kind of phantom existence. In practice, its

A sacred document of a thousand pages written by the finger of God is a burden too insupportable for frail mankind, whether it is read or no. It is by far the easier course not to read, to let others read, and to endure the prick of conscience that one does not read oneself. In truth, it is not wonderful that timid and tentative efforts were made here and there, and quite late in time, to forbid Bible reading; rather it is wonderful that Mother Church was not more fertile in expedients for enabling her children to avoid approach to this burning mountain. The best book of edification and comfort must indeed become a devouring fire if it is to have God for its author;[1] moreover, the questionings, the doubts, and the difficulties aroused by its contents, and above all by its discrepancies, must disturb and perplex the man who is at all earnest and conscientious. Away then with these oracles into the remotest cupboard of the sacristy! Better that a man should die without the Bible than of the Bible! And yet the Bible does demand that man should read it.

consequences are either not drawn at all, or only in a half-hearted way, because they simply cannot be drawn ; human life could not endure them.

[1] Innocent III. had some suspicion of this when he wrote (1199) to the Christians of the diocese of Metz in reference to the question of Bible reading by the laity (in the vulgar tongue): "Tanta est divinae scripturae profunditas, ut non solum simplices et illiterati, sed etiam prudentes et docti non plene sufficiant ad ipsius intelligentiam indagandam . . . *unde recte fuit olim in lege divina statutam ut bestia quae montem tetigerit, lapidetur,* ne videlicet simplex aliquis et indoctus praesumat ad sublimitatem scripturae sacrae pertingere vel eam aliis praedicare."

But the Church became bold and ingenious; side by side with the Bible she set up a rule of faith, and then announced that this rule contained the full essence of Holy Scripture, and that the spiritual not the literal sense of the Bible was the true sense. The relief that this brought was simply incalculable; for this spiritual sense was in fact her own experience, her own religious thought and practice. Now she was rid of the terror of terrors! By means of allegory and of authoritative doctrine—which itself included a large element of her own independent creation as well as the reflex of the fundamental historical facts—the Church delivered herself from Holy Scripture in so far as it pressed upon her as a crushing burden.

But then came the Reformation, which shattered authoritative doctrine and the allegorical method, and brought Scripture again into the foreground. It is true that from another point of view the Reformation strengthened the authority of dogma, and from the *analogia fidei* fashioned an allegorical method of its own; but against the authority of Mother Church, which had become an insupportable tyranny, the Reformation had nothing to oppose but the authority of Scripture. The Reformers intended, of course, to follow what was primitive and original in place of what was late and corrupt, to be disciples of Jesus instead of being slaves of the Pope; but with the Scripture as the fundamental document of primitive Christian life men found themselves also caught in the dead letter of its thousand pages. Luther, it is true, felt the necessity of freeing himself from the incubus of the Bible in its every word, and in bold, courageous faith he set himself again and again to thrust it from him; but the time had not yet come for the knowledge that would have supplied him with a fulcrum for firm leverage. It was grandly audacious to assert that the Scripture was only authoritative in so far as it pointed to Christ; it was still more audacious to assert that faith, even in using Scripture, need only follow her own law: yet Luther could not really justify these propositions so long as he was faced by a document inspired in every word. Protestantism as Luther bequeathed it to his successors remained involved in most acute contradiction. It claimed to know nothing save Christ and Him crucified, and at the same time to be the absolute religion of the Bible.

Christian faith and a Christian Church existed before ever there was a New Testament. Lessing did not indeed discover this historical fact, but he first recognised its decisive importance, and with the power of genius established it as current truth. Never has a simpler incident had a grander result. From this time dates the gradual dissolution of orthodox Protestantism; henceforth it could free itself from the burden of the letter, the burden of the Bible, to receive in exchange the Bible as the fundamental historical document of religion and a book of comfort that knows no terror. The complete freedom and liberty of man, bound only by the service of God, the ideal that moved before the eyes of Luther, was now no longer kept in bondage by the authority of a voluminous and despotic document.

As is well known, Lessing himself in his controversy with Goeze[1] developed the consequences of his discovery only tentatively and very cautiously both in general and in reference to the New Testament. As to the reason of this procedure opinions vary; we cannot here enter into the question.[2] However, towards the close the controversy narrowed itself down to the problem of the relation of the Creed to Holy Scripture, and in this connection Lessing published in the year 1778 the treatise, *A Necessary Answer to a very Unnecessary Question of Herr Goeze, Chief Pastor in Hamburg.*[3] This treatise, which starts from the question *whether the Christian religion could still exist even if the Bible were absolutely lost, if it had been long ago lost, if it had never existed,* leads up to twenty propositions concerning the historical relation of Creed and Scripture. These propositions expound Lessing's fundamental thought that the rule of Faith is more ancient than the New Testament, and that the Church at first developed and grew without the New Testament. The thought itself is historically correct, and has shattered the tyranny of ancient Protestant dogma, but the propositions in themselves rest upon a very question-

[1] *Cf.* above all Erich Schmidt, *Lessing,* Bd. ii.[2] (1899), S. 248 ff., 273 ff., 296 ff., 313 ff.

[2] *Cf.* E. Schmidt, S. 294 ff. The treatment here is excellent.

[3] Hempel's edition, Bd. xvi. S. 213–218.

able foundation; few only of them, taken in the letter, can be held to be historical; most of them are set forth in far too general and careless fashion, while a very considerable part of them is simply false. We have here an opportunity of studying how the proof of a great conception may break down in detail although the conception itself may be essentially correct. Lessing, it is true, concluded his propositions with the astounding assertion: "I have gathered these propositions from my own careful and constant reading of the Fathers of the first four centuries, and in defence and examination of them I am in the position to meet the most learned patristic scholars. The best-read scholar has had in this connection no further sources of information than myself. The best-read cannot accordingly know more than I, neither is it true that in order to deal thoroughly with all these questions such deep and extensive knowledge is required as many indeed imagine and would gladly persuade the world."

The ninth of these propositions runs as follows: "*The laymen of the primitive Church might not even read the books of the New Testament, not at least without the permission of the presbyter who had them in his keeping*";[1]

[1] Moreover, in the "Axiomata" (viii., Bd. xvi. S. 124): "Manuscripts [of the Bible] were scarcest in the first and second centuries, and indeed so scarce that a large community would only possess a single codex, which the presbyters of the community kept under lock and key, and which no one might read without their special permission. . . . It is an absolute fact that the Bible, even before the ninth century, was never in the hands of the ordinary layman. The ordinary layman never learned more from it than the clergy chose to impart."

and again the tenth: "*It was indeed accounted no slight offence in the laymen of the primitive Church if they gave greater credence to the written word of an apostle than to the living word of their bishop*"; and the twelfth: "*During the first four centuries the Christian religion was never based upon the writings of the New Testament; the most that can be asserted is that these were used as a subsidiary means of explanation and corroboration.*"

These remarkable statements stand only in a very loose connection with the main thesis which Lessing wished to prove—he could indeed have absolutely dispensed with them in his proof—and they could not but arouse in those who were thoroughly acquainted with the literature of the Early Church feelings of absolute astonishment. It is true that a great critic, Semler, had already asserted similar views in regard to the ninth proposition, but he spoke only incidentally, and the passage lies hidden in the body of his works.[1] Lessing's controversy with Goeze, however, attracted the notice of the theological world, and men now read the objectionable propositions in plain German

---

[1] Semler, *Comment. de antiquo statu ecclesiae*, p. 37: "Erant isti omnes libri [the Holy Scriptures] in manibus doctorum et ministrorum, non puerorum, mulierum, populi universi." P. 68: "Vel hinc existimare licet, quam absit a vero, quod plerique adhuc putant, librorum sacrorum usum fuisse et populo communem." P. 71: "Nemini catechumenorum usum sacrorum librorum fuisse liberum." We may indeed suppose that Lessing's position was not independent of these statements of Semler; for it can scarcely be believed that the two men arrived independently at such a false and paradoxical conclusion.

speech and in the most distinct and clear-cut formulation.

The most learned German patristic scholar of the time was Chr. W. Franz Walch of Göttingen; his renown was world-wide. He roused himself to reply, and in the very next year after the *Necessary Answer to a very Unnecessary Question* there appeared a work from him entitled: *A Critical Investigation of the Use of the Holy Scriptures among the Early Christians of the first four centuries.*[1]

In the second chapter (S. 26–163) a perfect cloud of witnesses for the unrestricted use of the Holy Scriptures (that is, for the early Protestant view of the Holy Scriptures) is most industriously collected; in the third and fourth chapters the evidence they afford is marshalled in order, and all the questions which stand in any connection with the main theme are discussed. The result is that these three theses of Lessing—though these only —are proved to be baseless, because all historical evidence is against them; so much so that the readers are simply left in absolute consternation that a man of the scholarship and fame of Lessing could have had the audacity to make such assertions. And yet Walch does not point the finger for the reader; he makes absolutely no mention of Lessing's name in these three chapters of his treatise. Only in the first introductory chapter does he mention him (and Semler), and with caustic severity expresses himself as follows: " Herr Hofrat Lessing, in

[1] Leipzig, 1779 (S. 221).

the controversy which he has carried on with Herr Pastor Goeze, has gone much further [than Semler] and has sketched out a completely new system of the rational basis of doctrine among the early Christians— a system which assigns to the primitive adherents of the Christian religion the same ideas concerning the books of the Bible, and particularly of the New Testament, as those held by himself. Only one part of this system does he share with Herr Semler; the greatest part is his own property in so strict a sense that even the most active champions of blind faith and the most violent opponents of the right of the people to read the Bible —those men of the Roman Church who wish to support their views by arguments from history—can advance no claim to them. Now all these statements are advanced without a show of proof, though they are accompanied by an assurance that the Hofrat is prepared to prove them all. I hope that no one will assume from these words of mine that my treatise has a polemical purpose, that I wish to refute the position of Dr Semler or of Hofrat Lessing. I cannot do this, because neither of them has so far given any reasons which can be answered. Rather I would assure my readers that my present intention is to investigate the question in cold blood and as calmly as if I had heard nothing of this controversy, and I would wish them to read what I have written in the like spirit."

The learned writer, in thus ranking Lessing with the most violent champions of blind faith, as indeed surpass-

2

ing them all, could not well have shown greater lack of appreciation.[1] But it is still more pitiful that Walch, because of his complete want of appreciation of Lessing's main thesis, so revolutionary, so triumphantly true, wished to prove far too much, and therefore has not only weakened the force but also obscured the import of that which he really has proved. His demonstration undoubtedly involves the complete refutation of Lessing's ninth proposition (also of the tenth and twelfth); but since Walch, in the evidence which he produces as to the use of Holy Scripture, does not everywhere distinguish between the public and private use—although the whole question in dispute is the relation of the latter to the former—and since he believed that he could also refute the remaining and much more important propositions of Lessing (concerning the relation of Creed to Scripture) by simply marshalling his evidence, without attempting to comprehend the essential point of the problem, he at once, and especially in conflict with a critic of the calibre of Lessing, laid himself open to the sharpest retorts and imperilled the success of his learned work in the points where he was in the right.

What did Lessing now do? Walch's book engaged his most active attention ; but he was not able to publish any reply—that is, we can only gather his answer from his literary remains. A man may not be held responsible for what is found in his literary remains ; in this

---

[1] The concluding passages of his book (S. 214 f.) show how seriously Walch meant this reproach against Lessing.

case, moreover, we can only regret that these fragments have remained mere fragments.

In the first place, in the fragment "Bibliolatrie" of the remains is found the following passage :[1] "Scarcely does Goeze see that I have resolved to take up the question in earnest than he proceeds to adopt his favourite tactics. He at once turns his back upon me, and with an impertinent cry of victory courageously retreats. 'But wait a while,' thinks the clerical hero; 'I will soon send another who will do for you.' And indeed a third combatant, whose learning and discretion would scarcely lead one to suppose that he knew more of Goeze than his name, has the loyalty to take his place — the place of Goeze! What can now prevent me from giving the name of this new combatant, seeing that his treatise lies before the eyes of the world? Professor Walch of Göttingen expressly states, in his *Critical Investigation of the Use of the Holy Scriptures* (S. 25), that he has not written against me. But I hold that his book is the more directed against me seeing that he gives so strange a reason for not having written against me. 'I cannot,' says the professor, 'have the polemical purpose of refuting Hofrat Lessing, because up to the present he has given no reasons that can be answered.' Seeing, then, that the professor cannot attack me, does he mean to take the precaution of removing out of the way weapons which I might be able to use? If I now

[1] Bd. xvii. S. 164 ff.

hasten to lay hold of some of these, who can complain of me? Surely not the professor at least. For I hasten at the same time to justify myself in his eyes. And in whose eyes can it be more fitting for me to justify myself than in the eyes of one whom the whole of Germany regards as the most competent umpire in these questions? Let him then be my judge; only let him first hear all that I have to say! Only let him learn of me, not from Goeze, but from myself! And even if Goeze's cause is the cause of the Church, let him at least distinguish between the cause and the advocate who sets himself to plead it."

After this introduction, in which Lessing's praise of Walch is not to be regarded as ironical—though he felt indeed justifiably injured by Walch's assurance that he was not thinking of him, — Lessing proceeds to sketch in full a comprehensive plan of an answer to Walch; the plan, however, is not here carried out.

In the manuscript, " Additional Notes to a Necessary Answer to a Most Unnecessary Question in the author's own hand," [1] is found (§ 19) the illuminating statement: " As the Creed is *regula fidei*, so the Scripture is *regula disciplinae*." With the help of this proposition Lessing, in his controversy with Walch, would have made honourable retreat in that wherein he was wrong,[2] and on the other hand would have been able to compel Walch to

---

[1] Bd. xvii. S. 170 ff.

[2] In his statement concerning the use of Holy Scripture.

a compromise on the main question.[1] But he himself
did not yet see so far as this.   In his literary remains
is found another short and fragmentary piece: "Concerning the Traditores.   From a letter of G. E. Lessing
to Dr Walch announcing a fuller treatise of the former."[2]
If I rightly understand the import of this fragment, it
was Lessing's intention to show that shortly before the
time of the Traditores, *i.e.* at the end of the third century,
a new conception of the Holy Scriptures (involving a
new method of use) had taken form among a section
of the Christians.   This new conception was the same
as that which, according to Lessing's original statement,
did not exist in the primitive Church.   If I am right,
Lessing, convinced by Walch's production of evidence
for the fourth century, was willing to confine his thesis
to the first three centuries.[3]   What he says concerning
the persecution of Diocletian is on the whole very good,
but his remarks against Walch are only superficially

---

[1] The relation of Creed and Scripture.

[2] Bd. xvii. S. 183 ff.

[3] This also follows from the conclusion of the next passage.   There
(S. 225 f.) Lessing, when in his examination of Walch's cloud of
witnesses he had come to Athanasius, writes thus: "Athanasius! and
who else! Simply men with whom begins the second period of the
Church and who can only be assigned to the fourth century.   If I may
confess the truth to your Worship, I should scarcely have thought of all
these in this connection.   It is true that I everywhere assert that my
propositions are true for the first four centuries.   But I really believed
that it was permissible to express oneself thus generally, though one
actually meant only the first period (up to Constantine and the Nicene
Council)."   We can only shake our heads, and the more so seeing that
Lessing himself adds: "Your Worship will now say that this narrower
limitation of my proposition is nothing else than a pitiful feint."

correct, and his attempt to prove that a new conception of the Bible and a new method of use arose
towards the end of the third century, had it been
carried into execution, would necessarily have proved a
complete failure.

Lastly, among the literary remains are found two
other fragments,[1] entitled, "So-called Letters to Dr
Walch," the second of which, carefully elaborated but
not completed, bears the title: "G. E. L. Concerning the Traditores.   Accompanied by a letter to His
Worship Dr C. W. F. Walch of Göttingen, concerning
his ʻ Critical Investigation of the Use of Holy Scripture
among the Early Christians of the first four centuries.ʼ
ὁ ἐλέγχων μετὰ παρρησίας εἰρηνοποιεῖ.   Berlin, 1780."
In this fragment there is no mention, however, made of
the Traditores; but a part only of the "letter" has
come down to us.[2] The chief subject, i.e. the treatise
concerning the Traditores, to which the "letter" was
intended to be an appendix, has accordingly come down
to us only in the short version of the fragment referred to
in the preceding paragraph.   This first shorter letter is
simply introductory, but from its character we can clearly
discern the spirit and temper in which Lessing intended
to compose his reply to Walch—respectful, peaceable,
and yet with firm conviction, just as we find in the
fragment "Bibliolatrie" above mentioned, passages of
which appear again word for word in this letter.

---

[1] Bd. xvii. S. 197 ff., S. 199–229.
[2] Not much of it, however, can be lacking.

Lessing gives here no hint that Walch has shaken him in his opinion, he only complains:[1] "[I am] one who has not infrequently experienced the strange misfortune to be misunderstood in the most extraordinary way by the very people to whom one might have believed that one's statements would be most welcome. This misfortune which dogs my footsteps has, I imagine, done me no little injury even with your Worship; for I might in the very first place complain that Dr Walch would rather learn of me from Goeze than from myself."

If Lessing in his reply would only have kept distinct from one another his two propositions that the Creed was independent of and older than the New Testament, and that the Holy Scriptures were not allowed to be read by the laity! They have almost nothing to do with one another, and the former proposition is as right as the latter is false. Did Lessing himself fail to see that they must be kept apart, or did he indeed see this, but only held the more firmly to his view after he had read Walch's treatise? At all events, he seems to have been convinced that he has not yielded to Walch. Yet he justifies his position only at the point where he was actually in the right—the point, namely, " that the early Christians did not derive their doctrines from the writings of the New Testament, but from an earlier source whence the New Testament, and, if I may venture the word, its canonicity, were themselves derived." He

[1] *Loc. cit.*, S. 199.

then proceeds in this "letter" to investigate in the most
scholarly fashion numerous passages from the Fathers ; [1]
but he is silent concerning his own ninth proposition, as
if this also were proved true by his demonstration that
the New Testament was not in point of time the primal
source of Christian doctrine. Moreover, all the passages
from the Fathers are not well handled ; indeed, a sentence
of Ignatius, which did not suit Lessing's case, is absolutely
falsified by a most audacious conjecture.[2]   And yet this
large fragment of a controversial treatise is certainly
worthy of the genius of Lessing : the amateur in early
Christian literature shows Walch, the learned patristic
scholar, how little he (Walch) had entered into the
essential spirit of his texts, but—nothing is said concerning the *use* of the Holy Scriptures by the laity.[3]

---

[1] Again at the very commencement reference is made to the significant
distinction between *regula fidei* and *regula disciplinae* ; but unfortunately the reader has no complete information as to the way in
which Lessing intended to develop this distinction. However, in the
statement that Walch's collection of passages from the Fathers showed
that the early Christians held the New Testament as the *regula disciplinae* (Lessing says: simply as *regula disciplinae*) there seems to lie
a significant admission, even if Lessing himself has not recognised it
as such.

[2] He allows himself to substitute ἐπισκόπῳ for εὐαγγελίῳ ; τοῖς
πρεσβυτέροις ἐκκλησίας ὡς ἀποστόλοις for τοῖς ἀποστόλοις ὡς πρεσβυτερίῳ
τῆς ἐκκλησίας ; and τοὺς διακόνους ἀγαπῶ ὡς προφήτας for τοὺς
προφήτας ἀγαπῶμεν in Ignat. *ad Ephes.* 5. Lightfoot here remarks:
"Lessing attempted to handle Ignatian criticism here and burnt his
fingers ; his emendation is an exhibition of reckless audacity, all the
more instructive as coming from a great man."

[3] Lessing himself often misses Walch's meaning and mistakes the
point of view under which Walch has adduced this or that quotation,
in that he follows only his own point of view. The tone of the polemic

On this point Walch is not only not refuted, but not even an attempt is made to refute him.

But Walch, in his collection of material, is quite uncritical, and above all devoid of historical sense. The meagreness of the historical imagination which guided him in his labours is painfully obvious in this no less than in his other works, and cannot be counter-balanced by that wonderful industry which Spittler applauds.[1] Besides, his distinction of historical periods is only superficial; in fact, the reader cannot learn from his treatise that Augustine and Jerome wrote under historical conditions different from those of Clement of Rome and Justin Martyr.

The question of the relation between Creed and Scripture has often been raised and thoroughly treated since the time of Lessing and Walch; but the question of the private use of Holy Scripture—subordinate, of course, when compared with the great central problem—

remains almost always worthy, except where Lessing sees himself forced to confine his thesis to the first three centuries (*vide supra*, p. 21, note 2), and on his retreat remarks that Walch must have known that when he spoke of the first four he meant only the first three centuries, but that then Walch's reply would have been reduced to a third of its size. Moreover, some bad mistakes in translation on the part of Walch are courteously corrected. Lessing announces that he can prove that all the women Bible readers mentioned in the Fathers were " probably deaconesses " (S. 212). Unfortunately, he does not present this proof. It certainly could not have brought him any credit.

[1] Indeed, no work teaches so clearly as this of Walch, with its meagreness of thought, that the last hour had struck for theology and historical investigation of this kind. But it also teaches us that a wonderful fund of historical erudition was carried with him to the grave.

has remained untouched during the 130 years that have passed. Walch saw what was right, but with all his learning he has given an unsatisfactory statement of the problem, and a demonstration that is unsatisfactory because it is burdened with so much that is doubtful. We are accordingly justified in taking up the question afresh and submitting it to a thorough examination in order to bring the abortive controversy between Lessing and Walch to its conclusion. And indeed it is with joy that one rushes to the assistance of a small man where he is in the right ; it is still the great man who carries off the palm of victory in the main battle.[1]

[1] I may be allowed a further note as to Walch's attitude as a theologian. While I was engaged in this treatise the *Fuldaer Geschichtsblätter*, 10. Jahrgang, 1911, came into my hands. In them S. 1 ff., 17 ff., 184 ff.) Professor Richter, the editor, has published articles entitled : " Ein Fuldaer Plan zur Wiedervereinigung der christlichen Konfessionen in Deutschland." On 10th June 1780, Pius VI., in a brief addressed to the Prince Bishop Henry VIII. of Fulda, bearing the title "Fuldaer Plan" or "Fuldaer Projekt," condemned a plan for the reunion of Christendom in Germany that had been the subject of careful thought and discussion in the Churches. Richter gives a detailed account of the project, according to the records of Fulda and other material, and then conclusively shows that, though the plan found support among the Benedictines of Fulda, it did not originate in Fulda or indeed among Catholics, but in Protestant circles. The originator was Professor Piderit of Kassel (born 1720), an opponent of rationalistic Biblical criticism, which, according to his conviction, "overthrew those doctrines upon which every rightly disposed Christian had hitherto based his salvation." Piderit was deeply moved by the pitiful condition of the Protestant Churches in consequence of the unrestrained innovations of the critics, and in this mood set himself to work for the reunion of the Christian sects in the German empire. After consultation with the Benedictines of Fulda, who were untouched by the new theories, and who of course

III

But there is another reason for devoting special attention to the question of the private use of the Holy Scriptures in the Early Church. The mystery-religions and other sacerdotal cults, in so far as they possess sacred writings, treat these as arcana, and either deny

upheld the doctrines of the Divinity of Christ and of the Inspiration of Holy Scripture in their integrity, he constructed in 1779 his plan of reunion, and in 1781 published it anonymously. Orthodox Protestantism was to be saved by reunion with Catholicism! Piderit naturally sought to win over confidentially other Protestant theologians to his plan. Bellisomi, the Papal Nuncio at Cologne, in a notice dated 27th April 1780, mentions that Walch of Göttingen, Leitz of Marburg, and three others had been won over (Richter, S. 187). Actually Walch! and that in 1779, the very year of the appearance of his *Critical Investigation*, which we have been discussing. In the preface of this treatise (S. 6) Walch gives expression to the same anxiety in the presence of the flood of rationalistic opinions which had moved Piderit: "May the Lord, who has given us His Word, preserve and guard it against all attempts to wrest it from the hands of the faithful or to make it contemptible in their eyes." But hitherto, so far as I know, there has been no suspicion that Walch did not trust solely to the power of the Word itself, but also looked round for assistance from Catholicism. What an extraordinary position for Protestantism! On the one hand Lessing deals Protestantism a fearful blow in that he plays off the *regula fidei* against the Scriptures, and so approaches a fundamental doctrine of Catholicism, while Walch secretly allies himself with a circle which would save orthodox Protestantism by reunion with Catholicism! Nicolai, with his suspicions of Jesuitism, does not seem to have been so mistaken after all. But as a matter of fact the situation was not really so dangerous; for, closely regarded, Lessing's thesis was far more dangerous to Catholicism than to Protestantism, and schemes for reunion were then (1780), as to-day, merely utopian, as was proved by the attitude of the Pope. The outcome of the scheme may be read in Richter's articles. It is not, however, pleasant to know that a man like Walch was secretly mixed up with it.

them altogether to the laity or only permit their use after a more or less lengthy period of preparation, and a succession of degrees of discipleship which has complete initiation as its aim and object. This principle is so deeply engrained in the nature of mystery and sacerdotal religions that it may be regarded as part of their essence. Now, it is certain that the Bible has never been treated in this way in the Catholic Churches; but seeing that at a comparatively early date these Churches acquired *also* characteristics belonging to mystery and sacerdotal religions, the question arises whether their use of the Bible was thereby affected, and if so, to what extent; nor can there be any doubt that the question is one of the first importance. If the use of the Bible in the Early Church was in no degree affected by this transformation, we are faced by an extraordinary fact, which may well incite us to inquire whether the ancient Catholic Church, in spite of its adoption of many characteristics of mystery and sacerdotal religions, is to be really regarded as a mystery-sect like other such sects. Any such thorough investigation of the distinctive attitude of the Christian religion must inevitably start with Judaism. We at once recognise that the case of the Law, and of the other books which were afterwards gathered into the Old Testament as the completion of the Law, is altogether different from that of the sacred books of mystery-religions. *The Law was both* regula fidei *and* regula disciplinae—*the latter, indeed, in yet higher degree than the former*—and it was the

immediate rule of life *for each individual Jew.* It
was therefore necessary that each individual should
have the closest possible acquaintance with the Law.
Thus the sacred volume, though it belonged originally to the Temple, soon belonged just as much to
the school, to the family, to the study, even though
private reading was not enjoined as a duty. We
indeed know that the Law and — though not so
frequently—the other sacred writings, through which
a man became " taught of God," were to be found
in Jewish homes. Of this fact the strange rule taught
by the Pharisees and scorned by the Sadducees, that
to touch the Holy Scriptures defiled the hands,[1] is
in itself a proof; and the same conclusion may be
drawn from the other ordinance that a book of the
Law might be bought with the proceeds of the sale of
other sacred writings, but not other sacred writings
with the proceeds of the sale of a book of the Law.[2]
Positive testimony to the private use of Holy Scripture
in the Greek and early Roman period is not, it is true,
great in amount, but it is quite sufficient. The testimony of 1 Macc. i. 56 ff. is quite clear and specially
valuable. Here we learn that Antiochus issued a
decree that every month search should be made, and
that everyone in whose possession the book of the Law

---

[1] This rule was naturally intended to guard the books from
profane and careless usage. The books of Homer did not defile the
hands ; *vide* Schürer, *Gesch. d. jüd. Volkes,* ii.³ S. 309 f., 311, 384 f.,
413.

[2] Megilla iii. 1 ; Schürer, ii.³ S. 311.

was found should be punished with death.[1] This decree presupposes a considerable circulation of the Law in private houses. As for the other sacred writings, it is sufficient to remember the Aethiopian eunuch who, returning from the feast at Jerusalem, read in his chariot the prophet Isaiah.[2] We have evidence to show that in imparting the knowledge of the Holy Scripture the Jews observed certain rules of a disciplinary character. Thus Gregory of Nazianzus (*Orat.*, ii. 48, T. i. p. 35) mentions with approval the report of Jewish scholars that it was a rule with the Hebrews of earlier days not to allow every man, regardless of age, to read every book of Holy Scripture, but to place in the hands of the young only those portions of Scripture whose literal sense commanded universal approval (the sentiment is somewhat Alexandrine in expression), and only after they had attained to the age of twenty-five years to permit them to read the whole Old Testament. Compare with this what Origen tells us of the scruples of Jewish teachers concerning the

---

[1] Afterwards the Roman power, in spite of its antipathy to books of magic, protected the Holy Scriptures (did it regard them as law books ?). A Roman soldier was punished with death because he had torn a book of the Law. Josephus, *Antiq.*, xx. 5, 4.

[2] Acts viii. 28. The importance of this anecdote for our purpose does not depend upon its historical accuracy, though this in essentials need not be called into question. In the Mishna (Jebamoth xvi. 7) we hear of a Levite who died in an inn. His luggage consisted of a knapsack and a book of the Law.

reading of the Song of Solomon by the young.[1] These disciplinary regulations have, however, simply nothing to do with the question of the absolute publicity of the Holy Scriptures. In Judaism the Bible was the book for every Jew; he heard it in the synagogue, but he was also expected to read it at home. This attitude of Judaism predetermined the history of the Bible in the Church.—What part had the laity of the Early Church in the Bible?—this is the subject of the following investigation. Other questions, such as the relation of Creed to Scripture, or the origin of the New Testament, will as far as possible be left on one side. I confine myself, like Walch, to the first four centuries (up to about 430 A.D.)—after that time there is no trace of anything really vital and original: I distinguish, however, three periods, bounded by the names of Irenaeus and Eusebius. I owe something to Walch's collection of material, but most of it was known to me years ago. I have for a long period had my attention fixed upon this question, as is shown by my other works, and especially by my *Missionsgeschichte*.[2]

---

[1] Origenes, *Proleg. in Cantic. Cant.* (T. xiv. p. 289, Lomm.): "Aiunt enim, observari etiam apud Hebraeos, quod, nisi quis ad aetatem perfectam maturamque pervenerit, libellum hunc ne quidem in manibus tenere permittatur." Compare also what follows. We give the whole passage further on.

[2] Vide *Missionsgeschichte*, 2. Aufl., i. S. 239, 317, 409, ii. S. 358, etc.

CHAPTER I

AMONG the Jewish Christians the private use of the
Holy Scriptures simply continued; for the fact that
they had become believers in the Messiahship of Jesus
had absolutely no other effect than to increase this use,
in so far as it was now necessary to study not only the
Law but also the Prophets and the Kethubim, seeing
that these afforded prophetic proofs of the Messiahship
of Jesus, and in so far as the religious independence of
the individual Christian was still greater than that of
the ordinary Jew (Acts ii. 17 ff.).

This use simply and easily passed over from the
Jewish to the Gentile Christians, for the Holy Scriptures
in the Greek translation were fully accessible to, and were
read by, the Jews of the Dispersion.   Moreover, we know
that among the Gentile Christians the order of public
worship and private and family discipline in matters
of religion and morality, took form in accordance with
the Jewish (Jewish Christian) models.

But though it is certain that the private use of the
Holy Scriptures among the Gentile Christians was limited

by no consideration of principle, rather that it was
suggested by inherited custom and common sense, still
it is also certain that at first and for a considerable
period of time this use was somewhat infrequent, simply
because of the lack of copies. This explains why
mention is never made of the private use in the epistles
of the New Testament. Timothy is exhorted to
"public reading";[1] it was from this public reading
that the community gained practically all its knowledge
of the Bible. It is true that Timothy himself "knew
from childhood the Holy Scriptures,"[2] and had thus
heard them in his own home; but he had a pious
Jewish mother. That St Paul did not in general count
upon private reading of the Holy Scriptures in his
communities follows conclusively from Col. iii. 16
(Eph. v. 19), where indeed mention is made of psalms
and hymns and spiritual songs, wherewith the individual
members should edify themselves and one another, but
nothing is said about the reading of Holy Scripture.
Nor can we, unfortunately, draw from the manner
in which the Apostle applies and makes use of the
Old Testament in his epistles any certain conclusions
as to the knowledge of the Bible in the communities;
still less as to the way in which that knowledge
had been gained. It is quite obvious that St Paul
makes distinctions—we need only compare the first
and second epistles to the Thessalonians—but we

---

[1] 1 Tim. iv. 13: πρόσεχε τῇ ἀναγνώσει, τῇ παρακλήσει, τῇ διδασκαλίᾳ.
[2] 2 Tim. iii. 15: ἀπὸ βρέφους ἱερὰ γράμματα οἶδας.

3

learn thence nothing that can help us in answering
our question.

The Gentile Christian St Luke shows in his works
at all events a very respectable knowledge of the Bible,
which cannot only have been acquired from what he
had heard in public worship, but must have been based
upon private study; indeed, he imitates the style of
the Septuagint with considerable skill. But in my
opinion he was probably in close touch with Judaism,
or at least with the disciples of the Baptist before he
became a Christian, though we cannot conclusively
prove this. Again, the question of the existence and
extent of private Bible reading ought not at any rate
to be made to depend upon the case of one who was
a literary man; the Bible knowledge of a man who
took up the pen to write books would naturally be far
in advance of that of the great majority of his brethren,
and such a case should therefore as a rule be excluded
from our investigation.

Before we proceed further, it will be in place to
sketch for ourselves cursorily the outward form in
which the Holy Scriptures were current at this period.
In the synagogues they existed as rolls preserved in
cloth coverings and in cases, and kept in an ark or
cupboard.[1] We must imagine them kept in a similar
way in private houses. Here the chief point to be
remembered is that the Scriptures were not united in

---

[1] *Vide* Schürer, ii.³ S. 449 f. Representations on tombstones have
come down to us.

one codex or volume, but that they consisted of several rolls (papyrus or parchment) separate from one another. It is true that at a very early period papyrus books also make their appearance, but they were exceptional; the roll predominated. Although the separate roll had its advantage in that it could be more easily purchased, the fact that the Scriptures did not exist in one volume had necessarily a detrimental influence in the history of the Canon. Zahn has given a full and illuminating discussion of this point in his *History of the Canon of the New Testament.*[1] As a rule, each considerable writing occupied a roll by itself—it can be proved from the textual history of the Gospels that they were often written and copied on separate rolls; moreover, the variation in the order of books has this for one of its reasons [2]—but large rolls were also to be found, comprising copies of several books of considerable size. And even when the parchment volume began to take the place of rolls (third and fourth centuries), the separate books written upon cheaper material could still be purchased. Thus for a comparatively small sum [3] a man could buy separate parts of the *Bibliotheca Divina.* It is true that, considering the scarcity of money among the lower middle class

[1] Bd. i. S. 60 ff. The student should read the whole section up to page 84.

[2] Leviticus comes before Numbers, not only in Melito's list and in the *Stichometria Mommsenia*, but also in a list of the Holy Scriptures belonging to the late Middle Ages in the monastery of Stam.

[3] *Vide* Birt, *Das antike Buchwesen*, 1882.

and the unsatisfactory conditions of the bookselling trade, St Augustine's complaint: "Ubi ipsos codices quaerimus? unde aut quando comparamus? a quibus sumimus"?[1] would have been heard in many quarters as frequently in the second as in the fourth century. Still, Augustine himself soon acquired a copy of the Pauline Epistles,[2] so that it could not have been so very difficult two or three centuries earlier for even poor men to obtain possession of books of the Holy Scriptures, if they made serious efforts to purchase them.[3]

This may also be proved—in spite of the almost complete absence of direct evidence for the period before Irenaeus—from the fact that the Scriptures of the Old Testament, as well as the Gospels and the Epistles of St Paul, which now appear side by side with them, became in high degree and to a wide extent the subject of study and controversy in the Christian communities. The writings of the Apostolic Fathers, but above all the great Gnostic movement, make it quite clear that these Scriptures were known to a comparatively large number of Christians, and that this knowledge could not have been derived solely from what they heard in public worship, but that the writings must have been also in their own hands. One need only read a letter like that

---

[1] *Confess.*, vi. 11, 18.

[2] *Ibid.*, viii. 12, 29.

[3] It was not everyone who could even make a copy; this would demand greater skill than would be gained from a merely elementary education.

of Ptolemy to Flora, or reflect upon the great Marcionite movement, in order to be forced to conclude that the Old Testament, the Gospels, and the Epistles of St Paul had a very wide circulation and were studied by multitudes of Christians.   There was indeed no lack of works which presented all that was most important in a shorter form—such as *The Teaching of the Twelve Apostles*, the *Antitheses* of Marcion for the Marcionite Church, and collections of sayings from the Old Testament in the interest of the doctrine of the uniqueness and unity of God, of ethics, and of the doctrine of future judgment,[1] etc. ;—still, it must have been the object of all Christian teachers to conduct and lead as many as possible of the members of the communities to the reading of the Holy Scriptures themselves.   The obscurity of Holy Scripture is almost never mentioned,[2] and there is absolutely no evidence that during this period a teacher ever for this reason dissuaded his pupils from reading Holy Scripture.   Rather we may assume, on the contrary, that the practice of the Jewish converts of Beroea, commended by St Luke (Acts xvii. 11: "They daily searched the Scriptures whether these things were so"), was both enjoined by the missionaries themselves and was carried out in the communities. Still, it is worthy of note that in "The Way of Life" (in the *Didache*) and in the practical concluding portion of

---

[1] Here also Judaism had in part led the way.

[2] The author of 2 Peter, in what he says of St Paul (iii. 15 f.), forms an exception.

the *Epistle of Barnabas* no express mention is made of
private Bible reading.   Those who could read and study
were indeed a small minority, and yet Ptolemy, for
example, presupposes in his pupil Flora a by no means
contemptible acquaintance with the books of Moses and
the Gospels, although she had not yet received the
(Gnostic) *Apostolic Tradition.*[1] It is a layman who
turns to the famous bishop, Melito of Sardis, with the
petition that he would "make for him a collection
of extracts from the Law and the Prophets referring
to our Saviour, and to our Faith in general," and
that he would besides give him authentic information
concerning the number and the order of the books of
the Old Testament.[2] This layman, whose religious
zeal is specially commended, would scarcely have asked
these questions if he had not already occupied himself in private with the Holy Scriptures.   It is true
that the layman Hermas, though he shows himself
to be a prophet and a prolific writer, evidently has
very little or no knowledge of the Holy Scriptures,
and such laymen were naturally always in the majority;
still, in this respect he stands alone among Christian
authors.   We may, moreover, learn from' his book
how a new revelation was made public among the
Christian communities.   Hermas had received such a
revelation, which he published in a book that was
addressed to all the *elect.* He himself is directed to
give it—that is, to read it—to the presbyters of his

[1] Epiph., *H.*, 31, 7.   [2] Euseb., *Hist. Eccl.*, iv. 26, 12.

(*i.e.* the Roman) Church, in order that these may give it wider circulation in the community.   Moreover, he is to make two copies.   One is intended for the presbyter who conducted foreign correspondence; he is to impart it to the "foreign cities," naturally by sending copies to the sister communities.   The other is to be kept by a certain Grapte, that she may from it exhort the widows and orphans.   This can only imply house-to-house visitation on the part of Grapte, who is to be regarded as one of the "widows" of the community. These directions are so instructive because they show that every divine revelation was made accessible to every individual Christian, that it was even brought into private houses and made known to the children.   We could not wish for a stronger proof of the complete publicity of the Word of God.

Clement of Rome (chap. liii.) testifies of the Corinthian Christians: "Ye know the Holy Scriptures, yea, your knowledge is laudable, and ye have deep insight into the oracles of God."   Though we may not take these words quite literally, still they show that good acquaintance with the Holy Scriptures, such as could only be gained by personal study, belonged to the ideal of a Christian community.   All Christians ought to be "taught of God," such as "search out what the Lord requires of us."[1]   This ideal could only be reached if they themselves, in so far as it was possible, made themselves acquainted with the divine Scriptures.   The

---

[1] Barn. xxi. 6.

tendency to religious independence which belonged to
the essence of Christianity, necessarily disposed the
individual to personal study of the Scriptures, and even
the gift of "the Spirit" could not dispense him from
this obligation—indeed, he was thereby impelled the
more earnestly to fulfil it; for it was in the ancient
prophecies that the New Prophecy found its source and
its vitality.

Polycarp coincides with Clement when he writes to
the Philippian Church (chap. xii.): "I trust that ye are
well exercised in the Holy Scriptures, and that nothing
is (there) hidden from you." This "exercise" also
points to personal study. The famous passage in the
Epistle of Ignatius to the Philadelphians (chap. viii.):
"I have heard some say: 'If I do not find it in the
Old Testament (τοῖς ἀρχαίοις), I do not believe it in
the Gospel'"—presupposes laymen who knew the
Scriptures. Also the author of the second Clementine
Epistle assumes his readers' good acquaintance with
the Scriptures when he writes (chap. xiv.): "I believe
that ye know very well that the living Church is the
body of Christ, and that 'the books' (of the Old
Testament) and the Apostles regard the Church not as
a temporal and earthly manifestation, but as one that
has come from above."

The publicity, the wide circulation, and the easy
accessibility of the Scriptures of the Old Testament [1]

[1] At first primitive Christianity was concerned exclusively with the
Scriptures of the Old Testament. Even the apologists, when speaking

are presupposed in the writings of all the apologists of the second century. Their demonstrations, their exhortations to read the Scriptures, would be incomprehensible if the use of the Holy Scriptures among the Christians had been confined to public worship. Let us consider the most important and pertinent passages.[1]

of Scriptures, mean only these. What Wrede says of Clement (*Unters. zum ersten Clemensbrief*, 1891, S. 75 f.) is true of all Christians of primitive times belonging to the Catholic Church : "Clement's treatment of Scripture depends entirely upon the axiom, accepted by all Christians, that the Old Testament is the unique sacred book, given by God to Christians and properly to Christians alone, whose words could claim absolute authority and formed the first and the most important foundation of all Christian παράδοσις. From a historical point of view it would be altogether unsatisfactory to say that the Jewish Old Testament—as a whole or in part—continued in force for the Christians as if its recognition implied some kind of previous reflection, and as if the possession of this heavenly and infallible book were not in the eyes of the Christians one of the most striking commendations of the new religion. It cannot be stated too emphatically that at that time there was not the slightest suspicion that in the future a second sacred volume would come into being with authority equal to, indeed greater than, the first." We cannot here describe how first separate Christian books, above all the Gospels and Apocalypses, then a collection of books, and at last a second Bible, found a place side by side with the first, and like it was also taken into private use ; if we did, this "excursus" would necessarily exceed in length our whole treatise. It must suffice to point out that the process which in the end so extraordinarily increased the volume of the ancient Scriptures by the addition of a second collection, though it had its beginnings in the first half of the second century, for the most part belonged to the second half of that century. It can be proved from testimony of the fourth century that certain writings of the Old Testament always stood in the foreground for private edification. The Kethubim, especially the Psalms, never resigned the first place in the private house to any other books.

[1] Appeal cannot be made to the most ancient of the authentic Latin Acts of the Martyrs, namely, the Acts of the Martyrs of Scili

Aristides, the earliest of the apologists, exhorts his
heathen readers after reading his own work to take
into their hands and to read the Holy Scriptures
themselves.[1] This appeal to the Holy Scriptures
runs through all the apologies from the earliest to
the latest,[2] and shows that their authors were united in
the belief that the regular way to become a convinced
Christian was to read the Holy Scriptures.[3] In this way

in Africa (A.D. 181). Here the Christian Speratus, when asked
by the Proconsul, "Quae sunt res in capsa vestra?" replies, "Libri
et epistulae Pauli viri iusti." (The ancient Greek version reads :
Ποῖαι πραγματεῖαι (ἐν) τοῖς ὑμετέροις ἀπόκεινται σκεύεσιν; ὁ ἅγιος
Σπερᾶτος εἶπεν. αἱ καθ' ἡμᾶς βίβλοι καὶ αἱ πρὸς ἐπὶ τούτοις ἐπιστολαὶ
Παύλου τοῦ ὁσίου ἀνδρός). Speratus seems to have been the leader of
the little band, and the "capsa" was not his own private property
(note the word "vestra"), but belonged to the community. We
cannot, therefore, here draw any conclusion as to the private use of
Holy Scripture.

[1] Apol., xvi.

[2] Pseudo-Justin, Orat. ad Graec., 5 ; so also the author of the Cohort.
ad Graec., 35. 36. 38.

[3] Tatian (Orat., chap. 29) gives the best summary of what the
Scriptures of the Old Testament had to say to a Greek, and what
impression they made upon him : Συνέβη γραφαῖς τισιν ἐντυχεῖν
βαρβαρικαῖς, πρεσβυτέραις μὲν ὡς πρὸς τὰ Ἑλλήνων δόγματα, θεοτέραις
δὲ ὡς πρὸς τὴν ἐκείνων πλάνην· καί μοι πεισθῆναι ταύταις συνέβη διά τε
τῶν λέξεων τὸ ἄτυφον καὶ τῶν εἰπόντων τὸ ἀνεπιτήδευτον καὶ τῆς τοῦ
παντὸς ποιήσεως τὸ εὐκατάληπτον καὶ τῶν μελλόντων προγνωστικὸν
καὶ τῶν παραγγελμάτων τὸ ἐξαίσιον καὶ τῶν ὅλων τὸ μοναρχικόν.
Θεοδιδάκτου (vide supra, Barn. xxi. 6: in the reading of the Holy
Scripture a man has God Himself for teacher) δέ μου γενομένης τῆς
ψυχῆς συνῆκα ὅτι τὰ μὲν καταδίκης ἔχει τρόπον, τὰ δὲ ὅτι λύει τὴν ἐν
κόσμῳ δουλείαν καὶ ἀρχόντων μὲν πολλῶν καὶ μυρίων ἀποσπᾷ τυράννων,
δίδωσι δὲ ἡμῖν οὐχ ὅπερ μὴ ἐλάβομεν, ἀλλ' ὅπερ λαβόντες ὑπὸ τῆς
πλάνης ἔχειν ἐκωλύθημεν. Compare also how Theophilus (ad Autol.,
i. 14 ; ii. 34) exhorts his heathen friend to read the Holy Scriptures :
Εἰ βούλει, καὶ σὺ ἔντυχε φιλοτίμως ταῖς προφητικαῖς γραφαῖς, καὶ αὐταί

Justin,[1] Tatian,[2] and Theophilus[3] expressly say that they themselves became Christians. Justin mentions incidentally that this reading was not without its dangers, seeing that the books of the Prophets were regarded as books of sorcery and magic by the authorities;[4] yet "we not only read them without fear, but we also offer them to you for study."[5]

σε τρανότερον ὁδηγήσουσιν κ.τ.λ. . . . . Τὸ λοιπὸν ἔστω σοι φιλοφρόνως ἐρευνᾷν τὰ τοῦ θεοῦ, λέγω δὲ τὰ διὰ τῶν προφητῶν ῥηθέντα·

[1] Dial., 7.

[2] Orat., 29. Philippus Sidetes professes to know that Athenagoras originally intended to combat Christianity, but that the reading of the Holy Scriptures turned him from a Saul into a Paul (Excerpta in Cod. Barocc. 142, fol. 216).

[3] Ad Autol., i. 14: Καὶ γὰρ ἐγὼ ἠπίστουν τοῦτο ἔσεσθαι, ἀλλὰ νῦν κατανοήσας αὐτὰ πιστεύω, ἅμα καὶ ἐπιτυχὼν ἱεραῖς γραφαῖς τῶν ἁγίων προφητῶν.

[4] We may not conclude from the words of Justin (see the following note) that there was an express decree of the Roman Government against the reading of the Scriptures of the Old Testament. Justin only assumes, and indeed with justice, that the laws against magic and books of magic could also be directed against these writings ("Qui de salute principis vel de summa reipublicae mathematicos, ariolos, aruspices, vaticinatores consulit, cum eo qui responderit capite punitur"; and "Libros magicae artis apud se neminem habere licet et si penes quoscumque reperti sint, bonis ademtis ambustisque his publice in insulam deportantur, humiliores capite puniuntur." Paul. Sentent., v., tit. 21, 23). Perhaps cases had already occurred.

[5] Justin, Apol., i. 44: Κατ' ἐνέργειαν τῶν φαύλων δαιμόνων θάνατος ὡρίσθη κατὰ τῶν τὰς Ὑστάσπου ἢ Σιβύλλης ἢ τῶν προφητῶν βίβλους ἀναγινωσκόντων, ὅπως διὰ τοῦ φόβου ἀποστρέψωσιν ἐντυγχάνοντας τοὺς ἀνθρώπους τῶν καλῶν γνῶσιν λαβεῖν, αὐτοῖς δὲ δουλεύοντας κατέχωσιν· ὅπερ εἰς τέλος οὐκ ἴσχυσαν πρᾶξαι. ἀφόβως μὲν γὰρ οὐ μόνον ἐντυγχάνομεν αὐταῖς, ἀλλὰ καὶ ὑμῖν ὡς ὁρᾶτε, εἰς ἐπίσκεψιν φέρομεν. Again, when Tatian tells us that Christian maidens "with the distaff" τὰ κατὰ θεὸν λαλοῦσιν ἐκφωνήματα (Orat., 33), he can only mean words of Scripture. He contrasts them with Sappho—τὸ γύναιον πορνικόν.

Justin is naïve enough to expect the emperors themselves to read them.[1] Athenagoras goes still further; he believes that he may assume that the emperors to whom he addresses his apology already know the Scriptures of the Old Testament, and he leaves it to them, on the ground of this knowledge which he begs them to refresh, to institute reforms in the matter of the process against the Christians.[2] This assumption may be only a *façon de parler*, but Athenagoras could not have made it if the Scriptures had not had a wide circulation. Justin does not mention whether his opponent Crescens the Cynic had read the teachings of Christ,[3] but he allows his other opponent, the Jew Trypho, to state expressly that he had made it his business himself to read the Gospel.[4] This is the earliest notice which we have of a Jew reading the Gospels. Yet the whole dialogue with Trypho (which has a historical foundation), and perhaps also the Fourth Gospel, presuppose controversies between Christians and Jews which were based upon a written Gospel that was read even by Jews. The first Greek of whom we know that he was thoroughly acquainted with the Christian Scriptures is Celsus,

---

[1] *Apol.*, i. 28.

[2] *Suppl.*, 9: Νομίζω καὶ ὑμᾶς φιλομαθεστάτους καὶ ἐπιστημονεστάτους ὄντας, οὐκ ἀνοήτους γεγονέναι οὔτε τῶν Ἡσαίου καὶ Ἱερεμίου καὶ τῶν λοιπῶν προφητῶν. . . . καταλείπω δὲ ὑμῖν, ἐπ' αὐτῶν τῶν βιβλίων γενομένοις, ἀκριβέστερον τὰς ἐκείνων ἐξετάσαι προφητείας, ὅπως μετὰ τοῦ προσήκοντος λογισμοῦ τὴν καθ' ἡμᾶς ἐπήρειαν ἀποσκευάσησθε.

[3] *Apol.*, ii. 3.

[4] *Dial.*, 10, 18: Ἐπειδὴ ἀνέγνως, ὦ Τρύφων, ὡς αὐτὸς ὁμολογήσας ἔφης, τὰ ὑπὸ τοῦ σωτῆρος ἡμῖν διδαχθέντα.

who wrote during the reign of Marcus Aurelius. It is not necessary to prove his very close acquaintance with the Gospels ;[1] and yet, though he had looked into so many Christian writings, he seems not to have known the Epistles of St Paul. He is, however, himself convinced that his knowledge of Christianity is based upon a complete investigation of the original documents : " I know all," he says.[2] He nowhere gives ground for the surmise that it had cost him any trouble to obtain the necessary books ; on the other hand, he does not describe the Christian religion as a religion of a " book " or of books. The enthusiastic character of the new religion stood for him in the foreground. Moreover, the Christian religion before the days of Calvin was never a religion of a book in the same sense and degree as Islam. It is, however, very noteworthy that already Celsus took offence at the poor form and the inferior style of the Holy Scriptures such as were fit only for the uneducated and barbarians, and that he makes invidious comparisons with the writings of Plato.[3] We shall see that this aspect of the Holy Scriptures presented difficulties to the Fathers, seeing that educated Christians also took offence at it.

Finally, we may with all due caution make use of the following consideration :—It cannot be proved that the

---

[1] The doubts of Origen are scarcely seriously meant.

[2] Origen, c. Cels., i. 12.

[3] Celsus apud Origen, vi. 1 f. Unfortunately Origen here gives only an extract. Concerning Christian conventicles in boudoirs and workrooms, vide Chap. III. p. 62 ff.

Scriptures of the Old Testament were translated into any other language except the Greek before the Christian era. This applies even to Syriac.[1] On the other hand, it is probable that the Old Testament was first translated into Latin not by Jews but by Christians,[2] and that these translations began to be made before the time of Irenaeus and Tertullian.[3] In the case of the Gospels the latter statement may be taken as proved for the Syriac as well as the Latin translations. It follows from this that the Christians from the very first were more zealous in translating the Scriptures than the Jews, and accordingly we may further conclude that this zeal was due partly at least to the earnest desire to place the Scriptures in the hands of the faithful for their private use; for in the case of public worship persons would surely have been found among the Christians, as they were among the Jews, who were capable of giving an oral interpretation

[1] *Vide* the article " Bibelübersetzungen " in Hauck's *Realenzykl.*, Bd. iii.[3] S. 169.

[2] Schürer, in his *Geschichte des judischen Volkes*, gives no evidence for a Jewish Latin Bible. One would think that, if it had ever existed, we must have heard something of it.

[3] Irenaeus speaks only of the Celts and Germans as people who believed without knowing and reading the Holy Scriptures, not of the Latins. It is possible that he did not mention these because he assumed that every Latin also understood Greek, yet it is not probable. Zahn (*Gesch. des NTlichen Kanons*, i. S. 31 ff., 51 ff.) has disputed the existence of Latin translations of books of the Bible before A.D. 200 ; but the evidence from Tertullian is against his theory. It also follows from Hippol. in Dan., ed. Bonwetsch, S. 338, that the Bible then existed in a Latin translation.

of the Scriptures.[1] There is accordingly not much direct evidence that can be produced for the private use of the Holy Scriptures during this period; but the fact that there is no evidence to the contrary is decisive. No change was made in the use which the Jews already made in private of the sacred volume; moreover, a Christian would naturally be more conversant with this volume than a Jew.

[1] The beginnings of the Latin Bible, especially of the Latin Old Testament, lie in complete obscurity. Even for Augustine this was so. He writes, indeed (*De doctrina Christ.*, ii. 11): "Qui scripturas ex Hebraea lingua in Graecam verterunt, numerari possunt, Latini autem interpretes nullo modo. Ut enim cuique *primis fidei temporibus* in manus venit codex Graecus et aliquantulum facultatis sibi utriusque linguae habere videbatur, ausus est interpretari" (compare the record of Papias concerning the translation of the Hebrew Logia of St Matthew in Eus., *Hist. Eccl.*, iii. 39), but what he says is of course not history but only conjecture. Even he at all events knows nothing of pre-Christian translations of the Old Testament into Latin. Further investigation must show whether or no the language (the vulgar Latin) forbids us to place the Latin translations earlier than the second century, and whether they do not afford internal evidence that the translators were Christians. Rönsch (*Itala und Vulgata*, 1875), perhaps rightly, does not even raise the question whether the Old Testament or some books of the same were not already translated into Latin by Jews.

CHAPTER II

BEHIND the great work of Irenaeus against the heretics, and still more behind Tertullian's tractate *De Prae-scriptione Haereticorum*, lie sad experiences of their authors in regard to the Holy Scriptures both of the Old and the New Testament. They must have learned from experience that these Scriptures were brought into the field to support stubborn and varied assaults upon the most precious beliefs of Catholic Christianity, and that the refutation of heretical exegesis was no easy matter and was often not altogether successful. Indeed, they must have been convinced that, if the absolute certainty which faith required was once placed in doubt, it could no longer, or only with difficulty, be re-established by an appeal to, and by interpretation of, Holy Scripture. During the second half of the second century the Holy Scriptures must have appeared to the more educated Christians of East and West like a tremendous battlefield whereon conflicts of the fiercest description were fought, where the strongest power, the Catholic Church, saw herself continually pressed hard by foes of different kinds,

48

who were, however, allied in opposition to herself. Under these circumstances the Church constructed two new strongholds, or rather now began to reconstruct them as central fortresses : these were the Apostolic rule of faith, and the Apostolic order of bishops as a guarantee of the truth. Into their safe keeping she committed religion itself, and from these she could now with new weapons also guard the great battlefield of the Holy Scriptures and could keep it within her range of fire, in that she at the same time set limits to this field by new definitions in regard to the compass of the new sacred writings (the foundation of the New Testament).[1]

One would imagine that it might have naturally occurred to the Church to cut at the root of these perilous disputes by withdrawing the Holy Scriptures from publicity, and to put an end to all controversy by declaring that these Scriptures were given solely to the Church, that is, to the clergy, and that profane hands had therefore absolutely nothing to do with them. It was forbidden to put the baptismal symbol in writing ; part of the public worship was withdrawn from profane eyes ; Baptism and the Lord's Supper were given the form of mysteries ; limits were set to the compass of Holy Scripture ; many other measures of the same

[1] *Vide* my *Dogmengeschichte*, i.⁴ S. 353–425. Kunze has published a comprehensive and original treatise, *Glaubensregel, heilige Schrift, und Taufbekenntniss* (1899), which has filled up certain gaps in earlier investigation, though it suffers somewhat from one-sidedness.

4

description were instituted. *Seeing that it was possible gradually to carry out all these changes in practically the whole of Eastern and Western Christendom,* it was evidently not from want of power that the Church did not withdraw the Bible from the laity, that she did not consign it exclusively to the clergy for their cautious use, and so deliver herself with *one* stroke from most troublesome and perilous disputes.

No one in the Church ever thought of this. Surely one of the most astounding facts in the internal history of the Church, and one which affords more conclusive testimony than any other that a by no means small measure of religious independence continued to be regarded as a matter of course, or—perhaps more correctly—that it was thought that no limits should be set to the edifying and sanctifying influence of the sacred writings! Even Tertullian, who of all the Fathers lays the greatest stress upon the rule of faith and had had in controversy the most bitter experience of the inconclusiveness and insecurity of the Catholic interpretation of Holy Scripture, even he does not for one moment think of forbidding or restricting the use of these writings by the laymen of the Church. He indeed denies that heretics have anything to do with the Scriptures, and declares it to be a piece of effrontery that these dare to express an opinion about them; he also warns Catholic Christians not to enter into a controversy with heretics concerning the Holy Scriptures; but this is the only restriction which he suggests. The thought that laymen should respectfully leave the Scriptures to the clergy lies altogether beyond his horizon; rather he teaches that they could read them, and ought to read them industriously, that they should search them with inquiring mind—ever, of course, under the guidance of the rule of faith.[1]

But even the one restriction which Tertullian so zealously urges upon his readers—namely, that they should not enter into controversy with heretics concerning the interpretation of Scripture, and consequently, when disputing with them, should dispense with Scriptural proofs—could not but prove to be a mere theoretical expedient which it was impossible to carry out in practice, and was even neglected by

---

[1] Tertullian's treatise, *De Praesc. Haer.* (see especially c. 8-12), is of such extreme importance because it has as its foil the author's hopelessness that anything could be accomplished against the heretics by means of the Scriptures. Tertullian therefore takes refuge in the rule of faith and the episcopate—that is, he appeals to the Apostolic teachers who guarantee the authenticity of the Creed. How easily it might have occurred to him to connect the Scriptures in the same way with the bishops and the Apostolic teachers! Nothing of the kind is, however, to be found in his pages! Rather the Scripture is for him an absolute entity, a thing by itself; and he is just as certain, indeed he holds as a matter of course, that what the Scripture says it says to everyone, and that every individual has direct access thereto. Just for this reason he is obliged to admit, in spite of all attempts at shuffling, that the command, "Quaerite (in Scripturis)," is addressed to all. In face of this treatise we can say that nothing is more certain than the conclusion that it did not belong to the clergy to give orders concerning the use of Holy Scripture. He could only advise and warn his readers against irreverent inquisitiveness in their searching of the Scriptures, lest they should in their searching lose their faith; there is not, however, the remotest shadow of the "saving expedient" of restricting the use of Scripture by means of the clergy.

Tertullian himself.[1] Irenaeus also seeks, indeed, to show that the proof for the truth of the Catholic conception of doctrine can be given without recourse to Holy Scripture ;[2] but he knows very well that in spite of this the Church cannot at any time and under any circumstances renounce the proof from Scripture, because the Holy Scriptures alone, and not the rule of faith, contain the direct *effata divina* by which all Catholic teaching must be tested. He knows this and he acts accordingly :[3] in his great work against the heretics the proof from Scripture occupies the largest room.[4] Nor do Clement of Alexandria, Hippolytus, and Origen think and act otherwise. Accordingly, during this period the use of Holy Scripture suffers no kind of restriction. Moreover, in spite of all sad experience, the fiction is still upheld that the meaning of Holy Scripture is absolutely clear and intelligible :[5] no other course was

[1] Compare his great work against Marcion and his other controversial works against heretics, in all of which the proof from Scripture is the main theme.

[2] In this aspect the Churches *sine literis*, the barbarian Churches, are to him of great importance.

[3] Iren., i., ii. fin., iii.–v.

[4] According to Irenaeus (iv. 33, 8), the "tractatio plenissima Scripturarum" and the "lectio sine falsatione" belonged to the most precious treasures of the Church.

[5] *Vide, e.g.*, Iren., ii. 27, 2 : "Cum itaque universae scripturae et prophetiae et evangelia, in aperto et sine ambiguitate et similiter ab omnibus audiri possint," etc. The views of the Alexandrian theologians are here more complicated ; but their conviction that the Scriptures had a secret signification which was only revealed to the true "Gnostic," and that a secret tradition derived from Christ stood side by side with the public tradition, does not affect the view that even these

possible if restriction of the use of Holy Scripture was not even to be thought of. It was only some Gnostic sects that had the discernment to describe some books of Scripture, or some portions of the same, as unintelligible to the layman, *i.e.* to him who was not a Gnostic.[1]

In this period we first begin to receive abundant evidence as to the extent of the private and domestic use of Holy Scripture, such as permits us to draw conclusions as to this use in earlier days. "Let a man take refuge in the Church," says Irenaeus; "let him be educated in her bosom and be nourished from the Holy Scriptures (*dominicae scripturae*)." What he means is clear from what follows: "The Church is planted like Paradise in this world; of every tree of this Paradise shall ye eat; that is, eat ye from every scripture of the Lord."[2] This implies an unrestricted use.[3] It might be supposed that this use was subject

Scriptures had an aspect wherein they were intelligible and accessible to all. The Alexandrians knew nothing of esoteric *Scripture.*

[1] *Vide* Iren., ii. 27, 3 (iii. 5 and elsewhere): "Quia enim de excogitato eorum qui contraria opinantur patre nihil aperte neque ipsa dictione (αὐτολεξεί) neque sine controversia in nulla omnino dictum sit scriptura, et ipsi testantur dicentes in absconso haec eadem salvatorem docuisse non omnes, sed aliquos discipulorum qui possunt capere, et per argumenta et aenigmata et parabolas ab eo significata intelligentibus." It is probable that the Valentinians, whose practice was to reveal their doctrines to their catechumens only by degrees, may have also kept portions of the Holy Scriptures in reserve; but we have no more definite information.

[2] Iren., v. 20, 2.

[3] There could have been no lack of manuscripts, seeing that Irenaeus states (v. 30, 1) that in the case of only one book, the Apocalypse of

to a certain oversight on the part of the presbyters, seeing that Irenaeus says (iv. 33, 1): "Post deinde et omnis sermo ei [the true believer] constabit, si et scripturas diligenter legerit apud eos qui in ecclesia sunt presbyteri, apud quos est apostolica doctrina."[1] But the words "apud eos, etc.," only express the necessary presupposition that the reader must belong to the Catholic Church, and cannot be understood in the sense that supervision was exercised over the reading of Scripture. If Irenaeus had intended this, he would have expressed himself otherwise, and would necessarily have insisted upon this rule in other passages of his work. He does not think of any control of Bible reading in particular, but of the great deposit of correct interpretation which is given to, and is the secure possession of, him alone who is in communion with the presbyters, the leaders of the Catholic and Apostolic Church. If this explanation does not commend itself, there can be only one other interpretation of the passage, namely, that the number of Bibles was still so small that a man was compelled to read those in the hands of the presbyters. This explanation is not, however, probable.

St John, he had consulted numerous manuscripts. He speaks of πάντες οἱ σπουδαῖοι καὶ ἀρχαῖοι ἀντίγραφοι of this book, and therefore knows of manuscripts of earlier and later date, and also distinguishes between better and worse exemplars. These could not all have belonged to his or other communities ; some of them must be supposed to have belonged to private persons.

[1] It is possible that this passage was in Lessing's mind when he composed his incorrect ninth proposition (*vide supra*, p. 14 f.).

The Holy Scriptures must, as far as possible, be read in communion with the presbyters *by each for himself* if he would advance in the Christian life—this is the opinion of Irenaeus, and this opinion is also shared by the other early Fathers of the Church.[1] This is especially clear when we hear Clement and Tertullian advise that married people should read the Holy Scriptures together. It is evident that we have here a rule of long standing for Christian families. Clement writes that married people should spend the day in prayer, reading (*i.e.* reading of the Holy Scriptures), and good works ;[2] and Tertullian, in reference to mixed marriages, which he disallows, asks the question : "Quae dei mentio, quae Christi invocatio, ubi fomenta fidei de scripturarum interjectione [interlectione ?]."[3] Thus Bible reading forms part of an ideal Christian life.

[1] Even Cyprian, with all his hierarchic opinions, forms no exception, for we learn nothing from his writings of any discord between Bible and hierarchy, or of hierarchy and Bible against the laity. In his treatise *De Zelo et Livore* (16) he writes: "Sit in manibus divina lectio, in sensibus dominica cogitatio." Similarly, Novatian (Pseudo-Cyprian) also concludes his *Adlocutio de bono pudicitiae* with the words: "Ego pauca dictavi, quoniam non est propositum volumina scribere . . . vos scripturas aspicite, exempla vobis de ipsis praeceptis huius rei maiora conquirite." The writer assumes, even though it be only the assumption of an ideal, that the Bible is in the hands of all. Whether in the famous inscription of Abercius (assuming its Catholic character) Abercius really relates that he took with him on his journey a copy of the Epistles of St Paul (just as the Ethiopian eunuch took the book of Isaiah) is of course doubtful (vide *Texte u. Unters.*, Bd. xii. H. 4ᵇ, S. 4 ff.).

[2] *Paedag.*, ii. 10, 96 : . . . ὁπηνίκα εὐχῆς καὶ ἀναγνώσεως καὶ τῶν μεθ' ἡμέραν εὐεργῶν ἔργων ὁ καιρός.

[3] *Ad Uxor.*, ii. 6. The context shows that the reference is to family life.

This also follows conclusively from the voluminous twelfth chapter of Clement's third book of the *Paedagogus*,[1] which affords to more advanced Christians guidance to a gradual advance in the knowledge of Holy Scripture by personal study. Clement also mentions the most fitting time for Bible reading—namely, before the chief meal of the day.[2] The same Father lays great emphasis upon the general accessibility of the Scriptures,[3] and though he believes that the deeper significance of Scripture is only revealed to the advanced Gnostic, still he teaches that its simple significance is plain to everyone,[4] and that each man must master the Scriptures if his faith is to have a sure foundation.[5]

Tertullian, in his *Apologeticus* (chap. 31), exhorts

---

[1] *Paedag.*, iii. 12, 87 : "Ὅσα μὲν οὖν οἴκοι παραφυλακτέον καὶ ὡς τὸν βίον ἐπανορθωτέον. Passages in the theological literature of this period, which incidentally presuppose private Bible reading, are very numerous. *Vide, e.g.*, Hippolyt. in Daniel iv. 15, p. 222 : Δεῖ πάντα ἄνθρωπον τὸν ἐντυγχάνοντα ταῖς θείαις γραφαῖς μιμεῖσθαι τὸν προφήτην Δανιήλ.

[2] *Strom.*, vii. 7, 49 : αἱ πρὸ τῆς ἑστιάσεως ἐντεύξεις τῶν γραφῶν. This was evidently an ancient custom, and had perhaps descended from Jewish times.

[3] *Strom.* i. 7, 38 : Διὰ τοῦτο Ἑλλήνων φωνῇ ἡρμηνεύθησαν αἱ γραφαί, ὡς μὴ πρόφασιν ἀγνοίας προβάλλεσθαι δυνηθῆναί ποτε αὐτούς. In *Strom.*, vii. 16, 97, the Holy Scriptures are called τὰ ἐν μέσῳ καὶ πρόχειρα. It is the more lamentable that the heretics introduce ψεύσματα and πλάσματα, ἵνα δὴ εὐλόγως δόξωσι μὴ προσίεσθαι τὰς γραφάς (*Strom.*, vii. 16, 99).

[4] Clement (*Strom.*, vi. 15, 131) refers to an event mentioned by Hermas, and then continues : Ἐδήλου δ' ἄρα τὴν μὲν γραφὴν πρόδηλον εἶναι πᾶσι κατὰ τὴν ψιλὴν ἀνάγνωσιν ἐκλαμβανομένην, καὶ ταύτην εἶναι τὴν πίστιν στοιχείων τάξιν ἔχουσαν.

[5] *Strom.*, vii. 16, 95. 96.

his heathen readers to consult the Holy Scriptures
"*quas neque ipsi subprimimus* et plerique casus ad
extraneos transferunt."[1]   He does not, indeed, believe
that they will follow his advice; for, says he, they of
set purpose shut themselves off from the truth and
cast it from them.   In his treatise *De testimonio Animae*
(chap. 1) he complains bitterly: "Tanto abest, ut
nostris litteris annuant homines, ad quas nemo venit
nisi iam Christianus."   This is an important statement.
Celsus was thus almost a white blackbird![2]   About
the year A.D. 200 the sacred writings of the Christians
were no more regarded as "literature" than the tracts
of the Salvation Army at the present time.   Nevertheless the statement, "ad quas nemo venit nisi iam
Christianus," is an exaggeration quite in Tertullian's
style; moreover, it was not only "plerique casus" that
made non-Christians acquainted with the Scriptures,
but the Christians took trouble ("non subprimimus")
to bring them to the knowledge of the Greeks wherever
there was any hope that they would be appreciated.[3]

[1] As a matter of curiosity, it may be mentioned that Walch (*loc. cit.*,
S. 52) here translates: "which prescribe so many special duties
towards those who are not Christians"!!   Lessing has already pointed
out this serious error in his letter to Walch.

[2] *Cf.* Norden, *Kunstprosa*, S. 517 f. : "One cannot set the number
of those heathen who read the New Testament at too low a figure. . . .
I think that I am not mistaken in stating that the heathen only read
the New Testament if they wished to refute it."

[3] Compare Justin's account of his own conversion.   The numerous
and carefully collected passages from the Bible in many of the apologies
are also to be regarded as extracts from the Bible for readers who
otherwise took no notice of that book.

Seeing that the Holy Scriptures, or parts of them, were to be found in many Christian families,[1] there was no difficulty about their accessibility.

The fact that the Holy Scriptures were constantly to be found in Christian homes, naturally of the more wealthy class, follows from numerous passages in the Christian literature of the third century. The passage which gives the fullest evidence on this point comes from the "Apostolic Didaskalia" preserved for us in the Syriac; we quote it here in place of many other passages. This passage is especially noteworthy because it shows that the aim of the Church was also to turn the attention of the more educated Christians to the Holy Scriptures, and by this means to satisfy their craving for literary culture, so that evil literature— whether it were really evil or simply profane—might be

---

[1] This fact, which is sufficiently certain, cannot, however, be proved from the treatise *De Corona*, i. The words, "Nec dubito quosdam [quasdam, H] scripturas [scriptore, D; secundum scripturas, B, sec. man.] emigrare, sarcinas expedire, fugae accingi de civitate in civitatem," cannot be translated, "that certain persons get rid of their Bibles." At a pinch "emigrare" could be taken as "emigrare facere" (with reference to Ps. li. 7, Vulg.); but if they themselves migrated, why should they not take their Bibles with them? Besides, this anxiety about copies of the Bible would have been natural during the persecution of Diocletian, not so a hundred years earlier. If the text is in order, of which I am not certain ("secundum" is a conjecture to remove a difficulty), one must, with Walch and others, translate "migrare" by "to overstep or exceed." How, while seeming to fulfil, they overstepped the ordinance of Matt. x. 24 is explained by Tertullian in a contemporary treatise: the ordinance was meant only for the Apostles. Tertullian chooses the word "emigrare" in view of the play upon words which follows.

banished from Christian homes. The passage runs as
follows :— [1]

" If thou art in good circumstances and needest not
to work for thy living, do not wander hither and thither
wasting your time, but be ever zealous to visit thy
brethren in the Faith. Meditate with them, and in-
struct thyself in the Living Word. If not, stay at
home and read in the Law, in the Book of Kings and
the Prophets, and in the Gospel which is their fulfil-
ment. Keep far from thyself all the books of the
heathen. For what wouldst thou with alien words or
with the laws and false prophecies which lead away the
youthful even from the Faith? What then dost thou
find wanting in the Word of God that thou rushest to
these heathen stories? If thou wouldst read history,
thou hast the book of the Kings ; if works of wise men
and philosophers, thou hast the Prophets, with whom
thou findest more wisdom and understanding than
with the wise and the philosophers ; for they are the
words of the One and only wise God. If thou desirest
poetry, thou hast the psalms of David ; if thou cravest
information concerning the beginnings of the world,
thou hast Genesis written by that great man Moses ;
if laws and ordinances, thou hast the Law, the glorious
book of God the Lord. Keep thyself wholly from
all those alien works, which are contrary (to Scripture).
Nevertheless when thou readest in the Law guard

[1] *Vide* Achelis and Flemming in *Texte u. Unters.*, Bd. xxv. Heft 1
(1904), S. 5 f.

thyself from the 'repetition of the Law' (the ceremonial Law); . . . for our Saviour is come for no
other reason than to fulfil the Law and to deliver us
from the bonds of the 'repetition of the Law.' . . .
Thou therefore, who art freed from this burden, read
the simple Law which agrees with the Gospel, and also
the Gospel itself and the Prophets, likewise the Book of
Kings that thou mayest know how many kings were
righteous and by the help of God the Lord attained to
renown even in this world and abided in God's promise
of eternal life. Those kings, however, who fell away
from God and served idols, according to their desert
came to fearful ruin by a speedy judgment, and were
deprived of the Kingdom of God, and instead of rest
suffer torment. This if thou so readest, thou wilt
greatly grow and increase in the Faith."

A new aspect of the efforts to extend the reading of
the Bible is here revealed to us. The aim was to
repress heathen literature, and it was hoped to attain
this end by means of the Bible, whose contents satisfied
such various and different needs.[1] Formal decrees

---

[1] Novatian, when warning his readers against visiting dramatic plays,
also points to the rich dramatic contents of Holy Scripture, the reading
of which could well take the place of the pleasure of the theatre;
vide *De Spect.*, 10: "Scripturis sacris incumbat Christianus fidelis:
ibi inveniet condigna fidei spectacula. videbit instituentem deum
mundum suum et cum ceteris animalibus homines illam admirabilem
fabricam melioremque facientem. spectabit mundum in deliciis suis(!),
iusta naufragia, piorum praemia impiorumque supplicia, maria populo
siccata et de petra rursus populo maria porrecta. spectabit de coelo
descendentes messes, non ex areis aratro impressas. inspiciet flumina
transitus siccas refrenatis aquarum agminibus exhibentia. videbit in

against reading the religious literature of the heathen
and the heretics were not issued by the Church before
the time of Constantine. But though historical and
philosophical literature was in general allowed—yet
even here with the Apostolical warning, "Beware
lest any man spoil you through philosophy"[1]—
and indeed could not be dispensed with in the
interests of necessary general culture and of apolo-
getics, it was nevertheless understood from the first
that a Christian, as a matter of course, must keep
aloof from the foul light literature of the times, from
frivolous and obscene dramas, from books of magic
and of strange religions. It was still more clearly
understood that he must avoid reading all heretical
literature. If he might not company with a heretic,
might not eat with him, might not greet him,[2] if
even the listening to heretical words should be for
him a thing intolerable,[3] still less might he read a

quibusdam fidem cum igne luctantem, religione superatas feras et in
mansuetudinem conversas. intuebitur et animas ab ipsa iam morte
revocatas. considerabit etiam de sepulcris ad mirabiles ipsorum con-
summatorum iam vitas corporum redactas. et in his omnibus iam
maius videbit spectaculum, diabolum illum, qui totum detriumphaverat
numdum sub pedibus Christi iacentem!" The Bible more interesting
and exciting than the play! Tertullian, in a similar connection,
does not refer clearly to private Bible reading, though he too says
(*De Spect.*, 29): "Si scenicae doctrinae delectant, satis nobis
litterarum est, satis versuum est, satis sentientiarum, satis etiam
canticorum, satis vocum, nec fabulae, sed veritates, nec strophae, sed
simplicitates."

[1] Col. ii. 8.
[2] 2 John 10 ; Tit. iii. 10 and elsewhere.
[3] *Vide* Polycarp *apud* Euseb., *Hist. Eccl.*, v. 20, 7.

heretic's books.[1] In this direction, indeed, a certain control, though not an organised control, was exercised even in our period, as an instructive story, which Dionysius the Great tells of himself, testifies.[2] The *Didaskalia*, moreover, teaches us that the beginnings of the efforts to thrust profane literature altogether aside fall into this period, and that the Bible was brought in to take its place. This would certainly have happened at an earlier date if there had been at that time urgent need for such regulations. But the number of educated

---

[1] As the Muratorian fragment teaches us, it was the custom even so early as A.D. 200 to add to the catalogue of the sacred writings received in the Church, either in an appendix or even in the text itself, descriptions of all that was rejected as heretical. Though these lists were in the first place drawn up to make known the books to be used in public worship, they were also meant to be in force for private reading. In the earlier days, however, wider bounds were given to private reading. Tertullian (*De Bapt.*, 17) repels an attempt to prove the right of woman to baptize from the Acta Pauli, showing that this book was a recent forgery, though written with a good intention; yet there is not one word to show that the book was not allowed to be read ("Quod si qui Pauli perperam scripta legunt, exemplum Theclae defendunt, etc.").

[2] Dionys., *Ep. ad Philem.*, *apud* Euseb., *Hist. Eccl.*, vii. 7 : Ἐγὼ δὲ καὶ τοῖς συντάγμασι καὶ ταῖς παραδόσεσι τῶν αἱρετικῶν ἐνέτυχον, χραίνων μέν μου πρὸς ὀλίγον τὴν ψυχὴν ταῖς παμμιάροις αὐτῶν ἐπιθυμήσεσιν, ὄνησιν δ' οὖν ἀπ' αὐτῶν ταύτην λαμβάνων, τὸ ἐξελέγχειν αὐτοὺς παρ' ἐμαυτῷ καὶ πολὺ πλέον βδελύττεσθαι. καὶ δή τινος ἀδελφοῦ τῶν πρεσβυτέρων [did he here exercise official control ?] με ἀπείργοντος καὶ δεδιττομένου συμφύρεσθαι τῷ τῆς πονηρίας αὐτῶν βορβόρῳ· λυμανεῖσθαι γὰρ τὴν ψυχὴν τὴν ἐμαυτοῦ, καὶ ἀληθῆ γε λέγοντος ὡς ᾐσθόμην· ὅραμα θεόπεμπτον προσελθὸν ἐπέρρωσέ με [such a drastic means was thus needed], καὶ λόγος πρός με γενόμενος προσέταξε διαρρήδην λέγων· Πᾶσιν ἐντύγχανε οἷς ἂν εἰς χεῖρας λάβοις· διευθύνειν γὰρ ἕκαστα καὶ δοκιμάζειν ἱκανὸς εἶ, καί σοι γέγονε τοῦτο ἐξ ἀρχῆς καὶ τῆς πίστεως αἴτιον [accordingly, Dionysius seems to have become a believer as the result of a com-

Christians was still comparatively small, and it is indeed probable that under such circumstances members of the Christian communities were proud rather than otherwise to greet as Christian brethren men who knew their Plato and Sophocles and had looked into all the sciences. In the second century, at all events, Justin still received in the Christian communities the title of "Philosopher," side by side with the honourable title "the Martyr."

From two passages in the pseudo-Clementine epistle *De Virginitate* we learn that into homes that possessed no Bible brethren would come and would hold a kind of "cottage lecture," in which they would read the Scriptures.[1] The writer is combating a scandal that

parative study of religions]. ἀπεδεξάμην τὸ δρᾶμα, ὡς ἀποστολικῇ φωνῇ συντρέχον τῇ λεγούσῃ πρὸς δυνατωτέρους [an apocryphal logion]· γίνεσθε δόκιμοι τραπεζῖται. We might also bring in here the story which Eusebius tells us (*Hist. Eccl.*, vi. 12) concerning Serapion, bishop of Antioch, and the community of Rhossus, relating to the Gospel of Peter. But it is, in my opinion, concerned not with private reading but with public lection. Lessing, moreover, might have sought support for his theory that Bible reading was always dependent upon the permission of the bishop or the clergy in this story. But the passage is not really appropriate for such a purpose; it only shows that the bishop decided the question when a controversy had arisen in the community as to whether or no the Gospel of Peter was a fit book for reading at public worship. In such cases the bishop would be appealed to, or would on his own initiative intervene as a matter of course.

[1] It is *a priori* certain that, side by side with the central services for public worship, smaller more or less informal assemblies continued to exist, wherein, among other things, sacred books would be read ; indeed, the central service in a special room grew out of the less formal services in private houses, and did not quite meet the needs which these

had crept in under the cloak of this practice, and he says of certain persons:[1] "Alii circumeunt per domos virginum fratrum aut sororum sub praetextu visitandi illos aut *legendi scripturas* aut exorcizandi eos aut docendi." And in another passage[2] we read: "Propterea non psallimus gentilibus neque Scripturas illis praelegimus." Hippolytus also assumes that a story

supplied, leaving out of account its relative infrequency. Ignatius refers to informal services which did not seem to him to be without danger; the existence of informal assemblies may be deduced from Hermas, *Vis.*, ii. 4, 3; and the existence of religious conventicles in which there was reading from Holy Scripture can be proved for the fourth and each following century. Zahn (*Gesch. des NTlichen Kanons*, ii. S. 111 f.) thinks that the words of the Muratorian fragment concerning the *Shepherd of Hermas* are to be referred to such informal assemblies: "legi eum quidem oportet, se publicare vero in ecclesia populo . . . in finem temporum non potest." But if the writer intended in this passage to distinguish between informal assembly and central public worship, he would necessarily, in my opinion, have expressed himself more clearly. We are therefore compelled to refer "legi" simply to private reading, which indeed thereby receives extraordinary emphasis, seeing that in the case of the book of Hermas private reading is not only allowed but even strongly commended. The meaning here can only be: "The prophecies and revelations of the Shepherd must ever abide in the memory of the faithful." This is, however, the only passage in the more ancient literature where it is plainly stated that writings which have no claim to canonical rank are to be still read, and where consequently private reading is called in to assistance. Moreover, this explanation of this passage comes to practically the same thing as Zahn's, if at least, with Jülicher (*Theol. Lit.-Ztg.*, 1889, col. 168), it is thought better to translate "oportet" by "may," not by "should" or "must."

[1] i. 10.

[2] ii. 6. Porphyry in *Macarius Magnes*, also bears witness to this house-to-house visitation of Christian teachers in order to read passages from the Scriptures (iii. 5): . . . ἀμέλει γοῦν χθές, οὐ πάλαι, γυναιξὶν εὐσχήμοσι ταῦτ' ἐπαναγινώσκοντες· Πώλησόν σου τὰ ὑπάρχοντα καὶ δὸς πτωχοῖς, καὶ ἕξεις θησαυρὸν ἐν οὐρανοῖς.

like that of Susanna was read far and wide:[1] "I now beseech you all who read this book, women and maidens, small and great, to imitate it, that ye also may receive your reward from God. . . . Ye men also, etc." The deepest and ultimate reason, however, why every Christian should read the Bible lies in this, that, just as everyone should speak to God as often as possible, so also everyone should *listen* to God as often as possible. *Oratio* and *lectio* belong together : so we read in countless passages from the later Fathers ; but Cyprian had already said it quite clearly. He writes to Donatus (c. 15): "Sit tibi vel oratio adsidua vel lectio ; nunc cum deo loquere, nunc deus tecum."[2]

That private Bible reading must have been very

---

[1] Comm. in Dan. i. 22, p. 34.

[2] Because the "lectio" presents God as the speaker, falsification of Scripture is the most grievous sin. It is, says Justin (*Dial.*, 73), worse than the setting up of the golden calf, than the sacrifices to Moloch and the slaying of the prophets. Nevertheless there was no lack of falsification, and the private circulation of the Scriptures fostered it. From this very Dialogue of Justin we learn of Christian interpolations in the Old Testament. From these we must naturally distinguish the cases wherein laymen undertook a revision of the texts of the Bible in the conviction that they were correcting them. The most important example is the text of Marcion, who indeed has corrected nothing but falsified everything. We hear that the Theodotians in Rome (*circa* A.D. 200) occupied themselves industriously with the sacred text ; unfortunately, we know no details ; it is, however, quite plain that they were concerned with manuscripts which were in private possession (Hippol. *apud* Euseb., *Hist. Eccl.*, v. 28, 15 *sq.*): ταῖς θείαις γραφαῖς ἀφόβως ἐπέβαλον τὰς χεῖρας, λέγοντες αὐτὰς διωρθωκέναι. καὶ ὅτι τοῦτο μὴ καταψευδόμενος αὐτῶν λέγω, ὁ βουλόμενος δύναται μαθεῖν. εἰ γάρ τις θελήσει συγκομίσας αὐτῶν ἑκάστου τὰ ἀντίγραφα ἐξετάζειν πρὸς ἄλληλα [this must have been possible, *i.e.* these critics must have published their recensions of the text), κατὰ πολὺ ἂν εὕροι διαφωνοῦντα [com-

5

common may be lastly established by a conclusion *a minore ad majus*—namely, from the wide circulation of Christian literature other than the books of the Bible. Here it is, of course, difficult to gain a clear and exact conception; but one has the impression that very much more in regard to the reading of theological and edifying books was required from the Christian laymen than from the laymen of other religions. Here also the spiritual character of this religion shows itself. How many theological works are dedicated to laymen, how quickly these books spread everywhere [1] and were really read even by laymen, how little of clerical character they show even so late as the third century! They were intended for *all* Christians, and even the most difficult of them are addressed to the whole of Christendom, even though only a small fraction could have been competent to read and understand them. Very significant in this connection are incidental remarks like that of Tertullian that the "gloriosissima multitudo psychicorum" are ignorant and have gained their knowledge of the new movement, together with

pare also what follows]. Arbitrary conjectures are judged to be sacrilege inspired by the daemons, because "the critics would wish to be wiser than the Holy Spirit." Compare also how Irenaeus judges those who had introduced and championed the variant 616 as the number of Antichrist (v. 30, 1). In the fourth century Sulpicius Severus writes (*Dial.*, i. 6): "Non est mirum, si in libris neotericis et recens scriptis fraus haeretica fuisset operata, quae in quibusdam locis non timuisset impetere evangelicam veritatem." Dionysius of Corinth had already made the same complaint (Euseb., *Hist. Eccl.*, iv. 23, 12).

[1] See the evidence adduced in my *Geschichte der Mission.*, i.[2] S. 314 f.

the regulations of the Paraclete, "*sola* forsitan *lectione*, non etiam intentione."[1] "*Sola lectione*"—it is strange indeed that they should have gained their know-ledge in this way, and we conclude therefrom that the knowledge of the Bible must have been still more widely spread.

In time it must, of course, have been more and more clearly seen that it was unwise to launch young and immature Christians rudderless upon the wide ocean of the Bible.   It was this that led Cyprian to publish his *Testimonia*, a systematised collection of Biblical quotations for the use of the " tirones," " quae legenti prosint ad prima fidei liniamenta formanda,"[2] a book which quickly gained wide circulation and had immense influence.   But Cyprian had not the slightest intention that his book was to take permanently the place of the Bible ; rather he meant that, as soon as his book had fulfilled its purpose, it was to give way to the Bible itself.[3] " Plus roboris tibi dabitur et magis ac magis intellectus cordis operabitur scrutanti scripturas veteres et novas plenius et universa librorum spiritualium volumina perlegenti, nam nos nunc de divinis fontibus implevimus modicum, quod tibi interim mitteremus, bibere uberius et saturari copiosius poteris, si tu quoque

[1] *De Jejunio*, 11.

[2] *Testim.*, Praef.

[3] The *Testimonia* still had their value even for one who had advanced to independent reading of the Bible, for every Christian was supposed to have at hand in concise form the Scriptural proof for the clauses of the Baptismal Creed, that is, the rule of faith ; *vide infra*, what Cyril of Jerusalem directs.

ad eosdem divinae plenitudinis fontes nobiscum pariter potaturus accesseris." It is also true of other works of the Fathers that they were intended to precede and lead up to reading of the Bible, though this is not expressly stated as it is in the introduction to Cyprian's *Testimonia*. Theoretically, the Bible was the one book, the only book of edification; but practically it presented, especially to readers in the Latin tongue, such serious difficulties in the way of comprehension, and so much that could only be rendered edifying by interpretation, that there was a great demand for books of edification apart from the demand for works of introduction to, and interpretation of, the Bible. We shall see in the next chapter what an important position, side by side with the Bible, the treatises and epistles of Cyprian attained in the fourth century.

Almost all that we have hitherto written concerning the private use of Holy Scripture receives ample support from the works of the great Biblical scholar Origen. I would, however, adduce from the multitude of pertinent passages those only which contain something of more special interest.

1. Origen speaks pretty frequently of the reading of Holy Scripture at home, and strongly commends it. It should be read every day,[1] and even one to two hours

---

[1] Hom. x. in Genes., 2 T. viii. (ed. Lommatzch), p. 218: "Rebecca quotidie veniebat ad puteos . . . docet quotidie venire ad puteos scripturarum, ad aquas spiritus sancti et haurire semper, etc."

seem to him too little to devote to Divine things.[1]
The latter remark shows him advancing along the path
which he has often enough trodden at other times, *i.e.*
he holds up before the general body of Christians an
ideal which can only be realised in the cloister. "Con-
versum esse ad dominum est, si his omnibus [sc. terrenis]
terga vertamus et studio, actibus, mente, sollicitudine
verbo dei operam demus et in lege eius die et nocte
meditemur, omissis omnibus deo vacemus, exerceamur
in testimoniis eius" (Hom. in Exod. xii. 27, 2 T. ix.
p. 143).

2. Origen speaks in several passages of the *taedium
verbi divini* among Christians; the reading of the
Scriptures in church and at home is distasteful to them,
indeed they do all they can to escape from it.[2] This
is one of the characteristics of a worldly popular
Christianity which we first find depicted in the works
of Origen and Cyprian, and which strikes us the more

[1] Hom. ii. in Num., 1 T. x. p. 19: "Sed et unusquisque nostrum
si de cibo et potu sollicitus sit et omnem curam in rebus saecularibus
gerat, unam vero aut duas horas ex integro die etiam deo deputet et ad
orationem veniat in ecclesiam vel in transitu verbum dei audiat,
praecipuam vero curam erga sollicitudinem saeculi et ventris expendat:
iste non complet mandatum, quod dicit, ut homo secundum ordinem
suum incedat." In reference to home reading see also Hom. xi.
in Gen., 3 T. viii. p. 231 ; xii. in Gen., 5 T. viii. p. 239 *sq.* ; Hom.
xii. in Exod., 2 T. ix. p. 143 *sq.* "Divina lectio" side by side
with "orationes assiduae" and "sermo doctrinae" ("non solum
in ecclesia audire verbum dei, sed in domibus vestris exerceri")
as "nutrimentum spiritus," Hom. xi. in Levit., 7 T. ix. p.
356.

[2] Hom. x. in Genes., 1 T. viii. p. 216 ; Hom. xii. in Exod., 2 T. ix.
p. 142 *sq.* ; Hom. xx. in Iesu Nave, 1 T. xi. p. 170.

forcibly because the earlier Fathers in their writings so seldom refer to it. Origen speaks of it with the deepest grief; for these people lose that daily renewing of the spirit which is the fruit of daily reading of the Bible.[1]

3. The fact that the style of the Biblical narratives and exhortations was not in accord with a more refined taste contributed somewhat to this *taedium verbi divini*. It is not only against Celsus[2] that Origen defends the unassuming form of the Bible (because it was the purpose of the Holy Spirit to be intelligible to those also who were uneducated and insignificant in the eyes of the world, and because mysteries lay hidden behind the outward form), but he also defends it in the Homilies.[3] In contrast with the *taedium verbi divini* felt by many Catholic Christians stands the opposite evil,

---

[1] Comment in Rom., lib. ix. 1 T. vii. p. 288. "Renovatur sensus noster per exercitia sapientiae et meditationem verbi dei et legis eius intelligentiam spiritualem, et quanto quis quotidie ex scripturarum proficit lectione, quanto altius intellectus eius accedit, tanto semper novus et quotidie novus efficitur."

[2] *Cont. Cels.*, vi. 1 f.

[3] *Vide, e.g.*, Hom. xv. in Gen., 1 T. viii. p. 259: "Quae observationes ostendunt scripturam divinam non, ut plurimis videtur, inerudito et agresti sermone compositam, sed secundum disciplinam divinae eruditionis aptatam, neque tantum historicis narrationibus, quantum rebus et sensibus mysticis servientem." Similarly in many other passages, *e.g.* Hom. viii. in Iesu Nave, 1 T. xi. p. 74: "Deprecamur vos non cum taedio vel fastidió ea, quae leguntur, audire pro eo quod minus delectabilis eorum videtur esse narratio." *De Princip.* iv. 1. 7. 26.

the "much searching" into the Scriptures of the
heretics, who thereby rush into perdition.[1]

4. As for the understanding of Holy Scripture,
Origen necessarily holds fast to the principle that the
Scriptures are quite accessible even to simple believers;
they must therefore have them daily at hand. The
thought, that priests and deacons as such are more
capable of understanding Scripture than laymen, is
absolutely alien to Origen. On the contrary, he states
openly that laymen could often be better exegetes
than the clergy, who often enough had the veil drawn
before their eyes.[2] But while he, on the other hand,
states that the Catholic Gnostic whose mind is en-
lightened by the Holy Spirit is alone capable of
entering into the depths of Holy Scripture,[3] the con-

---

[1] Hom. iv. in Levit., 5 T. ix. p. 223: "Est ergo ostendere, qui
multum quaerendo invenit perditionem: ut verbi gratia dicamus:
haeretici ad construenda et defendenda dogmata sua multum perquirunt
et discutiunt in scripturis divinis ut inveniant perditionem." Similarly
Tertullian, in his treatise *De Praescr. Haeret.*

[2] Hom. ii. in Num., 1 T. x. p. 19: "Saepe accidit ut is, qui
humilem sensum gerit et abjectum et qui terrena sapit, excelsum
sacerdotii gradum vel cathedram doctoris insideat, et ille qui spiritualis
est et a terrena conversatione tam liber, ut possit examinare omnia et
ipse a nemine iudicari, vel inferioris ministerii ordinem teneat vel
etiam in plebeia multitudine relinquatur, etc." Origen here speaks
from his own experience.

[3] *Cf.* Greg. Thaumat., *Panegyr. in Orig.*, c. 15. He says that
Origen himself as an expounder of the Bible drew from the same
source of inspiring power as the prophets. As for the obscurities
of Scripture, Gregory advances the hypothesis that they are so
because our souls are unworthy to understand them, and that we
have lost through the Fall the power of understanding what is really
clear.

science of the great scientific teacher also reacts to the
claim of the simple and immature believers, and he
recommends them to read the books that were easier
and accessible to their understanding. He writes:— [1]
"Inter homines sunt quaedam differentiae in appe-
tendis cibis, et alius quidem, qui bene sanus est et
habitudine corporis valens, fortem cibum requirit et
credit confiditque se edere omnia, velut robustissimi
quique athletarum. si quis vero infirmiorem se sentit
et invalidum, delectatur oleribus et fortem cibum pro

---

[1] Hom. xxvii. in Num., 1 T. x. p. 332 f. Referring especially to the
Song of Songs he speaks as follows (Prolog. in Cantic. Cant., T. xiv.
p. 288 *sq.*): "Primo scire nos oportet, quoniam, sicut puerilis aetas
non movetur ad amorem passibilem, ita nec ad capienda quidem verba
haec parvula et infantilis interioris hominis aetas admittitur, illorum
scilicet, qui lacte in Christo aluntur, non cibo forti, et qui nunc primum
rationabile et sine dolo lac concupiscunt. . . . Parvuli si veniant ad
haec loca, potest fieri, ut nihil quidem ex hac scriptura proficiant nec
tamen valde laedantur, vel ipsa quae scripta sunt legentes, vel quae ad
explanationem eorum dicenda sunt recensentes. si vero aliquis
accesserit, qui secundum carnem tantummodo vir est, huic tali non
parum ex hac scriptura discriminis periculique nascetur . . . occasione
divinae scripturae commoveri et incitari videbitur ad libidinem
carnis. ob hoc ergo moneo et consilium do omni, qui nondum
carnis et sanguinis molestiis caret neque ab affectu naturae materialis
abscedit, ut a lectione libelli huius eorumque quae in eo dicentur
penitus temperat. aiunt enim observari etiam apud Hebraeos,
quod, nisi quis ad aetatem perfectam maturamque pervenerit,
libellum hunc ne quidem in manibus tenere permittatur. sed et
illud ab iis accepimus custodiri, quandoquidem moris est apud eos,
omnes scripturas a doctoribus et a sapientibus tradi pueris simul
et eas, quas δευτερώσεις appellant, ad ultimum quattuor ista [scil.
retineri], i.e. principium Genesis, in quo mundi creatura describitur,
et Ezechielis prophetae principia, in quibus de Cherubim refertur, et
finem, in quo templi aedificatio continetur, et hunc Cantici Canticorum librum."

sui infirmitate corporis non recipit. si vero sit aliquis
parvulus, etiamsi voce indicare non possit, re tamen
ipsa nullam aliam quam lactis requirit alimoniam. . . .
Sicut in nutrimentis corporis multas dedimus differentias,
ita et natura rationabilis, quae ratione et verbo dei
pascitur, non omnis uno atque eodem verbo nutritur.
unde ad similitudinem corporalis exempli est aliquibus
etiam in verbo dei cibus lactis: apertior scilicet
simpliciorque doctrina, ut de moralibus esse solet, quae
praeberi consuevit iis, qui initia habent in divinis
studiis et prima eruditionis rationabilis elementa
suscipiunt. his ergo cum recitatur talis aliqua
divinorum voluminum lectio, in qua non videatur
aliquid obscurum, libenter accipiunt, verbi causa, ut
est libellus *Hester* aut *Iudith* vel etiam *Tobiae* aut
mandata *Sapientiae*. si vero legatur ei liber *Levitici*,
offenditur continuo animus et quasi non suum refugit
cibum. . . . Sed et alius, cum leguntur *Evangelia*
vel *Apostolus* aut *Psalmi*, laetus suscipit, libenter
amplectitur et velut remedia quaedam infirmitatis
suae inde colligens gaudet. huic si legatur *Numer-
orum* liber et ista maxime loca, quae nunc habemus
in manibus (Num. xxxiii.), nihil haec ad utilitatem
nihil ad infirmitatis suae remedium aut animae salutem
prodesse iudicabit." Here we are told in plain
words what we otherwise could only conjecture, that
the Old Testament Apocrypha formed the first stage
in Bible reading, the Psalms, Gospels, and Epistles
the second, while the remaining books of the Bible

took their place in order as further stages.[1] May it
not be that this temporal precedence of the Apocrypha
in Alexandria and elsewhere existed in late Judaism,
and thence passed over into the practice of the Church?
This preparatory course was by no means in every aspect
a fortunate one for the development of the Christian
character. How many may have carefully read only
these books during their catechumenate, and afterwards
have assimilated only fragments of the remaining books!
This was not, of course, what Origen meant; he wished
that a man, in his course of progressive reading, should
not shrink back even from the difficult and obscure
passages of Holy Scripture, for indeed even in that
which is not understood there lies power for good.[2]

---

[1] Origen (Comm. in Matth., T. iii. p. 40) cannot be referring to the
whole Old Testament, but only to the more difficult books of the same,
when he urges that a man should not read only the books of the New
Testament: Συνάγειν παντὶ τρόπῳ πειρατέον ἐν τῇ καρδίᾳ ἡμῶν διὰ τοῦ
προσέχειν τῇ ἀναγνώσει, τῇ παρακλήσει, τῇ διδασκαλίᾳ καὶ ἐν τῷ νόμῳ
κυρίου μελετᾶν ἡμέρας καὶ νυκτός, οὐ μόνον τὰ καινὰ τῶν εὐαγγελίων
καὶ τῶν ἀποστόλων καὶ τῆς ἀποκαλύψεως αὐτῶν λόγια, ἀλλὰ καὶ παλαιὰ
τοῦ σκιὰν ἔχοντος τῶν μελλόντων ἀγαθῶν νόμου καὶ τῶν ἀκολούθως
αὐτοῖς προφητευσάντων προφητῶν.

[2] Compare Hom. xx. in Iesu Nave, 1 T. xi. p. 170 sq. Here Origen
beautifully and truly shows how "taedium" may arise from the fact
that the passage read is not understood, but he exhorts the reader or
hearer to strive to understand, in the hope that even what is more
difficult will become clear. He proceeds to say that even the sound
of sacred words in the ear, though their sense may be obscure, is
beneficial; he reminds his readers of the power of the mere words of
heathen magic: how much greater must be the effect of sacred words!
We have here truly antique feeling! Origen, indeed, often astonishes
us by saying things which show that he shared much of the superstitious feeling of his times.

We hear of Origen himself [1] that he, " exercised already from childhood in the Holy Scriptures, had laid a good foundation for the teaching of the Faith. He had, moreover, spent no slight labour in their study, for his father, besides seeing that his son was instructed in the usual subjects of study, made a special point of instruction in the Scriptures. He incited him to practise himself above all in the doctrines of religion in preference to study of Greek learning, *and made him each day learn and say by heart some passages* (ἐκμαθήσεις καὶ ἐπαγγελίας, *scil.* of Holy Scripture). This was in no way distasteful to the boy ; he indeed undertook the task with the greatest joy. He was not satisfied with the simple and superficial reading of Holy Scripture, but he strove to go further and, child as he was, to search out its deeper significance, so that he even perplexed his father with his questions as to the significance of divinely inspired Scripture." We have here a glimpse into the home of an ordinary Christian citizen : the children daily hear the Scriptures read and learn passages of them by heart. A Bible was not only in the home : the Bible was the principal text-book of education ; the chief aim in the whole training of a child was that he should be taught to understand the Bible.

Porphyry, the great opponent and rival of Origen, conducted his forcible attack upon Christianity as an attack upon the Bible. If we compare the plan of his great work—so far as we can form an opinion from its fragments

[1] *Vide* Euseb., *Hist. Eccl.*, vi. 2, 6 *sq.*

—with the entirely different plan of Celsus' polemical treatise, it is at once obvious that the great book of Christendom had in the course of eighty years won a position so fundamental and central that Christianity could only be judged by it, and that it was now in the fullest sense accessible to the public. Porphyry had not to drag hidden mysteries into the light; his business was to refute by stringent historical and philosophical criticism the public documents of Christianity. He therefore never pretends to enlighten the educated public concerning the nature of Christianity, as if this were concealed by the Christians; his intention is only to display before the eyes of this public, which will not take the trouble to study this religion, its pitiful and utter worthlessness. From this fact we can judge of the degree of publicity of the Christian sacred writings.[1]

[1] Hierocles, in his controversial treatise, adopts exactly the same procedure as Porphyry: in order to refute the Christians he makes an assault on the Bible: "in libris suis ita falsitatem Scripturae sacrae arguere conatus est, tamquam sibi esset tota contraria. nam quaedam capita quae, repugnare sibi videbantur exposuit adeo multa, adeo intima enumerans, ut aliquando ex eadem disciplina fuisse videbatur . . . nisi forte casu in manus eius divinae litterae inciderunt. quae igitur temeritas erat id audere dissolvere quod illi nemo interpretatus est." Hierocles also laid emphasis on the barbaric style of the Scriptures: " discipulos Christi rudes et indoctos fuisse testatus est" (Lactant. v. 2). One may besides raise the question whether one reason that Porphyry and Hierocles investigated the Bible so microscopically and attacked it so bitterly was because they knew that educated Greeks were beginning to devote sympathetic attention to the Bible or to parts of it—indeed, that Neoplatonic philosophers were beginning to study Moses and St John with zeal and approval, and

Wealthy Christians also contributed to this publicity by having Bibles copied at their own expense and by giving them or lending them to their poorer brothers and sisters. Thus we are told of Pamphilus, an older contemporary and the venerated friend of Eusebius (Hieron., *adv. Ruf.*, i. 9): "Scripturas sanctas non ad legendum tantum sed et adhabendum tribuebat promptissime, nec solum viris sed et feminis, quas vidisset lectioni deditas, unde et multos codices praeparabat, ut, cum necessitas poposcisset, volentibus largiretur." Pamphilus thus had Bibles copied to keep in stock.

At the close of the period which we are now considering stand Arnobius and Lactantius; both are laymen, and both learnt their Christianity from the Holy Scriptures. Arnobius defends the Scriptures

---

to make formal quotations from them (*vide* my *Missionsgeschichte*, i.[2] S. 415: Numenius read and quoted from the Old Testament with great respect, Amelius from the Gospel of St John). Celsus had already been obliged to admit that there were things even to be commended in the sacred Scriptures of the Christians and in the sayings of Jesus, but he believed that all these could be explained away by the supposition of plagiarism from Plato. This easy theory fell into the background in the succeeding period; the books then became only the more "dangerous," especially for philosophers who believed in a revelation. Moreover, Porphyry himself, before he wrote his great work against the Christians, thought much more favourably of some parts of the Bible, and speaks of them with appreciation in his book, *Philosophy from the Oracles*. He had thus himself experienced the attraction of the Bible, and had for a time exerted himself to promote mutual understanding and reconciliation. Is not his frantic zeal against St John and St Paul (*vide* the Philosopher in *Macarius Magnes*.) to be explained from the fact that he wished at any price to repress the increasing interest which Greeks were beginning to feel in these authors !

from the charge, firstly, that they are false and that
their history is mere invention; secondly, that they
were written by rude and unlearned men ("et id circo
non facili auditione credenda") and swarmed with
barbarisms and solecisms.[1] It is possible that these
charges were based upon the work of Porphyry,
though it is not necessary to assume this, for the
Holy Scriptures were already much discussed, and
the same reproaches were to be heard from the
lips even of members of the Christian communities.
The charge of barbaric style applied to the Latin
Bible in much higher degree than to the Greek Bible,
and must have been deeply felt by everyone. From
the work of Arnobius we have the impression that the
discussion of the Bible had become a public controversy
in the great world of literature, and we gain the same
impression also from Lactantius. This could only have
happened if the Bible was in the hands of a multitude
of people. Lactantius also is compelled to deal with

---

[1] Arnob., i. 55 sq., ii. 6 : " Ab indoctis hominibus et rudibus scripta
sunt." "Barbarismis, soloecismis obsitae sunt res vestrae et vitiorum
deformitate pollutae." A similar judgment also prevented the youthful
Augustine from entering deeply into the Scriptures : "incessu humilis
. . . visa mihi indigna quam Tullianae dignitati compararem." As a
matter of fact, the style was in many places dreadful ; many verses
gave no sense at all, because the translator did not himself understand
them : e.g. Baruch ii. 29 ran, in helpless word-for-word translation :
" Dicens : si non audieritis vocis meae, si sonos magnos hagminis iste
avertatur in minima in gentibus, hubi dispergam ibi." A correspondence between St Paul and Seneca was forged, with a view to removing
the stumbling-blocks afforded by the style of the Pauline epistles in
the Latin version.

the charge that the Bible was written in a rude and poor style.[1] Here again the defence is that " the Bible is meant for the common people."[2] He further remarks that other works of Christian literature also found no favour among the cultured—a proof in itself that they were noticed. "Cyprianus a doctis huius saeculi, quibus forte scripta eius innotuerunt derideri solet." "Audivi ego," he continues, "quendam hominem sane disertum, qui eum immutata una litera 'Coprianum' vocaret, quasi quod elegans ingenium et melioribus rebus aptum ad aniles fabulas contulisset. quodsi accidit hoc ei cuius eloquentia non insuavis est, quid tandem putemus accidere eis quorum sermo ieiunus est et ingratus?"[3] Finally Lactantius finds himself forced to admit that the Bible was written in a poor style, and therefore needed explanation if it was to do its work; there was, however, a lack of experienced teachers fitted to deal with people of culture.[4]

The Bible is difficult in places, the Bible is not

[1] Lactant., v. 1.

[2] Loc. cit., "ut ad populum."

[3] Cf. also Epitome 57 (62): "Inde est quod scriptis caelestibus, quia videntur incompta, non facile credunt, qui aut ipsi sunt diserti aut diserta legere malunt: non quaerunt vera, sed dulcia, immo illis haec videntur verissima, quae auribus blandiuntur"; vide also vi. 21: "Homines litterati, cum ad religionem dei accesserint, ab aliquo imperito doctore fundati, minus credunt."

[4] Loc. cit., v. 2, 4. Cyprian also, according to Lactantius, used the wrong method in dealing with Demetrianus: "dilatis paulisper divinis lectionibus," which of course could make no impression upon the man; he ought to have pressed him first with arguments appealing to the intellect.

attractive in form, from the Bible heretics derive their
godless doctrines—nevertheless it must remain the
great public book of Christendom, to which all men
must be introduced and with which all must make
themselves acquainted by daily reading. This was the
conviction of the Church, a conviction that nothing
could shake. That she acted according, to this conviction is proved by the persecution under Diocletian
and his colleagues, which was at the same time in
express form a persecution of the Bible.[1] The State
sought to destroy the Church by the destruction of its
buildings, its officials, and the Bible: in these it saw
the foundations of the Church. This is the best proof
of the position which the Bible occupied among
Christians, and of the publicity which it had already
gained in the outside world.[2]

The copies of the Bible were sought for at first in
the Churches and demanded from the clergy; indeed, it
is possible that an actual edict ran: "ut libros deificos
peterent (extorquerent) *de manu episcoporum et presby-
terorum.*"[3] The object was to destroy the Church as an

[1] Augustin., *Contr. Cresc.*, iii. 26: "persecutio codicum tradendorum."
[2] No alteration had taken place in its position among Christians—
Lessing's attempt to prove such an alteration in this period remained,
and will always remain, abortive. *Vide* the fragment, "Von den
Traditores," *Werke*, Bd. xvii. S. 183 ff. ; to the general world, however,
the Bible, of course, meant something much more than it did two
generations previously.
[3] *Acta S. Felic.* ; Euseb., *Hist. Eccl.*, viii. 2, reports generally : τὰς
μὲν ἐκκλησίας εἰς ἔδαφος φέρειν, τὰς δὲ γραφὰς ἀφανεῖς πυρὶ γενέσθαι.
In the *Acta purg. Felicis* (*Optati Opp.*, p. 198, ed. Ziwsa) we read:
"ut quascumque scripturas haberent Christiani, incendio traderent."

organism in all its elements, but for the moment to leave the laity and all that belonged to them untouched. Accordingly, strictly speaking, only those Bibles came into account that belonged to the communities;[1] the Holy Scriptures, however, especially in heathen eyes, were not regarded as private books, and the laymen who possessed such books, possessed in them something which was in theory the property of the religious community. Thus the executive officials could here proceed according to their discretion : they could extend their search to the laity, or they could confine themselves to a search among the clergy. It soon necessarily followed that special attention was paid to the houses of the deacons and lectors, as, indeed, we learn from our sources of information. In many cases probably the clergy alone suffered from this persecution[2] (and some of them became traditores);[3] but in other cases we hear that laymen also were compelled to give up their

[1] Ephraem Syrus, *Serm.* iii., *De fide*, thinks only of these where he speaks of the persecution against the Bible.

[2] The proconsul in Carthage did not wish to force an entrance into the home of the bishop, but contented himself with searching the Church (*vide* August., *Brev. coll. die* iii. c. 13).

[3] Not only the Bibles, but all written documents (together with the furniture of the Church), were asked for ; indeed, the officials would not have been able to distinguish ; vide *Gesta apud Zenophil*, p. 186 (*Optati Opp.*, ed. Ziwsa). It may be conjectured that the opinion that the delivery of Bibles to the officials was a terrible crime was due to superstitious ideas ; this may be partly true, but loyalty to the faith itself forbade the delivery. Moreover, even pious Christians of the fourth and fifth centuries, such as Augustine, and especially Optatus in his seventh book, offered excuses for the traditores.

6

Bibles; for the object was the destruction of all Bibles, and laymen were frequently left unmolested because it was often supposed that they had no such books in their possession. We are not here concerned with these transactions, though the numbers of the Bibles for individual churches, and the information concerning the "Libraries of the Churches," is most interesting; [1]

[1] We cannot always decide whether some of these Bibles were always kept in the houses of the clergy or whether they were brought there as a temporary measure. The most important information is to be found in the *Gesta apud Zenophilum*. The information there given concerning the confiscation of the Scriptures in the community of Cirta is unfortunately of little use, because we do not learn anything of the contents of the thirty-seven volumes which were confiscated. Certainly they were not *complete* Bibles; we can only say that the "codex unus pernimius major" may have been either an Old or a New Testament. It is even possible that the manuscripts did not all of them contain portions of the Bible; some may have contained liturgical matter. The account runs as follows (p. 187 *sq.*): "Felix flamen perpetuus curator reipublicae dixit: proferte scripturas, quas habetis, ut praeceptis imperatorum et iussioni parere possimus [the scene is a Church; the furniture had been already given up]. Catullinus protulit *codicem unum pernimium maiorem.*" In answer to the question where the other books were, the deacons answered that they were in the possession of the lectors. "Et cum ventum est ad domum Eugeni [lectoris] . . . . protulit Eugenius *codices quattuor.*" . . . "et cum ventum fuisset ad domum Felicis sarsoris [lectoris] protulit *codices quinque,* et cum ventum esset ad domum Victorini, protulit *codices octo,* et cum ventum fuisset ad domum Proiecti, protulit *codices V. maiores et minores II.*, et cum ad grammatici domum ventum fuisset. . . . Victor grammaticus [lector] obtulit *codices II. et quiniones quattuor.* Felix flamen perpetuus curator reipublicae Victori dixit: profer scripturas; plus habes. Victor grammaticus dixit: si plus habuissem, dedissem. et cum ventum fuisset ad domum Eutici Caesariensis [lectoris], Felix Euticio dixit: profer scripturas, quas habes. . . . Euticius dixit: non habeo. Felix dixit: professio tua actis haeret. et cum ventum fuisset ad domum Coddeonis [lectoris], protulit uxor eius *codices sex.* Felix dixit: quaere, ne plus habeatis, profer.

not many, however, of the accounts go into details,
though they give abundant evidence in general. The
most interesting are the Acts of Agape, Chionia, and
their companions. Chionia in answer to the question:
" Have ye any of the commentaries, parchments, or books
of the godless Christians ? " replied: " We have none;
the reigning emperors have taken them all away from us."
In the case of Irene it is proved that she had secreted
a large number of parchments, books, lists, " codicilli et
paginae scripturarum," and had declared that she knew
nothing of them. When asked whether since then they
had not read the Scriptures together, the women
answered: " No, we did not dare to do so; it was the
greatest grief to us that we could no longer read them
by day and night as we ever were accustomed until last
year, when we hid them." [1]

Many of the laity could console themselves for the
loss of their Bibles, for many passages were fixed
firmly in their memory. Eusebius tells us from his own
knowledge of a blind Egyptian, John by name, who was
banished to Palestine,[2] that " he possessed whole books of
the Holy Scriptures not on tables of stone, as the divine
Apostle says, nor on skins of beasts or on paper, which
moth and time can devour, but . . . in his heart, so

mulier respondit: non habeo. Felix Bovi servo publico dixit: intra
et quaere, ne plus habeat. servus publicus dixit: quaesivi et non
inveni. Felix Victorino, Silvano et Caroso [fossoribus] dixit: si quid
minus factum fuerit, vos contingit periculum."

[1] Optatus (i. 13) knows of laymen also who were traditores.

[2] Euseb., *De Mart. Pal.*, 13.

that, as from a rich literary treasure, he could, ever
as he wished, repeat now passages from the Law
and the Prophets, now from the historical books,
now from the Gospels and the Apostolic epistles."
In antiquity there was much learning by heart,
and much also from the Bible was committed to
memory. Eusebius incidentally informs us that
Christian children began by learning the canticles of
the Bible.[1]

In the Church before the time of Constantine the
Bible had a different, because much more important,
position from that occupied by books of revelation
and religion in the heathen cults. It was the book
of faith, of discipline, of life, and of knowledge for
each and all, and theologians of the school of
Origen regarded it as God's second creation, ranking with the creation of the world. According to
the principle of the Church, absolutely all her
members ought to be "taught of God," *i.e.* ought
to live in the Bible and find there the daily food
of their souls. It was only the hard facts of existence that prevented this ideal from being realised.
The Church was never content with reading the
Scriptures to her children at public worship, rather she
exhorted each and all—man and woman, small and
great—to read the Bible daily. Eusebius desires that
even the beginner, who had only just come into close
touch with Christianity, should at once be made

[1] Euseb., *Praepar. Evang.*, xii. 20.

acquainted with the Scriptures.[1] In this period the Pauline motto, "Faith comes from preaching," was completed by the other, "Faith comes from reading." Neither did the Christians in their procedure pay too much heed to the warning of our Lord : "Give not that which is holy to the dogs, neither cast ye your pearls before swine "; they wished rather to do too much than too little. No doubt a powerful stimulus was thus given to the extension of the art of reading, and therein of education. The Church was compelled to lay stress upon Bible reading because, according to her doctrine, souls could be lost through *want of knowledge*,[2] and so she became the great elementary school-mistress of the Greeks and the Romans.[3] And not of these peoples

---

[1] Euseb., *Praepar. Evang.*, xii. 3 : Παρ' ἡμῖν τοῖς μὲν ἄρτι εἰσαγομένοις καὶ τὴν ἕξιν ἀτελέσιν, ὡς ἂν τὰς ψυχὰς νηπίοις, ἁπλούστερον ἢ ἐν ταῖς θείαις γραφαῖς ἀνάγνωσις παραδίδοται μετὰ τοῦ δεῖν πιστεύειν ὡς θεοῦ λόγοις τοῖς ἐμφερομένοις παρακελεύεσθαι.

[2] This is a most important point of difference from other religions. In spite of the inroads of mystery and sacrament, the Christian religion held fast to the conviction that every Christian must *know* what he believed, and must therefore in some degree possess an intellectual understanding of his religion ; *vide* Optatus, vii. 1, p. 165 : "Lex [the Bible] non magis pro doctrina quam pro futuro iudicio scripta esse videtur, ut sciat peccator quid pati possit, si minus iuste vixerit." Thus the Christian Church approximated to the attitude of the schools of contemporary religious philosophy, as was very soon noticed. Cyril of Jerusalem expressed in plain words the danger of ignorance of the Holy Scriptures, and gives the Creed as a substitute ; *vide infra*.

[3] This was the more important, seeing that in the second and still more in the third century not only higher but also elementary education went terribly downhill. Hence the increase in the number of those who could not read.

only. The Church, especially the Greek Church—for
the Latin Church proceeded otherwise,—pressed on to
translation of the Bible into other tongues, and by thus
neglecting her own national prerogative laid the foundations of national literature among peoples that
hitherto had possessed no literature, and in some cases
were even without the knowledge of writing. All this
came about because the Greeks demanded that the
Bible must be read. The beginnings of the Coptic
version of the Bible fall already into our period; the
Armenian and Gothic versions must have followed soon
afterwards.

Naturally, even so early as this period the Bible, after
heathen fashion, was pressed into the service of superstition, much more frequently, indeed, than the very
scanty evidence would imply. We learn incidentally
that Julius Africanus, in his *Cestoi*, gave as a receipt
for keeping wine from going sour that one should place
in the vessel an apple upon which had been scratched
the words: "Taste and see how gracious the Lord is";
we hear of verses from the Bible being used as phylac-
teries; of exorcisms by means of words of Scripture,
and suchlike; but we may well conjecture that of a
great multitude of instances of this kind only a few
have come down to us. But the worst of all is that even
a theologian such as Origen should have sympathised
with the magical use of the sacred Word.[1] But such

[1] *Vide supra*, p. 74, note 2. I give the passage in full because of
its importance (Hom. xx. 1 in Iesu Nave): "Verum tamen etiam

superstitious misuse was only to be expected as a matter of course in a time full of superstition, when men could only comprehend sacred things as magical charms.[1]

illud admoneo, non parum ex hoc ipso utilitatis animae conferri, quod aures nostras, licet obscura videantur, penetrant. si enim creditum est a gentibus, quod quaedam carmina, quas praecantationes appellant, quibus istud artis est, insusurrantes, nominibus quibusdam compellatis, quae ne illi quidem, qui invocant, norunt, ex solo vocis sono vel sopiunt serpentes vel etiam de cavernis protrahunt abstrusis. saepe autem et in corporibus humanis tumores vel fervores aut alia huiuscemodi voce sola reprimere dicuntur, interdum etiam animae stuporem quendam sensus infligere, ubi tamen Christi non restiterit fides : quanto magis totius praecantationis et carminis validiorem et potentiorem ducendam credimus quamcumque illam scripturae sanctae vel sermonum vel nominum appellationem ! sicut enim apud infideles contrariae virtutes, audientes illa vel illa nomina in carminibus vel praecantationibus adsunt et exhibent famulatum et dant operam in hoc, ad quod invocari se ex illo vel ex illo nomine senserint, . . . eo magis utique coelestes virtutes et angeli dei, qui nobiscum sunt, videntes faciem eius libenter et grate accipiunt, si semper verba scripturae et horum nominum appellationes velut carmina quaedam et praecantationes ex nostro ore promamus. *quia etsi nos non intelligimus, quae de ore proferimus, illae tamen virtutes, quae nobis adsunt, intelligunt et velut carmine quodam invitatae adesse nobis et ferre auxilium delectantur.*"

[1] If we wished to be in the fashion we should be forced to speak of this use as the " religionsgeschichtlich," or as that which is " religionsgeschichtlich" important ; but it is really unimportant and without interest. The use of the Bible which is " religionsgeschichtlich " important is that wherein the Christian religion distinguishes itself from other religions in its attitude towards its sacred writings. Optatus, in his great work, lib. vii., attacks a too exaggerated veneration for the book of the Bible (he is of course influenced by his desire to rehabilitate the traditores as much as possible). He declares (c. i.) that the real Bible, so to say, is that which is written in the heart, and that that which is written on paper or parchment stands only in the second line (p. 163) ; also that the Law (the Bible) was not given " ut ipsa pro deo coleretur" (p. 165); moreover (*loc. cit.*), that it is not written that Abraham heard the Scripture and believed, but that " Abraham believed

Yet the really great and important point was this, that
the Bible played so tremendous a part as the book for
faith, for morals, for inward and spiritual life, and that
men were required to understand this book, however
limited that understanding might well be.[1] If the
Church defined the Bible as the collection of *effata
divina,* indeed as a collection of oracles; if she even used
the Bible for inquiring into the future; if in increasing
measure she tolerated or even encouraged all kinds of
superstition in connection with the Bible as with the
sacraments, still in the main she sought in the Bible
something quite different from what the heathen sought
in their books of religion: she read in it the grand
progress of history from the Creation to the turning-

God, and it was reckoned to him for righteousness"; again, that man
was not made for the Holy Scripture, but the Holy Scripture for man
(p. 166); and finally, that a man must die for God: he is not called upon
to die for the Bible (*loc. cit.*).

[1] Among the Latins this requirement during our period still lies in
the background (there were no exegetes before Victorinus of Pettau to
afford guidance); among the Greeks it received the sharpest emphasis
from Origen. *The study of the Bible which he required of itself must
drive a man into the cloister.* "Tu ergo si volueris filium tuum scire
literas, quas liberales vocant, scire grammaticam vel rhetoricam disciplinam, numquid non ab omnibus eum vacuum et liberum reddis?
numquid non omissis ceteris huic uni studio dare operam facis?
paedagogos, magistros, libros, impensas, nihil prorsus deesse facis, quod
usque perfectum propositi studii opus reportet. quis nostrum ita se ad
divinae legis studia convertit? quis nostrum ita operam dedit? quis
tanto studio ac labore divina quaerit studia, quanto quaesivit humana?
et quid conquerimur, si, quod non didicimus, ignoramus? aliqui
vestrum ut recitari audierint, quae leguntur, statim discedunt. nulla
ex his, quae dicta sunt, inquisitio ad invicem, nulla collatio." (Hom.
xii. in Exod., 2 T. ix. p. 143.)

point of the ages; she read it as the fundamental
document of redemption and salvation for all mankind,
which claimed the most devoted study and zealous
application of the understanding; and she drew from
it all power for a holy and blissful life. And for this
very reason she gave it the greatest publicity.

During the last decade Egypt has opened up to us
fragments of the books of the Bible in exemplars of
the third century. The most comprehensive and most
important of these fragments, an almost complete copy
of Genesis, lies in the Royal Library of Berlin, and will
be published shortly.[1] The circulation of the Bible
received a fresh impulse from Constantine,[2] and continued to increase after his time.

---

[1] Many smaller fragments have been published by Grenfell and Hunt.
[2] *Vide* Euseb., *Vit. Constant.*, iv. 36 *sq.*

CHAPTER III

AT the end of this period Theodoret (*Graec. affect. cur*, v.)[1] writes as follows: "All the heralds of the truth, to wit the Prophets and Apostles, though unendowed with the Greek gift of eloquence, were yet filled with true wisdom, brought to all nations both Hellenic and barbarian the divine doctrine, and filled all lands and seas with their *writings*, whose content is virtue and piety. And now all men having renounced the follies of the philosophers, feast upon the doctrines of fishermen and publicans and reverence the words of the Tent-maker. Of the Italian and Ionic and Eleatic schools they no longer know even the names; for time has obliterated their memory; but of the prophets, who lived 1500 years earlier than these, they are ever speaking. Yea more, they know those who lived long before the prophets—Abraham and his children; yea, men still more ancient and famed for their good life, such as Abel, Enoch, and Noah. Of the Seven Wise Men and their successors, who lived

[1] *Opp.*, ed. Schulze, T. iv. p. 887 *sq.*

after the time of the prophets, even Greek-speaking
people no longer know the names. The names of
Matthew and Bartholomew and James, and indeed of
Moses, David, and Isaiah, and of the other Apostles and
Prophets, they know as customary names for children,
even though they may deride them as barbarous. . . .
Yet such scoffers are but few in number; they are
easily counted; they also lack Hellenic eloquence; their
every word manifests the barbarian. . . . Only tell me
—whom Xenophanes of Colophon, whom Parmenides
the Eleatic, whom Protagoras and Melissus, whom
Pythagoras or Anaxagoras, whom Speusippus or
Xenocrates, whom Anaximander or Anaximenes, whom
Arkesilaus or Philolaus have left as successors in their
schools? Who stands (to-day) at the head of the Stoic
school? Who champions the doctrine of the Stagirite?
Who governs according to the *Laws* of Plato? Who
swears by his *Republic*? Ye can produce no single
teacher of these doctrines; while we can point to the
doctrines of the Apostles and Prophets as now standing
in force; *for all lands upon which the sun shines are filled
with them; and what was once said in the Hebrew language
is now translated not only into Greek but also into Latin,
Egyptian, Persian, Indian, Armenian, Scythian, and
Sauromatian—in short, into the languages of all nations.*[1]
Plato the wise, who composed numerous works concerning the immortality of the soul, was not able

---

[1] *Cf.* the Homilies of St Chrysostom (*Opp.*, T. iii. p. 71 *sq.*) concerning
the benefit of Bible reading; Augustine, *De Doctrina Christ.*, ii. 5.

to convince even his own pupil Aristotle; our fishermen,
publicans, and tent-makers have convinced both Greeks
as well as Romans and Egyptians, and in a word all
nations, of the immortality and self-consciousness of
the soul. . . . And it is not only teachers of the Church
who know these doctrines, but also tent-makers, smiths,
wool-workers, and other artisans; women besides, not
only the educated but also workwomen and midwives,
indeed even slaves; and not only citizens but also
countrymen possess this knowledge.   Miners, herdsmen,
and gardeners are to be found who speak of the divine
Trinity and of the Creation of the world, and who
understand the nature of man much better than Aristotle and Plato; moreover, they practise virtue, they
avoid what is evil and fear the coming Judgment.
All this they have learned from none other than
men whom ye call 'Barbarophonoi.' . . . Marvel
also at the breviloquence of the Divine Oracles
and their power, and learn the truth of the Divine
Doctrine!"

The Bible has taken the place of Greek literature,
more especially of the philosophic literature; the Bible
is translated into all languages! This statement is
here proclaimed by Theodoret in words which are
indeed most exaggerated, and whose triumphant arro-
gance challenges criticism, which nevertheless answer
in the main to the facts of the situation that had
been reached in the reign of Theodosius II. Private
Bible reading undoubtedly had a great share in

this result, even though, as is very probable, no translations had been made into Indian, Scythian, and Sauromatian, or at the most only translations of Church lections.

During this period also, when the ancient Church reached its zenith of energy and prosperity, absolutely no restriction was laid upon private Bible reading; rather the duty was, if possible, still more energetically commended and sharply emphasised than in the previous century. The exhortation to Bible reading is unqualified; its benefit is regarded as absolute for everyone. Disciplinary suggestions in reference to the right choice of books of the Bible, and complaints of its misuse by self-conceited laymen, of which we shall speak later, are more rare, and still less frequently do we hear anything of the opinion that a Christian can reach so advanced a stage in the spiritual life as to be able to dispense with Bible reading.

It would be altogether superfluous to collect the innumerable passages from the writings of the Greek Fathers of the fourth century which testify to, or commend, the practice of private reading of the Bible. Here the attitude of the Latin half of Christendom was remarkably different. The Latin Church then and long afterwards took no pains to have the Bible translated into the "barbarian" tongues—there never existed a Punic Bible, nor, for many centuries afterwards, a Frank, a Celtic, an Anglo-Saxon Bible. Neither did this Church itself, either then or in the following generations, really make itself at home with its own Latin Bible. Even Jerome's immortal work, his translation of the Bible, made little difference in this respect. The more cultivated Latin could take absolutely no pleasure in the vulgar idiom of the old translations; moreover, the whole realm of thought and the mental horizon of the Bible were and remained for him very much less intelligible and more remote than for the Greek, saturated as he was with the Oriental spirit. Uneducated Latins were, however, relatively more numerous than uneducated Greeks, and the multitude of those who could not read increased in spite of all the efforts of the Church. Under such circumstances, exhortations to Bible reading on the part of preachers and writers are much less frequent in the West than in the East. It is worthy of note that Zeno of Verona, for example, in the large number of his sermons which we possess, never once, so far as I know, exhorts his hearers to read the Bible; nor is it otherwise with other preachers.[1] The excuse, " I am not a monk and therefore need not read the Bible," was during our period as loudly advanced in Antioch as in Rome; but we do not hear that it was so vigorously combated by the Western clergy as it was by St Chrysostom, though even in the West individual

[1] In the extraordinary propaganda which Martin of Tours carried on in favour of Christianity in Central France, which was still practically heathen, Bible reading evidently plays no part, although we receive incidental testimony that he himself regularly read the Bible (*Vita*, 26); he was not, however, a Biblical scholar.

champions were not wanting. Such an one was Sulpicius Severus, who championed the cause of the Latin Bible, and its reading against the fashionable and cultivated circles of Aquitania.[1] In the preface to his *Chronicles of the World*, he says that he has extracted this work, beginning with the Creation of the world, from the Bible, not that his readers should neglect the Bible, but on the contrary that they should be led to read it; "for all the mysteries of divine things can only be drawn from the sources themselves."[2] Evidently the Bible had little circulation in the class of readers to which Sulpicius addresses himself.

We might spare ourselves the trouble of collecting passages which only bear witness to the fact that Christians were exhorted to read the Bible and that the practice of Bible reading was widely spread in the Greek Churches. Yet these passages often throw interesting light upon the manner and circumstances of Bible reading and contain information which is historically important. Such passages we now proceed to collect and illustrate.

[1] Their refinement and sensitiveness in regard to linguistic barbarisms: Sulp. Sev., *Dial.*, i. 27.

[2] *Chron.*, i. 1: "Ea quae de sacris voluminibus breviata digessimus, non ita legentibus auctor accesserim, ut praetermissis his, unde derivata sunt, appetantur: nisi cum illa quis familiariter noverit, hic recognoscat quae ibi legerit: etenim universa divinarum rerum mysteria non nisi ex ipsis fontibus hauriri queunt."

§ 1.—Remarks concerning the Circulation of Religious Literature, the Market for Bibles, Sumptuous Copies of the Bible, the Keeping of Bibles, Superstitions connected with the Bible.

The intensive use and the extensive circulation of the Bible or of its separate parts cannot be better illustrated than by what Sulpicius Severus relates concerning the circulation of his own little book, the *Vita S. Martini.*[1] If this was the fortune of the dry tree, how much more of the green tree of Holy Scripture! Sulpicius makes his interlocutor Postumius speak as follows: "Numquam a dextera mea liber ister discedit, nam si agnoscis, ecce—et aperit librum, qui veste latebat—en ipsum! hic mihi, inquit, terra ac mari comes, hic in peregrinatione tota socius et consolator fuit. sed referam tibi sane, quo liber iste penetrarit, et quam nullus fere in orbe terrarum locus sit, ubi non materia tam felicis historiae pervulgata teneatur. primus eum Romanae urbi vir studiosissimus tui Paulinus invexit; deinde cum tota certatim urbe raperetur, exultantes librarios vidi, quod nihil ab his quaestiosius haberetur, siquidem nihil illo promptius, nihil carius venderetur. hic navigationis meae cursum longe ante praegressus, cum ad Africam veni, iam per totam Carthaginem legebatur. solus eum Cyrenensis ille presbyter non habebat, sed me largiente descripsit. nam quid ego de Alexandria loquar? ubi paene omni-

[1] *Dial.*, i. 23 (*cf.* iii. 17).

bus magis quam tibi notus est.   hic Aegyptum, Nitriam,
Thebaidam ac tota Memphitica regna transivit.   hunc
ego in eremo a quodam sene legi vidi, etc."   We hear
just the same of the extent of the circulation of the *Vita
Antonii* of Athanasius almost from the very moment of
its appearance.[1]   In Rome the publishers at once made
their profit from Sulpicius' little book.   The books of
the Bible were in increasing measure "a much better
selling article."   We have to thank Mommsen for a
catalogue drawn up by a publisher of Bibles in A.D. 359,[2]
in which the number of stichoi is given for each book
in order that the purchaser might not be cheated by
unprincipled booksellers.[3]   We cannot here discuss
the contents of this catalogue, but it is most interesting
that, together with the books of the Bible, it gives only
the works of Cyprian, again also with the number
of stichoi.   This is not accidental.   The writings of

---

[1] This book was already being read in Treves about the year 380
(August., *Confess.*, viii. 6, 15). Sulpicius (*Dial.*, i. 8) reports of the
works of Jerome: "Hieronymus per totum orbem legitur."
Theodoret (*Hist. Eccl.*, i. 20) suppressed more than 200 copies of
the Diatessaron in his diocese, and introduced copies of the separated
gospels in their place. This of itself shows what a number of copies
he had at his disposal. Optatus (vii. 1) speaks thus of the complete
Bible : "Librorum milia ubique recitantur . . . bibliothecae refertae
sunt libris ; nihil deest ecclesiae ; per loca singula divinum sonat ubique
praeconium ; non silent ora lectorum ; manus omnium codicibus
plenae sunt." The wide circulation of the Bible is for Augustine
an important apologetic argument ; vide *Confess.*, vi. 5, 7.

[2] *Hermes*, 1885, S. 142–156 ; 1890, S. 636–638 (printed in *Ges.
Schriften*, vii. S. 283 ff.).

[3] These omitted the stichoi ("avaritiae causa") so as to make
fancy prices.

Cyprian enjoyed in the fourth century a quasi-canonical reputation in the West,[1] and side by side with the Bible went to form the special religious and devotional writings and the theological standard works of Latin Christendom, which was so poor in this branch of literature;[2] their popularity, indeed, was the greater seeing that the Bible was often so unintelligible and so badly translated. There is no doubt that these lists of books were drawn up to meet the demand of private customers.

Of course it was not only in Rome, but also in every other important city, that the Bible and books of the Bible were on sale. For Antioch we have the testimony of Chrysostom, for Asia Minor and Milan that of Augustine. The former, in his third homily on Lazarus, develops the thought that for every Christian the Bible was the same as the tool to the artisan; therefore each Christian must buy a Bible and ought never to sell it.[3] Even poverty is here no excuse; for if the poor man has only a few tools that by his work he may support his life, then the Bible, as the most important tool, must always be among them; only the absolutely destitute are excused; they must and they can supply

---

[1] *Vide* my *Literaturgeschichte*, i. S. 701 ff. One passage may suffice. St Jerome, ep. 107, 12, writes, after he had given an earnest exhortation to read the Bible: "Cypriani opuscula semper in manu teneat."

[2] And yet only a part of Cyprian's treatises and epistles were really suitable for edification. We thus see how great was the lack of religious and devotional literature in the West.

[3] *Opp.*, T. i. p. 738.

the want of a Bible by diligent listening to the lections at public worship.[1] It is scandalous that in the majority of wealthy homes no Bible is to be found, or only Bibles bound richly and written in gold on the finest parchment, only for show, which are never read but lie idle in their cases.[2] "I do not say this to prevent you from buying books; rather I commend it with all my heart."[3] He who cannot buy a complete Bible ought at least to purchase a New Testament.[4] We find St Augustine in Milan earnestly studying the Epistles of St Paul,[5] which he had purchased, and at that time he also possessed the Psalms at the very least. He expressly states that there was no lack of Bibles offered for public sale.[6]

Poorer Christians who could write naturally copied for themselves parts of the Bible, like Hilarion, whose

[1] Hom. xi. (x.) in Joh., *Opp.*, viii. p. 63.

[2] St Jerome also speaks of these sumptuously bound Bibles (*vide, e.g.*, ep. 107, 12 : "Pro gemmis et serico divinos codices amet, in quibus non auri et pellis Babylonicae pictura, sed ad fidem placeat emendata et condita distinctio"; ep. 22, 32: "Inficiuntur membranae colore purpureo; aurum liquescit in literas, gemmis codices vestiuntur, et nudus ante fores earum Christus emoritur"). Such Bibles have come down to us—for example, the Gospel Codex of Rossano. The production of great and sumptuous volumes of the Bible could not have begun long before the time of Constantine. He himself gave attention to providing the Churches with fine copies of the Bible. Codex Sinaiticus and Codex Vaticanus, dating from the fourth century, are of this kind.

[3] Hom. xxxii. (xxxi.) in Joh., *Opp.*, viii. p. 187 *sq.*

[4] Hom. ix. in ep. Coloss., *Opp.*, xi. p. 391.

[5] *Confess.*, viii. 6, 14 ; 12, 29.

[6] Sermo i. in Ps. xxxvi., *Opp.*, iv. p. 194.

life is written by St Jerome, who copied the Gospels
for himself. They then possessed in these copies a
property with which they might realise money in time
of need.[1]

Pious people, however, did not part from their
Bibles. Thus Hilarion kept his copy of the Gospels
with him until death;[2] thus Augustine in the hour
of deepest spiritual conflict took his St Paul with
him into the garden; thus Paulinus of Nola writes
of one Martinianus who had saved himself from a
shipwreck :—[3]

> Dilecte frater, accipe et lauda deum
> sanctumque fratrem amplectere :
> ut adlabentem portui sensit ratem
> stridente harena litoris,

[1] *Vita Hilar.*, 35, 36, 44 : "Hilarion ascendit classem quae Siciliam
navigabat . . . venundato evangeliorum codice, quem manu sua adole-
scens scripserat, dare naulum disposuit . . . obtulit nauclero evangelium
pro subvectione sua . . . noluit accipere, maxime cum videret illum
excepto illo codice et his quibus vestitus erat amplius nihil habere . . .
Hilarion LXXX. aetatis suae anno quasi testamentum scripsit epistolam
omnes divitias Hesychio derelinquens, evangelium et tunicam sacceam,
cucullam et palliolum."

[2] In reference to the work of the copyists, compare Hieron., ep. 71,
5 : "Opuscula mea ad describendum hominibus tuis dedi et descripta
vidi in chartaceis codicibus ac frequenter admonui, ut conferrent dili-
gentius et emendarent. ego enim tanta volumina prae frequentia com-
meantium et peregrinorum turbis relegere non potui . . . Unde si
paragrammata repereris vel minus aliqua descripta sunt, quae sensum
legentis impediant, non mihi debes imputare, sed tuis et imperitiae
notariorum librariorumque incuriae, qui scribunt non quod inveniunt,
sed quod intelligunt, et dum alienos errores emendare nituntur,
ostendunt suos."

[3] *Carm.*, xxiv. v. 265 *sq.* (*Opp.*, ed. Hartel, ii. p. 215).

abeunte somno fit sui tandem memor
recipitque sese, expergitur
et adiacentes pectori tangit suo
epistolas apostoli
hunc in pavore codicem sed nesciens
rebus relictis sumpserat,
vel ille codex spiritu vivens sacro
non sentienti adhaeserat.

Consciously or unconsciously, in this rescue of the volume of St Paul a superstitious motive may have been at work. We often hear of sacred and devotional works being worn on the breast;[1] Chrysostom testifies that women and children hung the Gospels around their necks as defensive charms.[2] He does not forbid this practice, but he does not like it: one ought rather to write the commands of the Gospel in one's memory. Yet he is convinced that the mere sight of the Bible in the home promotes good resolutions and deters one from evil, and that the very touch of the book of the Gospels of itself awakens the heart.[3] In this period we also meet with the practice of taking oracles from the Bible—we may not, perhaps, reckon *Confess.*, viii. 12, 29, as an instance,

[1] St Jerome (ep. 60, 11) speaks thus of a favourite book: "Illum oculis, illum manibus, illum *sinu*, illum ore tenebat"; also *vide supra*, p. 96.

[2] Hom. xix. ad populum Antioch., *Opp.*, ii. p. 197; *cf.* Hom. lxxii. in Matth., *Opp.*, vii. p. 703. Examples of psalms and texts from the Bible written as charms during our period have come down to us. Rabulas of Edessa, in his canons for priests and clergy, forbids the writing of charms. *Vide* Bickell, *Ausgewählte Schriften der syrischen Kirchenväter* (Kempten, 1874), S. 232.

[3] Hom. iii. de Lazaro, *Opp.*, i. p. 739.

and yet this moving story does fall under this head. The practice was for the most part quietly tolerated by the Church, but there are many instances of condemnation. Among the canons for monks drawn up by Rabulas of Edessa, the nineteenth runs: "No monk on the behalf of any person shall seek for an oracle from passages of the Bible."[1] We may also reckon under the head of superstition the fact that men and women believed that in certain sexual conditions they ought not to touch the Bible.[2] The author of the *Apostolic Constitutions*, however, writes against this belief.[3]

It was felt that copies of the Bible in the home should be treated with great respect, but accidents which injured them could not be avoided. With the express motive of palliating the crime of those traditores who had delivered up Bibles to be destroyed, Optatus[4] describes the many other different ways in which private copies of the Bible might perish: "Non minus videmus neglegentiam frequenter operari quam necessitas operata est. nam si membranae aut libri, quibus scriptura

---

[1] *Vide* Bickell, *loc. cit.*, S. 228.

[2] We note here the influence of the Jewish laws of purity, which, through the medium of the Old Testament, began to penetrate into the Churches during the fourth century.

[3] *Const. App.*, vi. 27 : Εἴ τινες παρατηρούμενοι φυλάσσουσιν ἔθιμα Ἰουδαϊκά, γονορροίας, ὀνειρώξεις, πλησιασμοὺς τοὺς κατὰ νόμον, λεγέτωσαν ἡμῖν εἰ ἐν αἷς ὥραις ἢ ἡμέραις ἔν τι τούτων ὑπομείνωσιν, παρατηροῦνται προσεύξασθαι ἢ εὐχαριστίας μεταλαβεῖν ἢ βιβλίου θιγεῖν. καὶ ἐὰν συνθῶνται, δῆλον ὡς τοῦ ἁγίου πνεύματος κενοὶ τυγχάνουσιν τοῦ ἀεὶ παραμένοντος τοῖς πιστοῖς.

[4] Lib. vii. 1, p. 166 *sq.*

legitima continetur, in totum debent inlaesa servari,
quasi non damnantur aliqui neglegentes, non est longe
tradere a male ponere aut male ferre. alter in domo
librum posuit, quae domus incendio concremata est:
damnetur, qui neglegenter posuit, si damnandus est, qui
postulandum librum territus dedit. damnentur etiam
illi, qui neglectas membranas aut libros ita posuerunt,
ut eos domesticae bestiolae, hoc est mures, ita corroserint,
ut legi non possint. damnetur et ille, qui ita in domo
posuit, ut nimietate pluviarum sic tecta aliqua stillicidia
deliquarent, ut omnia humore oblitterata legi non
possint. damnentur et illi, qui ferentes libros legis
temerarii se rapacibus undis fluminum crediderunt et se
liberari cupientes scripturas in undis e suis manibus
dimiserunt."

§ 2.—Canonical, Apocryphal, and Heretical Writings in Private Use

The danger that an absolutely heretical book should
appear among the writings to be read *at public worship*
was practically non-existent during the fourth century,
but in most Churches there was still much to be
done in defining the boundary between canonical and
apocryphal books. In the Greek Church the work
of definition went quietly and steadily forward; in the
Latin Church, however, it progressed by leaps and
bounds. In the fourth century the latter Church was
for the first time simply overwhelmed by a flood of
pretentious writings quite unknown to her in earlier

days, and now appearing in translations.[1] These writings caused the more trouble in that they appeared suddenly and bore renowned names on their title-pages, and still more because men of sufficient learning to deal adequately with these books were too often lacking in the Church of the West. Under such conditions the severest measures were appropriate, and they were adopted more especially by the Roman bishops from Damasus onwards. In spite of this, many more apocryphal works have been preserved in the Latin language than in the Greek; for during the fourth and fifth centuries the Greek Churches so "purged" their libraries that, except the Bible and the most approved works of the Fathers, almost nothing else was left.[2] In this point also we see that the Greek Church, with the emperors and their edicts against books at its disposal,[3] was the leading Church in the ancient days.[4]

[1] Not only from the side of Manichæism, but from all sides.

[2] In the Churches of the Orient in the strict sense of the word it was otherwise; they reserved to themselves still more apocryphal works than the Latin Churches.

[3] Constantine prohibited the writings of Porphyry and Arius (Socrat., *Hist. Eccl.*, i. 9); after that time there was a continuous succession of prohibitive edicts. Arcadius ordered that the books of the Eunomians should be burned; if anyone refused to deliver them up, he was to be punished with death (Theod., *Cod.*, xvi. 5, 34).

[4] As Reuter especially has shown in his *Augustin-Studien*, even Augustine regarded the Greek Church, when compared with the Latin, as the leading Church and as setting the pattern for the others. Under this presupposition the development of the authority of Rome first appears in its proper light. Rome was not the East—that is, the decisive authority—but Rome was Rome.

In regard to private reading, the strict rule generally prevailed which Cyril of Jerusalem formulates in the words: "Nothing that is not read in the Churches should be read *privatim*."[1] Seeing that not only he, but also many other Fathers of the Eastern and Western Churches, thought it necessary, whether in their catechetical instructions or elsewhere, to publish lists of the canonical books name by name, and then to exclude apocryphal books either in general or with mention of their names, we conclude that this procedure can only imply that the practice of private reading was widely spread. As the practice prevailed and was furthered by both theologians and bishops with all the means in their power, it necessarily followed that the laity must receive more accurate information concerning the number and the titles of the canonical books. It would lead us much too far were we to give all the passages where such information is given; these are quoted in abundance and in convenient form in the greater works on the history of the Canon (especially that of Zahn). Here we would only draw attention to the fact that these lists also applied to the private reading of laymen and monks. St Basil repeats St Cyril's rule when he says: "The monk must read the genuine books of Holy Scripture, but not

---

[1] *Catech.*, iv. 36 (ed. Reischl): Ὅσαν μὲν ἐν ἐκκλησίαις μὴ ἀναγινώσκεται, ταῦτα μηδὲ κατὰ σαυτὸν ἀναγίνωσκε; cf. c. 33 : καί μοι μηδὲν τῶν ἀποκρύφων ἀναγίνωσκε.

the apocryphal books."[1] "Deceive not thy soul with strange books," is the warning of Gregory of Nazianzen.[2] "Avoid all apocryphal books," writes Jerome.[3]

Here and there, indeed, people spoke as if a man had need of nothing but his Bible, and ought to read nothing else, so that the ordinance of Julian, that Christians were to have no dealings with Hellenic literature but were to read their Matthew, seemed to meet their own wishes. But as in our period no formal ordinance of the Church forbidding Christians to read Greek literature was ever issued, so Christian theologians did not even think of giving up their reading of this literature,[4] and they felt Julian's prohibitive edict as a heavy blow,[5] even though some acted as if it did not affect them, because the Bible was all-sufficient. Of course the situation was not clearly defined, and at any time it might be objected against a teacher that he devoted too much attention to, or that he even noticed, heathen authors. We know what

[1] Sermo *De asc. discipl.*, 1 T. ii. p. 212 (Garnier).

[2] *Carm.*, xxxiii., T. ii. p. 98.

[3] Ep. 107, 12: "Caveat omnia apocrypha"; *cf.* Augustin., *De doctrina Chr.*, ii. 8 *sq.*

[4] Least of all those of the school of Origen. Compare how broad-mindedly Basil in his twentieth oration treats the question how young people could read heathen authors with profit. It is to him self-evident (*vide* c. 2) that the reading of good heathen books must precede the study of the Bible.

[5] *Cf.*, also, the very pertinent question he addressed to the Christians (Κατὰ Χριστιανῶν, p. 204, ed. Neumann): Τοῦ χάριν ὑμεῖς τῶν παρ' Ἕλλησι παρεσθίετε μαθημάτων, εἴπερ αὐτάρκης ὑμῖν ἐστιν ἡ τῶν ὑμετέρων γραφῶν ἀνάγνωσις ; καίτοι κρεῖττον ἐκείνων εἴργειν τοὺς ἀνθρώπους ἢ τῆς τῶν ἱεροθύτων ἐδωδῆς.

happened in the case of Jerome : how he wished to withdraw himself from the ancient literature, and yet found
that he could not give up the old authors, and how he
was reproached by others, above all by his former friend
Rufinus. He was, of course, in a very awkward position ;
for he was a monk, and as a monk he was altogether
restricted to the reading of Holy Scripture—monkish
decorum at that time required this ; and yet not only
his scientific mind, but also a disposition whose innate
worldliness was kept in suppression, demanded other food.
Nor could he refrain from interlarding his discourses
with such expressions as " my Virgil," " my Horace,"
" my Cicero," and from showing how vain he was of his
learning ; and thus he reaped the just recompense of
blame and hostility. Rufinus in particular reproaches
him for making a parade of long quotations from
classical authors even before matrons and young women,
for whom the Bible alone ought to have been the sole
source of edification.[1] Still, profane literature fared
better than heretical writings.[2]

In increasing measure apocryphal books, even though
they were innocent, indeed even though they were
edifying, met with the same treatment as heretical

[1] *Cf.* Book ii. of the *Invectives* of Rufinus ; also Hieron., ep. 22, 29.
30 ; 70, 2.
[2] With the prohibition of the *Thalia* of Arius by the Nicene Council
begins the long series of ecclesiastical edicts against heretical writings.
In turn the books of Origen, Nestorius, Eutyches, and others were
forbidden. Since 400 A.D. both Church and State waged a war of
extermination against the Gnostic literature, which had long ago been
rejected.

books.[1] Laymen and monks were strictly warned to refrain from them in their private reading. But at the end of the fourth century there appeared in the Spanish Church a man, namely Priscillian, who contended with all his might for the right of reading good (that is, prophetical) apocryphal books (of the Old Testament). His chief argument was that even the Apostles had read these books, and with the greatest industry and acuteness he collected abundant evidence in support of his statement.[2] His opponents energetically upheld the principle of the sufficiency of the canonical Scriptures: "plus legisse peccare est." He disputed this sufficiency:[3] from an historical point of view the books of the Old Testament required to be completed from other prophetical writings, such as Enoch, the apocryphal books of Ezra, etc. (p. 47). "Si quaero," he writes (p. 51), "quod Christiani hominis est, si quod ecclesiasticae dispositionis, si quod dei Christi est, in his invenio qui deum praedicant, in his invenio qui profetant. non est timor, fides est, quod diligimus meliora et deteriora respuimus, unum inter

---

[1] The apocryphal writings accordingly met with the same fortune as the schismatical sects.

[2] Vide his Treatise iii. (Liber de fide et apocryphis), p. 44 sq., ed. Schepps. Priscillian, indeed, concealed behind his demand that free reading of the apocrypha should be allowed all kinds of peculiar dogmatic ideas; but he would not have anything to do with the "stulta haereticorum dogmata."

[3] He never disputed the unique importance of Holy Scripture; vide p. 52: "Facile natura hominum obligata saeculo fidem perderet si ad praedicationem divini nominis scripturarum testimonia non haberet."

ista servantes, ut—quoniam in huiusmodi libris, quos
extra canonicorum librorum numerum ad legendi
laborem diligentia retentabat atque ad conprobanda
ea quae scripta in canone legimus adsumpti sunt,
haereticorum in pleraque sensus invadens pugnam
catholicis parans falsare maluit quam tenere—illam
apostolicam feramus iure sententiam, omnem spiritum
qui negat Jesum de deo non esse et omnem spiritum
qui confitetur Christum Jesum de deo esse, sicut scriptum
est : nemo enim dicit in spiritu sancto anathema Jesu
et nemo nisi in spiritu sancto loquitur dominum Jesum."
Therefore he continues (p. 52) : " Qualiter pauca ex his
[apocryphis prophetarum] legentes culpabiles sumus,
cum magis ob hoc rei sumus, quod omnia quae de deo
sunt profetata non legimus ? non dubito autem quem-
quam ex his qui calumnias potius quam fidem diligunt
esse dicturum : ultra nihil quaeras ! sufficit te legere
quod in canone scriptum est. cuius quidem verbis
facile ingenio humanae naturae quae otium potius
quam laborem requirit adsurgerem, nisi me Lucae
evangelistae testimonium perurgeret dicentis in actibus
apostolorum : 'at discipuli pariter conferebant inter se
scripturas, si ita esset,' quemadmodum locutus fuerat
ad eos Paulus, et ea quorum cognitionem volo testimonium prophetiae in canone accepisse cognosco. quamvis
enim crimen sit apostolicis non credidisse sermonibus,
non est tamen damnabilis culpae firmamentum fidei
scriptorum probatione construere et nihil in quo nos
infirmes redarguitio diaboli faciat reservare. potuit

enim sermo divinus, quoniam ipsius erat omne quod dixerat, tamquam ab se loquens non scriptum ab alio dicere, sed ex se ipse proferre; dicens autem scriptum esse, necessaria proponens nobis legendi sollicitudinem, et suam de quo profetatum fuerat gloriam et illius qui profetaverat debitam posteritati gratiam non omisit. ergo certe inter utrosque utrisque debitor sum, ut et illum qui ad memoriam divinam profetaverit legam et deo credam. quis enim non delectetur Christum ante saecula non a paucis, sed ab omnibus profetatum ? "

I have given these quotations in full because the two principles for which Priscillian contended are of the highest importance: (1) Prophecy extends beyond the circle of canonical Scripture; (2) the circle of the canonical books and that of books to be read are not coincident.[1]   But he in vain set himself to oppose a development which had already almost reached maturity.[2]   In itself it was no great loss that the

---

[1] In reference to this point Priscillian indeed struck the note: "Ubi libertas, ibi Christus" (p. 55).

[2] Origen (Prolog. in Cantic. Cant., T. xiv. p. 325) had already written as follows: "Apocryphae: pro eo, quod multa in iis corrupta et contra fidem veram inveniuntur a maioribus tradita, non placuit iis dari locum nec admitti ad auctoritatem. supra nos est pronuntiare de talibus, illud tamen palam est, multa vel ab apostolis vel ab evangelistis exempla esse prolata et Novo Testamento inserta, quae in his scripturis, quas canonicas habemus, nunquam legimus, in apocryphis tamen inveniuntur et evidenter ex ipsis ostenduntur assumpta. sed ne sic quidem locus apocryphis dandus est, non enim transeundi sunt termini quos statuerunt patres nostri. potuit enim fieri, ut apostoli vel evangelistae sancto spiritu repleti sciverint, quid assumendum ex illis esset scripturis quidve refutandum ; nobis autem non est absque periculo aliquid tale praesumere, quibus non est tanta spiritus abundantia."

"Apocrypha" gradually vanished from private reading, even the *Shepherd of Hermas*, which had for a long period possessed important patrons,[1] and the Apocalypse of Enoch, for the rejection of which from the canon Tertullian once was inclined to blame the Jews in their hostility to Christ.[2] In the interests of freedom, however, it is to be deplored that the sphere of private reading became ever more and more restricted.[3] Moreover, with the disappearance of the middle term which was afforded in the apocryphal prophetical writings, the

---

[1] And *Hermas* never quite disappeared in the West, as is shown by the number of manuscripts which exist.

[2] "Cum Enoch scriptura etiam de domino praedicarit, a nobis quidem nihil omnino reiciendum est quod pertineat ad nos. et legimus omnem scripturam aedificationi habilem divinitus inspirari. a Iudaeis potest iam videri propterea reiecta, sicut et cetera fere quae Christum sonant" (*De Cultu. Fem.*, i. 3). Priscillian may have known of his precursor (*cf.* also Tertullian's further observations).

[3] Sulpicius Severus (*Dial.*, i. 6 *sq.*) informs us of a reaction against the prohibition of the books of Origen (by an Alexandrian synod of the year 399). Sulpicius describes this reaction as if the monks had revolted against the *bishops*; but this belongs to the tendency of his work: really the monks stood some on one side, some on the other. The champions of Origen asserted that he was a "tractator scripturarum sacrarum peritissimus," that he was not responsible for the falsifications of his books, moreover that readers could easily distinguish the false from the true. The opponents retorted: "Recte etiam universa cum pravis et cum ipso auctore damnantur, *quia satis superque sufficerent libri quos ecclesia recepisset*; respuendam esse penitus lectionem, quae plus esset nocitura insipientibus quam profutura sapientibus." Sulpicius, moreover, expresses his disapproval that, because the authority of the bishops did not suffice, the Prefect was summoned to their assistance "scaevo exemplo ad regendam ecclesiae disciplinam." St Jerome (ep. 119, 11) tells us that he read heretical writings that he might pick out what was good in them; so also Theophilus of Alexandria (Socrat., *Hist. Eccl.*, vi. 15). But even as early as the fifth century this excuse was no longer allowed to pass.

canonical books could not but appear more and more out of touch with human history and all earthly conditions.

§ 3.—VARIETIES IN THE PRACTICE OF PRIVATE BIBLE READING

In this period also it was the hearing the Bible read aloud that continued to give the greatest impetus to the practice of Bible reading. Besides the lections in the principal service of Divine worship, there were the lections in subsidiary services, in family worship,[1] and in private Bible classes. These classes were specially commended by St Chrysostom and other public teachers.[2] We learn incidentally that the libraries which were attached to many churches, and were placed in separate outbuildings, were also accessible to laymen, who could here either read the Bible or hear it read.[3]

[1] Common *oratio* and *lectio*—both always together—in the family circle are presupposed by Chrysostom and other Fathers.

[2] Chrysostom, Hom. vi. in Genes., T. iv. p. 48 : a man ought to call his neighbours together and to read the Bible with them.

[3] *Vide* Paulin. of Nola, ep. 32 (description of the church of Nola), 12 : "Totum vero extra concham basilicae spatium alto et lacunato culmine geminis utrimque porticibus dilatatur, quibus duplex per singulos arcus columnarum ordo dirigitur. cubicula intra porticus quaterna longis basilicae lateribus inserta secretis orantium vel in lege domini meditantium, etc."; *cf.* 16 : "In secretariis vero duobus, quae supra dixi circa absidam esse, hi versus indicant officia singulorum." A dextra abside :

Hic locus est, veneranda penus qua conditur et qua
Promitur alma sacri pompa ministerii.

A sinistra eiusdem :

Si quem sancta tenet meditandi in lege voluntas
Hic poterit residens sacris intendere libris."

The Church was ever most anxious that the Bible should be open and accessible even to the heathen;[1] for she had again and again learned by experience that the Bible was her best missionary. The conversions of Hilary[2] and Victorinus in Rome[3] were notable examples; these men had been led to the Church by the Holy Scriptures. Of course the Old Testament, if it was read without guidance, presented very great difficulties:[4] many stories and sayings in the Gospel appeared at first childish, the theological arguments of the epistles were often unintelligible, and the style of most of the books was not very attractive.[5] Yet

---

[1] Naturally, the New Testament was also given to every Jew who wished to read it ; vide, e.g., Epiph., 30, 11.

[2] De Trinit., i. 5, 10.

[3] Augustin., Confess., viii. 2, 4.

[4] How many, like Augustine, may have been led by the Old Testament to Manichæism instead of to the Church! Among the Fathers of the fourth century, St Ambrose, with his practical mind, points out most clearly the dangers of Bible reading (without guidance or with false guidance); vide, e.g., De Paradiso, 58 (i. p. 318, Schenkl): "Gentilis, si quis scripturas accipiat, legit: 'oculum pro oculo, etc.,' legit etiam: 'si scandalizaverit te dextera tua abscide illam,' non intelligit sensum non advertit divini sermonis arcana, peius labitur quam si non legisset." Augustine (De Catech. Rud., 8) says that on the authority of canonical Scripture, which certainly contains the purest truth, many have introduced a mass of destructive doctrines ; but he charitably adds that one must pardon the human weakness of these men if they (at least) afterwards show themselves accessible to instruction.

[5] There was no cessation of the efforts to defend, or rather to excuse, the style of the Bible, to explain its lack of adornment, and to make for it a virtue out of necessity. From Eusebius up to Theodoret (Graec. cur. affect.), pertinent evidence lies before us. The arguments are always the same as those which we have already found in the earlier Fathers: the Holy Spirit must necessarily avoid worldly rhetoric and

8

the Church gladly accepted the scoffing and the mis-
understandings as part of her bargain; for she knew
that a book like Genesis, that religious poems like the
Psalms, and that the profound thought of the first
chapter of St John and of many other passages in the
apostolic writings would as a rule triumphantly over-
come all difficulties and objections.   St Augustine
expressly states that educated men who gave in their
names as catechumens had for the most part a considerable knowledge of the Holy Scriptures, and that

fine speaking; He must speak simply and so as to be intelligible to
all; behind the obscurities there lie grand mysteries; what the words
lack in adornment is compensated for by their truth and power; etc.
(Hieron., ep. 48 [49], 4: "Eloquentiam quam pro Christo in Cicerone
contemnis, in parvulis ne requiras.   ecclesiastica interpretatio etiamsi
habet eloquii venustatem, dissimulare eam debet et fugere, ut non
otiosis philosophorum scholis paucisque discipulis, sed universo loquatur
hominum generi.")   Nevertheless, here and there attempts were made
to replace in paraphrasing, if not in the text itself, a vulgar word by
one more refined, and an obscure sentence by one that was clearer (as
St Luke had done with St Mark).   But it was necessary to be
careful.   Socrates (*Hist. Eccl.*, i. 12) tells us that Triphyllius, when
preaching before a Cyprian synod, referred to the story of the Healing
of the Paralytic and used the word σκίμπους instead of the vulgar
word κράββατον.   His colleague the Bishop Spyridion at once
rebuked him: "Art thou perchance better than He who spoke the
word κράββατον because thou art ashamed to use such words?"
Augustine says (*De Catech. Rud.*, 9) that for God's ears there is no
other voice than the loving devotion of the heart; He pays no heed
to mistakes in language; it is not a question of "bona dictio" but of
"benedictio"; scoffing is quite misplaced if here and there officers and
ministers of the Church pray to God with barbarous expressions or in
false syntax, or do not understand their own words and pronounce
them wrongly.   "I do not say that these things should not be
corrected; for the people must say Amen to what they clearly understand; but they must be endured with charity."

in their case the only requisite was admission to the sacraments. "If they come from the schools of the grammarians and rhetoricians they must be directed to listen attentively to the Bible": "ne sordeat eis solidum eloquium."[1]

The Bible appeared, and is often so described by the Fathers, as God's great proclamation to mankind, as the open letter directed to every man which must not only be read but earnestly studied by everyone. Therefore no one can do too much in private reading. Every blessing for the understanding and for the life is promised as the fruit of Bible reading, and especially of private Bible reading.[2] The Bible is the " treasury " of salvation; it affords the *vitalia* and the *pabulum*

[1] *De Catech. Rud.*, 8 *sq.* Here and elsewhere we also learn that not only the Bible but sometimes other Christian writings ripened with some the determination to become Christians: "If it is seen that (an educated person who has become a catechumen) has been moved thereto by the reading whether of the canonical Scriptures or of some other good books, then at the beginning of instruction one can say something in praise of those books. . . . Further, one must also endeavour to make the catechumen tell what author he studies most and what are his favourite works, and which of them has brought him to make up his mind to join the Church. When we have gained this information, if we ourselves know these books, or at least understand, from the good report they enjoy in the Church, that they proceed from the pen of some reputable Catholic, we must express our joyful approval; if, however, he has fallen upon heretical books and has adopted from them heretical views in the ignorant belief that they are Catholic, then, etc."

[2] The Emperor Julian, it is true, found that no one was the better for reading the Bible; *vide* κατὰ Χριστιανῶν, p. 206 : "The following will be a proof. Choose from among yourselves lads, and let them be brought up on your literature : if when they become men they prove more useful as slaves, account me a mere babbler and cynic."

of the soul; it is *succus et esca vitae*; it grips, it awakens, it elevates the inward man; it is the greatest shield against sin; it teaches us to speak good words; it arms the reader against the assaults of heresy; it frees the soul from the curse of ignorance; it attracts the heart from earthly cares; yea, even in this life it makes the light of God shine upon the soul of the reader, and after it has made him a man by means of the Old Testament, it makes him an angel by means of the New Testament. The last figure comes from St Chrysostom,[1] who indeed devoted a homily, "Quod utilis sit lectio scripturarum,"[2] to this special subject. He, the great man of the Bible of the fourth century, loved to dwell upon the first Psalm in connection with continuous Bible reading; he teaches that the Christian should be like the tree planted by the streams of water, so that "day and night" he might draw his nourishment from the Bible. This "day and night" is also repeated by other Fathers, and the Ethiopian eunuch who read even on his journey is again and again quoted as an example and model for Christians. Where monks and nuns are mentioned, this "semper" receives special emphasis, and St Jerome thinks that he is giving his friend the highest possible praise when he says of him: "Lectione adsidua et meditatione diuturna pectus suum bibliothecam fecerat Christi."[3]

[1] *Synops. Script.*, *vide* T. vi. p. 317. *Cf.* Hieronymus, ep. 53, 10: reading the Scriptures = to be in the Kingdom of Heaven.

[2] T. iii. p. 71 *sq.*

[3] Ep. 60, 10.

Monks and nuns—in the second half of the fourth century it becomes absolutely clear that moral and spiritual demands which, according to theory, were addressed to all Christians are more and more being restricted to these alone. *But indeed the claims of theory necessarily drove the consistent Christian into the cloister*, as the conversion of St Augustine and many other similar cases most clearly show. But while St Jerome already directs his exhortations to Christians of the first and second class, St Chrysostom, a truly great man, contends with all the power of heart and will, and devotes every resource of oratory to the establishing of one simple and strict ideal for all Christians. In this contest no weapon seems to him to be more powerful than the Bible. In the midst of a great metropolis filled with Christians who were Christians only in name, he never wearies in his endeavour to plant the Bible in the home, in the firm conviction that, if he can only establish regular reading of the Scriptures in the family and among individuals, he is thus laying a solid foundation for a truly Christian life.

But the fact that this exhortation is so constantly repeated,[1] of itself clearly shows that as a rule his seed was sown on stony ground,[2] and the objections which he seeks to refute were very insistent. "We are not

[1] Not only in the church, but also by private admonition when individuals sought advice from him.

[2] Unfortunately, it is quite impossible to give with any approach to accuracy the number of Bibles in private possession in proportion to the size of the community, say in Antioch. According to some passages in

118 BIBLE READING IN THE EARLY CHURCH

monks," some objected, showing therewith that they
applied the new distinction between laymen and monks
as a balm to their consciences.[1] "I am tied down as
a government official to the courts; I have to give my
attention to public business; I carry on a trade; I
must look after my wife and children and servants; in
short, I am a man of the world; it is not my business
to read the Bible; that is the business of people who
have renounced the world and devote themselves to
a lonely life upon the tops of the mountains."[2]
"What is worst of all and ruins everything," cries
St Chrysostom, "is this, that ye believe that Bible
reading is purely a matter for monks, while ye need
it far more than they."[3] Others declared that they

Chrysostom, it seems to have been small. "Which of you takes up a
Christian book at home . . . ! Dice are to be found in most homes, but
not books, at least only in few homes " (Hom. xxxii. [xxxi.] in Ioann.,
T. viii. 187 *sq.*). According to other passages it appears to have been
otherwise, and in the complaints of a pastor the condition of his flock is
often painted in too dark a light. That many hermits possessed no
Bible we may naturally assume, and indeed learn incidentally from
Augustine, *De Doctrina Christ.*, i. 39.

[1] Two hundred years earlier laymen felt themselves relieved in their
religious, moral, and ecclesiastical duties by the distinction between
clergy and laity, which then first came to sharp expression, and they
shuffled off the fulfilling of the commandments of Christ upon the
clergy; we learn this from the angry complaints of Tertullian; *vide
De Exhort. Cast.*, 7; *De Monog.*, 11, 12: "Cum extollimur et inflamur
adversus clerum, tunc unum omnes sumus, tunc omnes sacerdotes, quia
sacerdotes nos deo et patri fecit. cum ad peraequationem disciplinae
sacerdotalis provocamur, deponimus infulas."

[2] Hom. iii. de Lazaro, T. i. p. 737; *cf.* Hom. xxi. in Genes., T. iv.
p. 189 *sq.*

[3] Hom. ii. in Matth., T. vii. p. 29 *sq.* "He who lives amid the distrac-
tions of much business has the greatest need of the help of the Bible."

would not read the Bible because they could not understand it, and therefore would derive no benefit from it.[1] Others said that they found absolutely no time for quiet Bible reading.[2] As for men of standing and of cultivated mind, we possess two beautiful examples of the tactful way in which the duty of reading Holy Scripture was presented to them by the bishops. St Augustine writes thus to the "Dominus illustris et meritus praestantissimus" Volusianus:[3]

"De salute tua, quam et in hoc saeculo et in Christo esse cupio, sanctae matris tuae votis sum fortasse etiam ipse non impar. unde meritis tuis reddens salutationis obsequium hortor, ut valeo, ut litterarum vere certeque sanctarum te curam non pigeat impendere. sincera enim et solida res est nec fucatis eloquiis ambit ad animum nec ullo linguae tectorio inane aliquid ac pendulum crepitat. multum movet non verborum sed rerum avidum et multum terret factura securum. praecipue apostolorum linguas exhortor ut legas; ex his enim ad cognoscendos prophetas excitaberis, quorum

[1] Hom. iii. de Lazaro, p. 739 sq.

[2] Some also seem to have complained that a quite new demand was being made of them (vide Hom. i. de Lazaro, i. p. 719). It is just possible, but not at all probable, that in connection with the advance of monasticism greater demands were made of the laity in regard to the Bible. Great stress was laid upon Bible reading long before the time of St Chrysostom, and the new demand which disturbed these people was not the simple requirement that the Bible should be read, but the regulation, by which the Bible was to be introduced into the home, that family worship with reading of the Scriptures should be held after supper and before retiring to rest (vide infra).

[3] Ep. 132.

testimoniis utuntur apostoli. si quid autem, vel cum legeris vel cum cogitas, tibi oritur quaestionis, in quo dissolvendo videar necessarius, scribe ut rescribam." What a tactful letter to a man who was evidently sincere!

Paulinus of Nola, in his letter to Jovius,[1] also has before him an official of high rank, who is to be cured of an outspoken disinclination to read the Holy Scriptures. Paulinus writes:

" Erige in summam sapientiae mentem tuam et ipsum veri luminis fomitem Christum pete, qui fideles animas inluminat et pectora casta perlabitur. quod et te ita sentire docuisti, licet pro excusatione praetenderis imparem te adhuc et ideo non capacem dei [scil. of Holy Scripture], quia terrenis rebus et curis obsessus ab altiore suspectu caelestium quasi nubibus interpositis arcearis. sed utinam ista tam vere possis obtendere, quam facunde potes. arguit enim ipsa facundiae tuae doctrinaeque fecunditas voluntatem tibi potius in sacris litteris parem quam aut vacationem aut facultatem abesse. non enim, opinor, dormiens aut aliud agens tantas oris aut pectoris divitias coegisti. omnium poetarum floribus spiras, omnium oratorum fluminibus exundas, philosophiae quoque fontibus irrigaris, peregrinis etiam dives litteris Romanum os Atticis favis imples. quaeso te, ubi tunc tributa sunt, cum Tullium et Demosthenem perlegis? vel iam usitatiorum de saturitate fastidiens lectionum Xenophontem, Plato-

<hr>
[1] Ep. 16 (p. 114 sq., Hartel).

nem, Catonem Varronemque perlectos revolvis multosque
praeterea, quorum nos forte nec nomina, tu etiam
volumina tenes? ut istis occuperis, inmunis et liber,
ut Christum hoc est sapientiam dei discas, tributarius
et occupatus es! vacat tibi ut et philosophus sis,
non vacat ut Christianus sis. verte potius sententiam,
verte facundiam. nam animi philosophiam non deponas
licet, dum eam fide condias et religione; conserta
utare sapientius, ut sis dei philosophus et dei vates,
non quaerendo sed imitando deum sapiens, ut non
lingua quam vita eruditus tam disseras magna quam
facias! esto Peripateticus deo, Pythagoreus mundo."

Here a fair amount of flattery is mingled with
irony and blame; but all is directed towards the one
object of refuting Jovius' objections and inciting him
to the study of the Bible.

High and low,[1] old and young, catechumens together
with the faithful, must read the Bible. In regard to
the introduction of catechumens to the study of Holy
Scripture, we possess abundant information in the
catechetical lectures of St Cyril of Jerusalem and
St Augustine's treatises, *De Catechizandis Rudibus* and
De Doctrina Christiana—information which finds its
completion in incidental remarks made by other
Fathers. It is interesting to notice that St Athanasius,
in his Festival letter of the year 367, after giving a

---

[1] Country people were as a rule excepted. Chrysostom (Hom. xix.
de Column.) praises the Christian peasants who dwelt around Antioch
and came to the church on feast-days. He speaks, indeed, of their
spiritual discourse, but never of their Bible reading.

list of the canonical books, remarks that there was another group of writings which did not belong to the Canon, but which the Fathers had determined to be suitable for catechumens, namely, the Wisdom of Solomon, Sirach, Esther, Judith, Tobit, the so-called *Teaching of the Apostles*, and *The Shepherd*. As early as the third century these books were set apart fort his purpose (*vide supra*, p. 73), a fact, indeed, which perhaps throws light upon the "oportet" of the Muratorian fragment (*vide supra*, p. 64).

The Fathers without scruple direct that children in Christian homes should be introduced to the Bible from the very earliest age. As a beginning in elementary education, little boys and girls should learn to put together Biblical names with their ivory letter blocks— the names could be chosen from the genealogies of our Lord in St Matthew and St Luke (!);—they should then be advanced to reading the Bible.[1] Girls from seven years onwards should learn the Psalms by heart, and should have read the Bible before the age of maturity.[2]

[1] Hieron., ep. 107, 4 *sq.* ; ep. 128, 1 (concerning the education of little Pacatula): "Interim modo litterarum elementa cognoscat, iungat syllabas, discat nomina, verba consociet . . . de matris pendeat collo, rapiat oscula propinquorum, *psalmos mercede decantet*, amet quos cogitur discere, ut non opus sit labor sed delectatio, non necessitas sed voluntas."

[2] Hieron., ep. 128, 3: "Cum autem virgunculam rudem et edentulam septimus aetatis annus exceperit et ceperit erubescere, scire quid taceat, dubitare quid dicat, discat memoriter psalterium et usque ad annos pubertatis libros Salomonis, Evangelia, Apostolos et Prophetas sui cordis thesaurum faciat." St Basil also exhorts a widow to nourish her growing daughter with the words of the Lord. Paulinus

The *Apostolic Constitutions* (iv. 11) gives the comprehensive direction: "Teach your children thoroughly the Word of the Lord . . . and place in their hands every book of Holy Scripture." Many Fathers—St Basil, for instance[1]—testify that they themselves from their very earliest youth were made acquainted with the Bible. Several Fathers insist that women no less than men should occupy themselves with the study of the Bible.[2]

Seeing that it is unfortunately impossible to occupy oneself continually with the Bible as one ought, one must make a practice of reading a daily portion.[3] Those who have entirely dedicated themselves to God should devote several hours to quiet meditation (in some private place), alternating prayer with reading.[4]

---

of Nola (*Carm.*, xxiv. 829 *sq.*) gives directions concerning the education of his young nephew; he is to travel through all the *libri sacri.* *Cf.* Chrysos., Hom. xxi. in Ep. ad Ephes., T. xi. p. 160.

[1] *Proaem. De iudicio dei*, T. ii. p. 213.

[2] I would here only refer to the many pertinent epistles of St Jerome to women and maidens, and the epistle of Pelagius to Demetrias. They are indeed concerned with nuns, or women who are about to become nuns; but they set forth the general Christian ideal. Also the letter to Celancia printed among the works of Jerome and Paulinus of Nola (Hartel, i. p. 436 *sq.*) is especially instructive; see especially c. 14: "Non tam frequenter recordanda sunt praecepta dei quam semper cogitanda. Sint ergo divinae scripturae semper in manibus et iugiter mente volvantur, nec sufficere tibi putes mandata dei memoria tenere et operibus oblivisci."

[3] Hieron., ep. 107, 9: "Reddat tibi pensum quotidie de scripturarum floribus carptum." Ep. 54, 11: "De scripturis sanctis habeto fixum versuum numerum; istud pensum domino tuo redde"; and many similar passages.

[4] Pelag., ep. ad Demetr. *Cf.* St Jerome's letters to nuns.

The rest should imitate them as far as possible, and go into similar retirement at certain fixed hours.[1] The reading of Scripture will not separate them from their family; indeed, it is only through meditation on the Bible that they will gain a right relation to the family. Regular Scripture reading after the chief meal (thus before retiring to rest) is recommended by several Fathers, though in Antioch at the time of St Chrysostom it was regarded as an innovation.[2] Caesarius recommends reading at table if it is impossible to read before meals.[3] Both he[4] and St Chrysostom[5] recommend that after divine service the lections that had been heard in church should be again read at home. St Chrysostom, indeed, always announced what lections he would read on the following Sunday, in order that the congregation might read them and think over them

---

[1] Paulin., ep. ad Celanciam, 24 i., p. 454 : "Ita habeto domus sollicitudinem, ut aliquam tamen vacationem animae tribuas. eligatur tibi oportunus et aliquantulum a familiae strepitu remotus locus, in quem tu velut in portum quasi ex multa tempestate curarum te recipias et excitatos foris cogitationum fluctus secreti tranquillitate componas. tantum tibi sit divinae lectionis studium, tam crebrae orationum vices, tam firma et pressa de futuris cogitatio, ut omnes reliqui temporis occupationes facile hac vacatione compenses. nec hoc ideo dicimus, quo te retrahamus a tuis, immo id agimus, ut ibi discas ibique mediteris qualem tuis te praebere debeas."

[2] *Vide supra*, p. 119 (Hom. i. de Lazaro, i. p. 719). Also Hieron., ep. 54, 11 : "Quando comedis, cogita quod statim tibi orandum, illico et legendum sit . . . nec ante quieti membra concedas, quam calathum pectoris tui hoc subtegmine impleveris. post scripturas sanctas doctorum hominum tractatus lege."

[3] Sermo cxli., among the sermons of St Augustine.

[4] *Loc. cit.*

[5] "With wife and children." Hom. v. in Matth., T. vii. p. 72 *sq.*

beforehand at home.[1] Exhortations not to read too much are rare; yet Pelagius warns Demetrias not to read so long as to be obliged to cease from weariness, and St Ambrose writes concerning his sister:[2] "Tu multiplicatis noctibus ac diebus innumera tempora sine cibo transigis, et si quando rogaris ut cibum sumas, paulisper deponis codicem, respondes illico: Non in pane solo vivit homo sed in omni verbo dei. Ipse epularum usus cibis obviis; ut edendi fastidio ieiunium desideretur: potus e fonte, fletus in prece, somnus in codice."

We often meet with the strong recommendation that a part of what was read, especially the Psalms, should be learned by heart.[3] In antiquity, moreover, reading and learning by heart were more closely connected than with us. In one of his sermons St Chrysostom complains bitterly: "Which among you that are assembled here can repeat a psalm or any other portion out of the Bible? Not one! And this is not all that is sad, for ye who are so slothful in divine things are only the more forward in the things of Satan. If anyone required of you Satanic odes or impure lays, he would find many who knew them well and would repeat them with pleasure.

---

[1] This advice is very often given in his homilies; he was evidently very anxious to introduce this custom; *vide* Hom. iii. de Lazaro, T. i. p. 737 and elsewhere.

[2] *De Virginibus*, iii. 4, 15. Similar remarks are made by St Jerome.

[3] This command applied to monks with double emphasis; but every Christian should commit this most essential book to memory, for in it is summed up all that is profitable in Holy Scripture.

What is your defence against such charges? Ye say: I am not a monk but a married man, a father, and must direct the business of my household."[1]

The Psalms are to be learned by heart—the Psalms, indeed, stand everywhere in the foreground of Bible reading.[2] The man begins with them when he is already a child, and they are to be his companions through life; for all that is profitable in Holy Scripture is found gathered together in the Psalms; for layman and monk[3] they are alike important. Here West and East are at one, and there is no need of quotations to prove it.[4] St Jerome even counsels pious and gifted

---

[1] Hom. ii. in Matth., T. vii. p. 29 *sq.* ; *vide supra*, p. 118.

[2] Psalms and *lectio* are also distinguished from one another ; *vide* Hieron., ep. 130, 11 : "nec in lectione nec in psalmis."

[3] Nuns: Hieron., ep. 108, 19, concerning the convent of Paula : "Mane, hora tertia, sexta, nona, vespere, noctis medio per ordinem psalterium cantabant."

[4] The praise of the Psalms is proclaimed in the fullest tones by Gregory of Nyssa (Tract. i., in psalm. inscr. 3, T. i. p. 263 *sq.*). He would show why the difficult teaching of the virtuous life, the proclamation of doctrines so mysterious, a theology veiled in dogma so unintelligible, are made so easy, so acceptable in the Psalms, that not only those who are more mature and practised in the spiritual life eagerly listen to their teaching, but also women as if it belonged only to them ; that children find in it the same pleasure as in their games, the aged the same satisfaction as in their staff and their repose ; that the joyful believe that the gift was meant only for them, while the sorrowful and unfortunate likewise think that it is for their sake that God has given this gracious boon. Even so, those who travel by land or sea and those who sit at home about their business, in short, all classes, men and women, sick and whole, count it loss if they have not this lofty teaching in their mouths. At our feasts, at our marriage revels, this philosophy is a part of our enjoyment, etc. Ambros., Praef. in Psal. i. enarr. 7 : "In libro Psalmorum profectus est omnium et

women and maidens to learn Hebrew, in order to be able to read the Psalms in the original, and his exhortation was not without effect.[1]

Starting from the Psalms, the reading of the Bible is to be gradually extended. Full use must be made of the many-sidedness of the Bible.[2] Many Fathers show that their mind is set upon an ordered course of reading,[3] though they do not go into details. Here St Jerome (ep. 107, 12) is the most precise in his recommendations; he draws up what is a veritable course of reading and instruction: "Discat primo Psalterium, his se cantis avocet et in Proverbiis Salomonis erudiatur ad vitam. in Ecclesiaste consuescat quae mundi sunt calcare. in Iob virtutis et patientiae exempla sectetur.

medicina quaedam salutis humanae. . . . Intra unum Psalmum (ps. 67) totam paternae historiae seriem accipit comprehensam . . . 8 : In Psalmis nobis non solum nascitur Jesus, sed etiam salutarem illam suscipit corporis passionem, quiescit, resurgit, ascendit ad caelum, sedet ad dexteram patris "; *cf.* § 9.

[1] Hieron., ep. 39, 1 (de Blaesilla): "Si Graece loquentem audiisses, Latine eam nescire putares ; si in Romanum sonum lingua se verterat, nihil omnino peregrini sermo redolebat. Iam vero quod in Origene quoque illo Graecia tota miratur, in paucis non dicam mensibus, sed diebus, ita Hebraeae linguae vicerat difficultates, ut in discendis canendisque Psalmis cum matre contenderet." Ep. 30 ; 33 ; 108, 19 (de Paula): "Non licebat cuiquam sororum ignorare psalmos et non de scripturis sanctis quotidie aliquid discere." Ep. 108, 26 : "Hebraeam linguam discere voluit et consecuta est, ita ut psalmos Hebraice, caneret et sermonem absque ulla Latinae linguae proprietate personaret. quod quidem usque hodie in sancta filia eius Eustochia cernimus."

[2] Pelagius, Ep. ad Demetr. But the reading of Scripture should not be "ad laborem," but "ad delectationem" (Hieron., ep. 130, 15).

[3] *Vide supra*, pp. 72 ff. ; 119 ff. Augustin., *ad Volusianum* and *De Doctr Christ.*, ii. 9.

ad Evangelia transeat, numquam ea positura de
manibus. Apostolorum Acta et epistolas tota cordis
imbibat voluntate. cumque pectoris sui cellarium his
opibus locupletaverit, mandet memoriae Prophetas,
Heptateuchum et Regum et Paralipomenom libros,
Esdrae quoque et Esther volumina. ad ultimum sine
periculo discat Canticum Canticorum, ne si in exordio
legerit, sub carnalibus verbis spiritualium nuptiarum
epithalamium non intelligens, vulneretur. caveat omnia
apocrypha . . . Cypriani opuscula semper in manu
teneat. Athanasii epistolas et Hilarii libros inoffenso
decurrat pede. illorum tractatibus, illorum delectetur
ingeniis, in quorum libris pietas fidei non vacillat.
ceteros sic legat, ut magis iudicet quam sequatur."
From St Jerome we thus derive the following course of
Bible reading: first the Kethubim (except the Song of
Solomon), *i.e.* the ethical writings form the commencement; then follow the Gospels; in the third place come
the Apostolic writings; in the fourth place, all the
remaining books of the Old Testament, with the
Prophets in the forefront; the course closes with the
Song of Solomon. The principles governing this course
are transparent.

But how confused must have been the poor head of
the layman—of the plain man or woman—that was thus
crammed with the Bible! How much could they understand? The Fathers do not disguise from themselves
the fact that much—and more especially the deeper
significance—must remain unintelligible to them. But

they console themselves with the following considerations: (1) The verbal sense on its ethical side, the narratives, and the Gospel stories and miracles are for the most part intelligible and can be at once assimilated when simply read,[1] and such simple reading is what God wills, who does not demand of us subtlety of intellect;[2] (2) God will Himself provide for further understanding according to the need of each; (3) even what is not understood is valuable for edification and promotes sanctification,[3] and even what seems to be unedifying, such as the lists of names and the genealogies, enshrines rich jewels of mystery;[4] (4) a man can advance himself in understanding of the Bible by asking questions of good teachers. As a matter of fact, interested laymen constantly availed themselves of this means, as is especially shown in the works of St Jerome and St Augustine. St Jerome was often overwhelmed with questions addressed to him concerning the Bible, more especially by his spiritual friends among the ladies of Rome. It is plain that at the end of the fourth and the beginning of the fifth century there was a spiritual awakening everywhere in connection with the growing adoption of monasticism by persons of education; this movement was in close

---

[1] *Vide* especially Chrysostom, Hom. iii. de Lazaro, T. i. p. 739 *sq.*

[2] *Vide, e.g.*, Ephraem, Sermo lxx. adv. scrutatores, T. iii. p. 193 (Syro-Lat., Assemani); Hieron. in Iesaj., L. iv., T. iii. p. 102.

[3] Chrysostom, *loc. cit.*

[4] Chrysostom, Hom. xxi. in Genes., T. iv. p. 181; Hom. ii. in Iesaj. vi. 2, T. vi. p. 109.

9

touch with the Bible; men wished to master the Bible that they might attain to the knowledge of God and deepen their spiritual life.[1]   Among those of lower social rank the movement was at work at an earlier date; but here also study of the Bible was now more strenuous than before.   Even among barbarians, friends of the Bible were not wanting.   "Jam Aegyptius Serapis factus est Christianus, Marnas Gazae luget inclusus et eversionem templi iugiter pertimescit.   de India, Perside, Aethiopia monachorum quotidie turbas suscipimus.   deposuit pharetras Armenius, *Hunni discunt psalterium*, Scythiae frigora fervent calore fidei: Getularum rutilus et flavus exercitus ecclesiarum circumfert tentoria."[2]   "Quis hoc crederet," cries St Jerome in one of his epistles,[3] "ut barbara Getarum lingua Hebraicam quaereret veritatem et dormitantibus, imo contendentibus Graecis ipsa Germania spiritus sancti eloquia scrutaretur?"

Such Bible reading has disadvantages; it tends to encourage faults which manifest themselves among all those whose knowledge of the Bible is gained through self-education or at the ordinary Bible-class, such as self-

---

[1] In connection with this movement, the great Bible-quaestiones literature makes its appearance partly as an independent branch (*cf.*, as the most ancient Latin work of the kind, the voluminous and valuable "Quaestiones" of Pseudo-Augustine on the two Testaments, which belongs to the end of the fourth century and proceeds perhaps from the Jewish-Christian Isaac: ed. Souter, 1908), partly in conjunction with more general works of the same kind.

[2] Hieron., ep. 107, 2.

[3] Ep. 106, 1.

conceit, spiritual pride, disdain of theological learning. These faults were not wanting in those early days, but they were rarely rebuked, from apprehension lest the Spirit might be quenched and Bible reading restricted. Only the three most important and most cultured Fathers—Augustine, Jerome, and Gregory of Nazianzen—ventured to speak words of warning. St Augustine, in the notable preface to his work, *De Doctrina Christiana*, gives most energetic expression to the thought that those who, in their Bible reading, trust solely to the spirit fall into error and cannot grasp the real sense of what they read, and that devoted study and accurate knowledge are thus indispensable. The spirit, he continues, is never found apart from the letter; therefore human guidance is necessary for the understanding of the Scriptures, for the letter implies learning. "Be it said in all seriousness: let each learn without self-conceit all that can only be learned from men, and let everyone who teaches others impart without self-conceit and envy all that he has received. Let us not tempt God, to whom we have given ourselves, in that we, led astray by the wiles of the Enemy and our own perversity, determine neither to go to church nor to read a book nor to listen to human reading or exhortation, not even that we may hear and learn about the Gospel. Must we then expect, in the body or out of the body, as the Apostle says, to be caught up into the third heaven and there to hear unspeakable words which no man can utter, or there to see the Lord Jesus Christ and to hear the Gospel from Him rather than from men?" St Augustine then refers very pertinently to the fact that even St Paul, though he had heard the voice from heaven, was yet sent to Ananias, and that the centurion Cornelius, though he was found worthy to receive the angelic visitation, yet needed St Peter to give him instruction. "All this could have been given by the Angel; but the dignity of human nature would have been compromised if God had made it appear that He did not wish His work ·to be proclaimed to man by man." . . . "If men learn nothing by human means, love, which binds men together in the bond of unity, would have no opportunity to draw souls together in mutual converse and to blend them with one another." The following passage, directed against these self-taught spiritualists, is most noteworthy: "They have good confidence in their gift from God whereby they can at once comprehend the obscurities of Holy Scripture, and they seek thereby not their own but God's glory. But if one of them himself reads and understands without human explanation, *why does he apply himself to give explanations to others, why does he not rather point them to God that they also may attain to insight not by human mediation but by direct divine inspiration?* Is it not perhaps because he fears that he may one day hear those words: 'Thou slothful servant, thou shouldest have given my money to the changers'? Seeing that these also impart their knowledge by word and writing,

I also am not deserving of their blame. . . . No one may treat anything except what is false as his own peculiar property."

In other fashion St Jerome makes the similar complaint that everyone imagined that he could interpret the Bible. Let his pointed and biting words speak for themselves:[1] "Sola scripturarum ars est, quam sibi omnes passim vindicant. 'Scribimus indocti doctique poëmata passim' [Horatius]. Hanc garrula anus, hanc delirus senex, hanc sophista verbosus, hanc universi praesumunt, lacerant, docent, antequam discant. alii adducto supercilio grandia verba trutinantes inter mulierculas de sacris literis philosophantur. alii discunt, proh pudor, a feminis, quod viros doceant, et ne parum hoc sit, quadam facilitate verborum, imo audacia edisserunt aliis, quod ipsi non intelligunt. taceo de mei similibus, qui si forte ad scripturas sanctas post saeculares literas venerint, et sermone composito aurem populi mulserint, quidquid dixerint, hoc legem dei putant, nec scire dignantur, quid prophetae, quid apostoli senserint, sed ad sensum suum incongrua aptant testimonia, quasi grande sit et non vitiossimum docendi genus, depravare sententias et ad voluntatem suam scripturam trahere repugnantem."[2]

[1] Ep. 53, 7.

[2] Cf. also Ep. 119, 11 ; 130, 17: "Certe si rudes saecularium literarum de tractatibus hominum disertorum quippiam legerint, verbositatem solam discunt absque notitia scripturarum, et iuxta vetus elogium: cum loqui nesciant, tacere non possunt docentque scripturas quas non intelligunt, et cum aliis persuaserint, eruditorum

But Gregory of Nazianzen is the only Father who declares in plain words that the whole of Holy Scripture is not meant for persons of all ages, that it is presumptuous folly to pretend to interpret the Bible without adequate knowledge, that by this means many dangerous errors have arisen, and that some ancient Hebrew teachers had judged that the whole Bible should not be made accessible to the faithful before they had reached the age of twenty-five years.[1] He does not, however, venture to accept or recommend this rule in plain terms. An attempt to introduce such restrictions into the Churches was evidently hopeless. Neither Augustine nor Jerome nor Gregory dreamed of compulsory rules limiting the reading of the Bible.

§ 4.—BIBLICAL THEOLOGY AND THE LAITY

The Church's science is Biblical science, and in principle she owns no other. The two founders of ecclesiastical theology, Justin and Valentinus (Ptolemy), created this science as in strict sense a theology of the Bible[2]—Justin as a theology of the Old Testament

sibi assumunt supercilium, prius imperitorum magistri quam doctorum discipuli. bonum est igitur obedire maioribus, parere perfectis et post regulas scripturarum vitae suae tramitem ab aliis discere nec praeceptore uti pessimo, scilicet praesumptione sua. De talibus feminis [he is therefore speaking of women] et apostolus loquitur."

[1] *Orat.* ii. 48, T. i. p. 35 ; *vide supra*, p. 30.

[2] In *Texte und Untersuch.*, Bd. xxviii., 2b, S. 3 ff. (1905), I have pointed out that it is possible that the Ptolemy of Justin's second apology is identical with Ptolemy the Gnostic. I am the more con-

with help from the Gospels; Ptolemy as a theology of the Gospels and the Pauline doctrine in antithesis to the Old Testament. The synthesis of the two was carried out by Irenaeus, Clement, and Origen, who made the theology of the Church the theology of both Testaments. The process first reached its completion with Origen,[1] and remained as he left it. St Augustine, in his work *De Doctrina Christiana*, *i.e.* "Concerning Christian Theology," understands ecclesiastical theology as being exclusively a theology of the Bible.

This is not the place to discuss the vast questions of the manner in which this science took form, of its principles, its organisation and development as a kind of Biblical alchemy in decided opposition to all knowledge based upon the intellect, though copious use was made of the same. Our sole concern is to establish the fact *that in the fourth century this theology was as exoteric as the Bible itself, which was meant to be read by everyone.* The prudent efforts of Origen to reserve Biblical theology for the "Gnostics," *i.e.* for theologians, were felt to be a serious encroachment upon the universality and the popular character of Christianity, and as such were rejected. This on the

firmed in my opinion since noticing how alike, in spite of all differences, is the attitude of both towards the Old Testament; *vide* my article concerning St Matt. v. 17 in the *Sitzungsber. der Preuss. Akademie*, 15th February 1912. I believe that Justin learned from Ptolemy as did Origen from Heracleon.

[1] *Vide* his work *De Principiis*, especially book iv.

one hand necessarily led to the fatal result that the worship of the letter, the orthodoxy of ordinary and monastic minds, sooner or later completely triumphed; yet on the other hand there was the good side that *in the early days of the Church the Bible was never handed over either to the priesthood or to some separate caste as their exclusive possession.* Biblical theology was *in principle* as accessible to the laity as to the clergy, and as a matter of fact laymen did participate in it.[1] There is a general disposition to paint the early history of the Church in too ecclesiastical colours, in that traits which belong to the Middle Ages are too hastily assigned to it. The ministration of public worship and of the sacraments lay in the hands of the priests; but the Bible together with Biblical theology were exoteric, it was intended that in these all, to the best of their powers, should exercise themselves. Compared with other religions, there was something of a paradox in the fact that the books were accessible to all; yet this very fact reveals an essential difference between the Christian religion (with the Jewish) and other religions:[2] each man is to be "taught of God," each for himself should daily

[1] Justin and other apologists were laymen; Origen as a layman laid the foundations of ecclesiastical dogmatics; the heads of the Alexandrian school were obliged to be laymen; it is doubtful whether Tertullian was a cleric; Augustine as a layman applied himself to ecclesiastical theology; and so forth.

[2] Islam, the daughter-religion of Christianity, treats the Koran in the same way.

listen to the Divine Voice in the Bible. Hence in
the early days Christianity never fully became a
mystery-religion.[1]

Together with the Bible the Church possesses the
Creed, the deposit of her faith and her tradition, as
a fundamental rule of belief. What is the relation
between Creed and Bible, or, in other words, between
tradition and the Bible? Volumes have been written
on this subject. At no period has the relation been
clearly realised. It is indeed obvious that the New
Testament "came in between"; for the *fides quae
creditur* was prior to the New Testament, and the
Old Testament was prior to the *fides*. It might be
said that the traditional *fides* was true because it could
be proved from Holy Scripture (or was derived from
Holy Scripture), or that the Scripture was inspired
because it bore testimony to the tenets of the
traditional *fides*. Both statements, forming as they
do an argument in a circle, were equally orthodox.
It was accounted correct to confirm the truth of the
Creed clause by clause by means of texts of Holy Scripture—every catechumen was supposed to be supplied
with a store of such texts[2]—and to regard the Creed
as a surrogate for the inexhaustible riches of Holy
Scripture, as an excerpt from Scripture convenient

[1] The rise of monasticism and of monastic theology was conditioned
by this fact.

[2] *Vide* the *Testimonia* of Cyprian, and especially the catechetical
lectures of Cyril of Jerusalem, Epiphan., *Ancorat.*, 199, etc.

and easy to handle.[1] On the other hand, it was as correct to regard the Creed as the complete epitome of religion ("a Christo per apostolos") and to recognise the actual possibility of a Christian life lived without the Scriptures and only in accordance with the rule of the *fides*. The traditional *fides* was, however, more acceptable to the officials of an ecclesiastical system than the Scriptures; for these ever kept alive the truth of the universal priesthood and afforded to the reader independent and free converse with God. The popular view concerning the relation between Holy Scripture and the Creed of the Church is reproduced by Vincentius of Lerinum in his *Commonitorium* (1 *sq.*), where he says that Holy Scripture is in itself all-sufficient; but, seeing that it is interpreted in various ways, and that thus many heresies and errors have arisen, it is therefore necessary to call in the Church's Creed as a guide to interpretation. According to this view, the Holy Scripture is superior to the Creed;

---

[1] Cyril, *Catech.*, v. 12: Πίστιν ἐν μαθήσει καὶ ἀπαγγελίᾳ κτῆσαι καὶ τήρησον μόνην, τὴν ὑπὸ τῆς ἐκκλησίας νυνί σοι παραδιδομένην, τὴν ἐκ πάσης γραφῆς ὠχυρωμένην. ἐπειδὴ γὰρ οὐ πάντες δύνανται τὰς γραφὰς ἀναγινώσκειν, ἀλλὰ τοὺς μὲν ἰδιωτεία, τοὺς δὲ ἀσχολία τις ἐμποδίζει πρὸς τὴν γνῶσιν· ὑπὲρ τοῦ μὴ τὴν ψυχὴν ἐξ ἀμαθίας ἀπολέσθαι ἐν ὀλίγοις τοῖς στίχοις τὸ πᾶν δόγμα τῆς πίστεως περιλαμβάνομεν . . . . καὶ τέως μὲν ἐπ' αὐτῆς τῆς λέξεως ἀκούων, μνημόνευσον τῆς πίστεως, ἐκδέχου δὲ κατὰ τὸν δέοντα καιρὸν τὴν ἀπὸ τῶν θείων γραφῶν περὶ ἕκαστον τῶν ἐγκειμένων σύστασιν· οὐ γὰρ ὡς ἔδοξεν ἀνθρώποις συνετέθη τὰ τῆς Πίστεως, ἀλλ' ἐκ πάσης γραφῆς τὰ καιριώτατα συλλεχθέντα μίαν ἀναπληροῖ τὴν τῆς Πίστεως διδασκαλίαν. Here the Creed is completely subordinated to Scripture; but the history of its origin is simply constructed without reference to the actual facts.

but in spite of the fact that so many Fathers are of a similar opinion, yet the Church of Rome has never been able to acquiesce in it.

St Augustine alone boldly makes a statement which implies a freedom even surpassing the freedom implied by the possession of the Scripture as opposed to the claims of ecclesiastical dogma. He writes (*De Doctrina Christiana*, i. 39): " *A man who bases himself upon Faith, Hope, and Love, and keeps firm hold of these, needs the Scripture only for the instruction of others. Thus many live by these three virtues without any books, even in the desert.*" The second sentence weakens the force of the first; yet St Augustine does not intend the first sentence to apply only to monks, as is shown by many passages of his works. He here understands by Faith, Hope, and Love a frame of mind that is not simply and solely obedience to the traditional *fides*, but lies in another sphere which he himself has discovered yet cannot adequately describe. What he says passes far beyond Origen's theory that the perfect " Gnostic " has no further need of ordinary means of grace and of knowledge, or rather the two views are not on the same plane. The pre-Augustinian period was dominated by two ideals—an authoritative Christianity of the Creed (the Apostolic deposit) and a Christianity of the Holy Scriptures equally authoritative, through enshrining an element of liberty. Both ideals were equally accessible to the laity. St Augustine denied neither the one nor the other, but he had so lived himself into

the spirit of the Psalms and of St Paul that he had
arrived at the vision of a state of Christian independence which had no further need of sacred writings.

Yet one more question, and the last: Do we find
that there existed in early days a lay theology distinct
from, or perhaps opposed to, the prevalent theology of
the Church? The question is to be answered in the
negative. It is indeed true that since the second
century two schools of theology, one "realistic" and
"literal," the other "idealistic" and "spiritual," stood
in strong opposition to one another: I have fully dealt
with these two schools and the history of their relation
with one another in my *History of Dogma*. It is also
true that the realistic and literal school derived then,
as always, part of its power from the simple and
fanatical believers among the uneducated laity (and
the monks); but the sides were never, or at least only
here and there, so divided as to constitute a cleavage
between clergy and laity. This statement holds good
for the Montanist, Monarchian, Eschatological, Origen-
istic, and other controversies. Laymen and monks
never had cause to complain that their obscurantist,
realistic, and "literal" views were unrepresented in the
public Forum of the Church, and that their corporeal
God, furnished with all parts and members, was destitute
of a champion there. More than once, indeed, in the
history of dogma the "scientific" faith of the theologians overcame and suppressed the naïve faith of the
majority of Christians, but as a rule this majority also

included the greater part of the clergy. After the close of the fourth century the great compromise was concluded between the two schools, and the monks as the champions of the naïve faith of the laity now celebrated their triumph. But although some priests, like Theophilus of Alexandria and Jerome, were compelled to capitulate, this triumph could be felt and regarded only as a victory over the theologians, not over the priests, for it was as theologians, not as priests, that they made their submission, and the ranks of the victors were led by priests, above all by Epiphanius. We have therefore no right to describe the priests as the vanquished, or to speak of a religion of the laity which then gained the victory.

We have greater justification for describing the position represented by the ecclesiastical historian Socrates [1] as a theology with definitely lay characteristics. In fact, an anti-clerical, indeed—so far as it was possible at that time—an undogmatic, type of Christianity here makes its appearance, and the Byzantine lawyer would not have expressed himself so unreservedly if a large number of persons had not shared in his opinions. But this position has no direct connection with the Bible. It was not deduced from the educated layman's study of the Bible, but was due to the influence of Origen and his school, as Socrates himself testifies. The theology of Origen had evoked among the educated laity a type of "liberal" Christianity which

[1] *Vide* my article in the 2nd edition of Hauck's *Encyclopaedia*.

held itself aloof from sacerdotal and dogmatic disputes—similar, indeed, to that type which came into being last century under the influence of the rationalistic movement and the philosophy of Hegel and Schleiermacher. In both instances the private use of Holy Scripture played absolutely no part, and in the second and third generations the study even of the writings of theologian and philosopher only to the very slightest degree contributed to a result which was principally due to the general diffusion of their ideas. Since we are only concerned with the private use of Holy Scripture, we are not called upon to investigate this Byzantine type of lay Christianity. It never gave the Church much trouble—unless, indeed, we regard the iconoclastic movement as a late offshoot from it.

MAIN CONCLUSIONS

1. According to the present teaching of the Roman Catholic Church, Holy Scripture is the property of the Church as a body, and she—*i.e.*, in the last instance, the Pope—is bound to administer this property dutifully according to her discretion, and to determine how and in what measure Holy Scripture is to be made accessible to the individual Christian.[1] As a result of our investiga-

---

[1] "Holy Scripture is not of itself the immediate rule of faith for the individual ; it, like tradition, is only mediated to the individual by the official ministry of the Church. To this ministry is committed the whole deposit of the Faith, whether written or oral, both for its own use and to be imparted to the faithful" (Wetzer und Weltes' *Kirchenlexicon*, Bd. x.[2] col. 1956).

tion we see that this claim of the Roman Catholic Church is an innovation. Neither in the first three centuries nor in the fourth was the Bible in any sense subordinate to the Church; accordingly, we cannot discover the slightest trace of a belief that the relations of the laity to the Holy Scriptures were different from, and more limited than, those of the clergy, or of any authoritative episcopal ordinance restricting laymen in their reading of the Bible. Such authoritative ordinances as are found refer only to the distinction to be made between canonical apocryphal and heretical writings; in addition to these we have, of course, instances of advice and guidance being given with a view to instructing the laity as to the best method of reading the Bible. Holy Scripture and the Church stood side by side as independent entities. The Bible belongs to the individual in the same sense as it belongs to the Church. Complication first came in when it was taught that Scripture must be interpreted in accordance with the rule of faith, yet of course no distinction was thereby created between clergy and laity in reference to the use of Holy Scripture.[1] Protestantism has thus the testimony of the Early Church on its side in not allowing the Church to dictate the relations between the individual and Holy Scripture. If the Church of Rome would only restrict herself to giving advice or

---

[1] It is obvious that this theory in actual working would necessarily lead to the subordination of Scripture to the Church, and thus to the clergy; but we cannot here dwell further upon this point.

warning in regard to the reading of the Bible, such an attitude could be reconciled with the attitude of the Early Church. But seeing that the official ministry of that Church asserts its right to enact binding ordinances in regard to the use of Scripture, and thus to bring the Scriptures into direct subjection to itself,[1] it follows that the claim of the Roman Catholic Church to be the Church of unaltered tradition breaks down in this, as in so many other points.

2. What has been said implies the refutation of Lessing's ninth thesis: " The layman of the Early Church might not even read the separate books of the New Testament, at least not without the permission of the presbyter, who had them in his keeping." Lessing himself afterwards limited his thesis to the first three centuries; but, as we have seen, it is as false for the earliest days as it is for the fourth century. Until about the end of the second century no New Testament was in existence, and the documentary evidence for this century is not very extensive. In this century, however, so far as concerns the Old Testament, the situation was not different from that in the third and fourth centuries, which means that the practice of the fourth century

---

[1] The later Greek Church, as in so many instances, has in practice followed the lead of the Roman Church (yet in a weak and half-hearted fashion); in theory her attitude is equally uncertain; the "Confessio Dosithei," qu. 1 (Kimmel, *Monumenta Fidei*, p. 465), which adopts entirely the Roman position, is not decisive: Τοῖς μὴ γεγυμνασ-μένοις . . . . ἡ καθολικὴ ἐκκλησία . . . . οὐ θεμιτὴν τὴν ἀνάγνωσιν εἶναι ἐντέλλεται, soon afterwards we read " ἀπηγορεύεται."

and even later was the same from the beginning.
Lessing's theory is not, however, only partly false, it is
false altogether; for laymen not only *might* read, but
they actually *did* read, Holy Scripture; the presbyters
had not to give any permission; the Holy Scriptures
were not in their " keeping," but were accessible to all,
and were in the hands of many Christians. Lessing's
great mistake cannot, however, detract from the undying
service he has rendered in a much more important
question, in that he perceived that the New Testament
as a book and as the recognised fundamental document
of the Christian religion originated in the *Church*.
But Lessing did not recognise that the Book from the
moment of its origin freed itself from all the conditions
of its birth, and at once claimed to be an *entirely independent and unconditioned authority*. This was indeed
only possible because the book at once took its place
beside the Old Testament, which occupied a position of
absolute and unquestionable independence because it
was more ancient than the Church.[1]

3. The proof that the Bible in the Early Church was
not a secret book but was accessible to all, and was
also much read in private, involves a point of peculiar

[1] The philosophic historian might therefore argue as follows :—Seeing
that the New Testament is an offspring of the Church, the Church of
the Middle Ages (*i.e.* the Council of Trent), in that it subordinated
Scripture to the Church, only did away with the fiction that the New
Testament was to be reverenced and treated as a book of independent
authority. Thus, though the Tridentine decrees did not restore the
ancient tradition, yet they took up the true historical position in regard

10

importance; it follows that the religion of the Early Church, however much of mystery and sacrament it gradually adopted, was, like Judaism, no mystery-religion. If the revelation of God—and according to Christian ideas the Bible included practically all instances of Divine revelation—was in its entirety accessible to all, if in regard to this revelation the priest was almost as much a "layman" as the layman himself, if no ecclesiastical law, no clerical interference was allowed to come between God speaking in the Bible and the soul of him who listened and read, then the religion is in principle no mystery-religion, to whatever extent it may have become such in its accessories. That it was not yet a mystery-religion even about the year 300 is shown in a striking way by the origin of monasticism; that it still preserved its essential character about the year 400 is shown by the fact that monasticism prevailed and continued to increase in strength.

If it is asked how it happened that Christianity was able to preserve in principle its distinctive character

to the New Testament, a position which lay behind tradition and was lost sight of from the very first. But this train of argument would only be conclusive if the Tridentine decrees had at the same time done away with the doctrine of the inspiration of the book, and had given scope for free investigation into the origin of the Canon. As this was not done, the decrees only created a new contradiction. Thus it is the free theology of Protestantism that was the first to discover the correct historical standpoint, and this theology declares—here showing itself more Catholic than the Pope himself—that the New Testament *qua* compilation is an offspring of the Catholic Church and is nothing else. Its separate parts share, of course, a common origin with the Catholic Church, all springing from the same soil.

and to defend its sacred writings from the encroachment of the priesthood amid a world of mystery-religion, we answer—it was because Christianity was the daughter of Judaism; it was because Christianity, in so far as it was distinct from Judaism, was more spiritual, more lucid, more free, more universal, more simple than that religion; and because, with even greater energy than Judaism, it strove to make not only the faith, but also the sacred discipline of the life, the central point of its system. Soon, indeed, the faith and the cultus attracted to themselves and acquiesced in very much that belonged to the mystery-religions, but the essential characteristics of Christianity—the belief in God as the Almighty Creator of heaven and earth, as the Father of mankind, as the Father of Jesus Christ, the good news addressed to *all* men, the faith in the Saviour of the world, the *regula disciplinae* for a new humanity—all these fundamental characteristics could not possibly be proclaimed in mysteries, and at the same time implied and demanded an unrestricted use of the Bible. This unrestricted right to listen daily to the direct voice of God might have proved the strongest bulwark of Christian independence, freedom, and equality, and a lasting defence against complete subjection to sacerdotalism and mystery. But as time went on the laity made less and less use of their privilege: *la médiocrité fonda l'autorité*; and when in the twelfth century a lay Christianity based upon the private reading of the Bible struggled into the light of day, it was now too late. The Church of priesthood and mystery—though even then it had not altogether become this—was now strong enough not only to crush this development, but also, unencumbered by the tradition of bygone centuries, to begin to take measures, at first cautiously and tentatively, with a view to withdrawing the Bible from the common people. Neither then nor afterwards did she deal thoroughly and decisively with this question, because half-measures were quite sufficient, and because it was necessary to preserve in appearance the sovereignty and the publicity of the Bible. The Reformation, however, measured by the standard of antiquity, has one of its chief justifications in the fact that it has restored the Bible to the common people, because it recognised the complete sovereignty and publicity of Holy Scripture as the inspired Word of God. Now, indeed, the dogma of inspiration can be no longer upheld, yet all that is Christian in these fundamental historical documents must be preserved; in power for edification no other book comes up to their standard, and no creed, no Church, has the right to decide what they contain and what they teach.

APPENDIX

(TO NOTE 4 UPON PAGE 126)

GREGORY of Nyssa relates that at feasts and marriage-festivals it was customary to extract amusement from the Psalms. The "Cenae" (Table-Talk), like the "Cena Cypriani" of the fourth or fifth century, and cursory remarks of Zeno of Verona (Tract. ii. 38), afford other instances of similar use of the Bible. The object was to imprint passages from the Bible on the memory, to make them amusing, and to incite to Bible reading: "The host offers you from his table precious bread and wine that he has brought out of his store-rooms. The 'three young men' arrange first to eat vegetables, which, to make them more palatable, they sprinkle with the salt of wisdom; Christ pours oil upon them; Moses prepares, in the haste in which it happened, a full-grown lamb of the first year; Abraham in his faith a fatted and well-dressed calf; Isaac in his innocence brings the oil and the wood; the patient Jacob offers sheep of different kinds; Joseph gives corn of all kinds if anyone has want. . . . Noah, the host of the Ark, refuses nothing that is asked for. Peter the fisherman presents rich supplies of sea-fish with wondrous condiment. Tobias the foreigner prepares and carefully fries the entrails of the fresh-water fish. John, the humble Forerunner in the garment of camels' hair, collects honey and locusts from the wilderness, and so forth." *Cf.* Harnack, *Texte u. Unters.*, Bd. xix., H. 3b, 1899; Brewer in the *Ztschr. f. kathol. Theol.*, 1904, S. 92; Hass, *Studien z. Heptateuchdichter Cyprian* (Berliner Diss.), 1912. Such jests and riddles from the Bible were popular in pietistic circles even in the last century, and were intended to promote Bible reading.

H. Achelis (*Das Christentum in den ersten drei Jahrhunderten*, ii. p. 105 f.), has also reminded me of Pseudo-Cyprian (Novatian), *adv. Jud.*, 10 (Christian children and peasants know the Bible and can give instruction in the Holy Scriptures); Euseb., *De Mart. Pal.*, 11 (the deacon Valens in Jerusalem knew the whole Bible by heart); *Can. Hippolyti*, 27 (every Christian should daily study the Scriptures, even though he has already heard them read at public worship); also of the constant reading of the Scriptures by the Therapeutae.

INDEX OF AUTHORS QUOTED

151

Sulpicius Severus, Dial. i. 6 f. :
66, 111.
Dial. i. 8 : 97.
  ,, i. 23 : 96.
  ,, i. 27 : 95.
  ,, iii. 17 : 96.

Tatianus, Orat. 29 : 42.
Orat. 33 : 43.
Tertullianus, de praescr. 8 ff.,
14 ff., 41 : 51.
Apol. 31 : 56.
de testim. 1 : 57.
de spect. 29 : 61.
de corona 1 : 58.
ad uxor. ii. 6 : 55.

Tertullianus, de bapt. 17 : 62.
de exhort. 7 : 118.
de cult. fem. i. 3 : 111.
de monog. 11, 12 : 118.
de jejunio 11 : 67.
Theodoretus, Graec. affect. cur.
v. : 90.
h. e. i. 20 : 97.
Theodos. Codex xvi. 5, 34 : 104.
Theophilus, ad Aut. i. 14 : 42.
ad Aut. ii. 34 : 42.

Vincentius, Commonit. 1 ff. : 138.

Zeno Veron. : 94, 149.
Zenophilus, Gesta apud : 82.

Further information of all kinds as to the *lectio privata* can be extracted from the following passages in the Epistles of St Jerome : Ep. 5, 2 ; 7, 2 ; 22, 17. 25 ; 29, 1 ; 31, 3 ; 34, 3 ; 38, 4 ; 43, 1 ; 43, 2. 3 ; 45, 2 ; 50, 1. 3 ; 52, 7 ; 53, 1. 3. 6. 9 ; 54, 13 ; 58, 6. 9 ; 60, 10 ; 65, 2 ; 66, 9 ; 68, 2 ; 75, 4 ; 77, 7. 9 ; 79, 9 ; 84, 8 ; 125, 11. 15. 16 ; 127, 4. 7 ; 128, 4 ; 130, 7. 20 ; 148, 14. 24.

INDEX OF SUBJECTS

155

Bible, literary controversies concerning, 78 f.
market value of copies, 35 f., 96 ff.
new birth through the Bible, 70 ; the Bible as a treasury, 115 ; as an instructor, 53, 69 ; as the greatest public revelation of the Divine Will, 115 ; not to be treated as God, 87 f. ; the second creation, 84 ; the tool for every Christian, 98 ; not to be touched in certain sexual conditions, 102.
not regarded as an obscure book, 37 ; explanation of its obscurity, 72.
not regarded as a secret book, 27 f., 56 f., 71 f. ; meant for all, 78 f., 113 (to be read by Jews and heathen), 135 f.
not regarded like the Koran, 45.
plagiarism, supposed, from Plato, 77.
means for preservation of copies of, 34 f., 81 f., 100 f.
takes place of profane literature, 58 ff.
prohibition of the Bible among Catholics, 1–8.
Protestant conception of, 1 ff., 8 f.
reverence due to copies of, 81 f., 101.
scarcity of copies of, 33, 117 f.
sumptuous copies of, 99.
superstitious use of, 86 ff., 101 f., 129.
surrender of (traditio), 81 f., 102.
Bible readers, a kind of philosophers, 85 ; peasants, 150.
women "Bible readers" all probably deaconesses, 25.
Bible reading, not yet recommended in the New Testament, 33, 38.
fruit of, 115 f.
useless according to Julian, 115.
and prayer, 55 f., 65, 69, etc.

Bible reading, at home, 55 f., 58 f., 66 f., 68 f., 75, 83 f., 98 f., 112, 117, 123 f., 149 f.
compensated for by public lection in cases of necessity, 98 f.
daily and continuous, 69 f., 74 f., 84 f., 115 f., 123, 150.
because one should every day hear God's voice, 65.
fixed times and hours for, 56, 68 f., 123 ff.
in Bible classes, 63 ff., 83.
to be combined with learning by heart, 75, 83 f., 122, 125, 150.
progressive course of, 72 f., 115 f., 122 f., 127 f., 134.
excuses against, 117 ff.
difficulties and dangers of, 113 f. ; conceit, pride, contempt of theology, 130 ff.
even children should make a beginning, 84, 122 f., 149 f.
importance in elementary education and in spreading the art of reading, 85 f.
in special rooms near the church, 122.
laymen say that it belongs to monks, 94, 117 f., 126.
of monks and nuns, 106 f., 116 f., 123, 125 f., 129 f.
more necessary for laymen than for monks, 118.
leads to monasticism, 69, 117.
is dreary, 69 f.
is not necessary for those who have arrived at the highest degree of spirituality, 93, 139 f.
less frequent with Latins than with Greeks, 93 ff.
whether controlled by the clergy, 53 f.
nothing to be read except the Bible, 106 f.
after supper, 119, 124.
before the chief meal, 56.

158 BIBLE READING IN THE EARLY CHURCH

PRINTED BY NEILL AND CO., LTD., EDINBURGH

A CATALOGUE OF
WILLIAMS & NORGATE'S
PUBLICATIONS

ADDIS (W. E., M.A.). Hebrew Religion to the Establishment of Judaism under Ezra. Crown 8vo, cloth. 4s. 6d. net. *See* Crown Theological Library, p. 34.

AINSWORTH DAVIS (J. R.) and H. J. FLEURE, B.Sc. Patella (the Common Limpet). With 4 Plates. 2s. 6d. net. *See* Liverpool Marine Biology Committee Memoirs, p. 39.

ALLIN (Rev. THOS.). Universalism asserted as the Hope of the Gospel on the Authority of Reason, the Fathers, and Holy Scripture. With a Preface by Edna Lyall, and a Letter from Canon Wilberforce. Crown 8vo, cloth. 2s. 6d. net.

ALVIELLA (Count GOBLET D'). Lectures on the Origin and the Growth of the Conception of God, as Illustrated by Anthropology and History. Translated by the Rev. P. H. Wicksteed. Hibbert Lectures 1891. Cloth, Library Ed., 10s. 6d. Popular Ed., 3s. 6d.

ANDREWS (CHARLES M'LEAN, Ph.D., L.H.D.). The Colonial Period. F'cap. 8vo, cloth. 2s. 6d. net.

ANGLICAN LIBERALISM. By Twelve Churchmen. Rev. Hubert Handley, Prof. F. C. Burkitt, M.A., D.D., Rev. J. R. Wilkinson, M.A., Rev. C. R. Shaw Stewart, M.A., Rev. Hastings Rashdall, D.Litt., D.C.L., Prof. Percy Gardner, D.Litt., LL.D., Sir C. T. Dyke Acland, Rev. A. J. Carlyle, M.A., Rev. H. G. Woods, D.D., Rev. A. A. Caldcott, D.Litt., D.D., Rev. W. D. Morrison, LL.D., Rev. A. L. Lilley, M.A. Crown 8vo, cloth. 4s. 6d. net.

ASHWORTH (J. H., D.Sc.). Arenicola (the Lug-Worm). With 8 Plates. 4s. 6d. net. *See* Liverpool Marine Biology Committee Memoirs, p. 39.

AVEBURY (Lord, D.C.L., F.R.S.). Prehistoric Times, as Illustrated by Ancient Remains and the Manners and Customs of Modern Savages. 6th Edition, revised, with 239 Illustrations, a large number of which are specially prepared for this Edition. Demy 8vo, cloth, gilt tops. Cheap Popular Edition, 7s. 6d. net.

AVESTI, PAHLAVI, and ANCIENT PERSIAN STUDIES in Honour of the late Shams-ul-Ulama Dastur Peshotanji Behramji Sanjana, M.A., Ph.D. Paper cover, 12s. 6d. net; cloth, 13s. 6d. net.

BACON (Professor B. W., LL.D., D.D.). The Making of the New Testament. F'cap. 8vo, cloth, 1s. net; leather, 2s. 6d. net. Forming Vol. 56 in the Home University Library; for list, *see* p. 38.

BACON (ROGER), the "Opus Majus" of. Edited, with Introduction and Analytical Table, by John Henry Bridges, Fellow of Royal College of Physicians, sometime Fellow of Oriel College. Complete in 3 vols., 31s. 6d. ; Vol. III. sold separately, 7s. 6d.

BAILEY (JOHN, M.A.). Dr Johnson and his Circle. F'cap. 8vo, cloth, 1s. net ; leather, 2s. 6d. Forming Vol. 64 in Home University Library ; for list, see p. 38.

BALSILLIE (DAVID, M.A.). An Examination of Professor Bergson's Philosophy. Crown 8vo, cloth. 5s. net.

BARRETT (Sir W. F., F.R.S.). Psychical Research. F'cap. 8vo, cloth, 1s. net ; leather, 2s. 6d. net. Forming Vol. 28 in the Home University Library ; for list, see p. 37.

BARRY (WILLIAM, D.D.). The Papacy and Modern Times (1303–1870). F'cap. 8vo, cloth, 1s. net ; leather, 2s. 6d. net. Forming Vol. 14 in the Home University Library; for list, see p. 37.

BAUR (F. C.). Church History of the First Three Centuries. Translated from the Third German Edition. Edited by Rev. Allan Menzies. 2 vols. 8vo, cloth. 12s.

——— **Paul, the Apostle of Jesus Christ, his Life and Work, his** Epistles and Doctrine. A Contribution to a Critical History of Primitive Christianity. Edited by Rev. Allan Menzies. 2nd Edition. 2 vols. 8vo, cloth. 12s.

BAYLEY (HAROLD). The Lost Language of Symbolism. With above 1400 symbols. 2 vols. Medium 8vo, cloth. 25s. net.

BEARD (Rev. Dr C.). Lectures on the Reformation of the Sixteenth Century in its Relation to Modern Thought and Knowledge. Hibbert Lectures, 1883. 8vo, cloth. 10s. 6d. Cheap Edition, 3rd Edition, 3s. 6d.

——— **The Universal Christ, and other Sermons.** Crown 8vo, cloth. 7s. 6d.

BEGBIE (HAROLD). See "Character and Life," p. 4.

BELLOC (HILAIRE, M.A.). The French Revolution. (With Maps.) F'cap. 8vo, cloth, 1s. net ; leather, 2s. 6d. net. Forming Vol. 3 in the Home University Library ; for list, see p. 37.

——— **Warfare in England.** (With Maps.) F'cap. 8vo, cloth, 1s. net ; leather, 2s. 6d. net. Vol. 51 in the Home University Library ; for list, see p. 38.

BENEDICT (F. E., Ph.D.). Elementary Organic Analysis. Small 8vo. Pages vi + 82. 15 Illustrations. 4s. 6d. net.

BERGEY (D. G.). Handbook of Practical Hygiene. Small 8vo. Pages v + 164. 6s. 6d. net.

BEVAN (Rev. J. O., M.A., F.G.S.). The Genesis and Evolution of the Individual Soul scientifically Treated. Including also Problems relating to Science and Immortality. Crown 8vo, cloth. 2s. 6d. net.

BIBLE. Translated by Samuel Sharpe, being a Revision of the Authorised English Version. 6th Edition of the Old, 10th Edition of the New Testament. 8vo, roan. 5s.

BILTZ (HENRY). The Practical Methods of determining Molecular Weights. Translated by Jones. Small 8vo. Pages viii + 245. 44 Illustrations. 8s. 6d. net.

BLACKBURN (HELEN). Women's Suffrage. A Record of the Women's Suffrage Movement in the British Isles, with a Biographical Sketch of Miss Becker. With portraits. Crown 8vo, cloth. 6s.

BOÏELLE (JAS.). French Composition through Lord Macaulay's English. Edited, with Notes, Hints, and Introduction, by the late James Boïelle, B.A. (Univ. Gall.), Officier d'Académie, Senior French Master, Dulwich College, etc., etc. Crown 8vo, cloth. Vol. I. Frederick the Great. 3s. Vol. II. Warren Hastings. 3s. Vol. III. Lord Clive. 3s.

—— *See* Victor Hugo, "Les Misérables" and "Notre Dame."

BOLTON. History of the Thermometer. 12mo. 96 pages. 6 Illustrations. 4s. 6d. net.

BOUSSET (Prof. WILHELM). Jesus. Trans. by Janet Penrose Trevelyan, and ed. by Rev. W. D. Morrison, LL.D. Cr. 8vo. 3s. 6d. net. Forming Vol. 14 in the Cr. Theological Library; *see* p. 34.

BOUTROUX (EMILE). Education and Ethics. Authorised Translation by Fred. Rothwell. Crown 8vo, cloth. 5s. net.

BRADLEY (A. G.). Canada. F'cap. 8vo, cloth, 1s. net; leather, 2s. 6d. net. Forming Vol. 34 in the Home University Library; *see* list, p. 37.

BRAUNS (Dr REINHARD). The Mineral Kingdom. The author is the well-known Professor of Mineralogy in the University of Bonn. Translated with additions by L. J. Spencer, M.A., F.G.S., Assistant in the Mineral Department of the British Museum. In demy 4to, comprising 91 full-page plates beautifully executed in colours, 73 of which are chromo-lithographs, 18 photographic reproductions, and 275 figures in the text. Bound in half-morocco. £2, 16s. net.

BREMOND (HENRI). The Mystery of Newman. With Introduction by the late Rev. George Tyrrell, M.A. Medium 8vo, cloth. 10s. 6d. net.

BREWSTER (H. B.). The Theories of Anarchy and of Law. A Midnight Debate. Crown 8vo, parchment. 5s.

—— The Prison. A Dialogue. Crown 8vo, parchment. 5s.
—— The Statuette and the Background. Crown 8vo, parchment. 4s.

BREWSTER (Prof. W. T.), Editor of The Home University Library; for list, *see* p. 37.

—— The Writing of English. F'cap. 8vo, cloth, 1s. net; leather, 2s. 6d. net. Forming Vol. 73 in Home University Library; for list, *see* p. 39.

BRUCE (ALEX., M.A., M.D., F.R.C.P.E.). A Topographical
Atlas of the Spinal Cord. F'cap. folio, half-leather. £2, 2s. net.
BRUCE (Dr W. S., F.R.S.E.). Polar Exploration. (With Maps.)
F'cap. 8vo, cloth, 1s. net ; leather, 2s. 6d. net. Forming Vol. 8
in the Home University Library ; for list, *see* p. 37.
BURKITT (Prof. F. C.). Euphemia and the Goth. With the
Acts of Martyrdom of the Confessors of Edessa. 21s. net. *See*
Text and Translation Society, p. 40.
BURY (Prof. J. B., Litt.D.). A History of Freedom of Thought.
F'cap. 8vo, 1s. net ; leather, 2s. 6d. net. Forming Vol. 74 in
Home University Library ; for list, *see* p. 39.
CAMPBELL (Rev. COLIN, D.D.) The First Three Gospels
in Greek. Arranged in parallel columns. 2nd Edition, Revised.
Crown 8vo, cloth. 3s. 6d. net.
CARPENTER (Rt. Rev. W. BOYD). Some Pages of My
Life. By the present Canon of Westminster and late Bishop of
Ripon. With portrait of the author as frontispiece, and other
interesting portraits. Medium 8vo, cloth, gilt top. 15s. net.
CARPENTER (Prof. J. E., LL.D.). Comparative Religion.
F'cap. 8vo, cloth, 1s. net ; leather, 2s. 6d. net. Forming Vol. 68
in Home University Library ; for list, *see* p. 38.
CARTWRIGHT (Captain) and His Labrador Journal. Edited by
Charles Wendell Townsend, M.D. With an Introduction by Dr
Wilfred T. Grenfell. With Illustrations from old engravings,
photographs and a map. Crown 8vo, cloth. 5s. net.
CECIL (Lord HUGH, M.A., M.P.). Conservatism. F'cap. 8vo,
cloth, 1s. net ; leather, 2s. 6d. net. Forming Vol. 11 in the Home
University Library ; for list, *see* p. 37.
CHADWICK (HERBERT CLIFTON). Antedon. With 7 Plates.
2s. 6d. net. *See* Liverpool Marine Biology Memoirs, p. 39.
—— **Echinus.** With 5 Plates. Price 2s. net. *See* Liverpool Marine
Biology Memoirs, p. 39.
CHANNING'S COMPLETE WORKS. Including "The Perfect
Life," with a Memoir. Centennial Edition. 4to Ed. Cloth. 7s. 6d.
CHAPMAN (Prof. S. J., M.A.). Elements of Political Economy.
F'cap. 8vo, cloth, 1s. net ; leather, 2s. 6d. net. Forming Vol.
59 in the Home University Library ; for list, *see* p. 38.
CHARACTER AND LIFE: A Symposium. By Dr Alfred
Russel Wallace, John A. Hobson, Harold Begbie, Walter Crane,
and the late Dr Emil Reich. Arranged by Percy L. Parker,
Editor of "Public Opinion." Crown 8vo, cloth. 3s. 6d. net.
CHESTERTON (G. K.). The Victorian Age in Literature.
F'cap. 8vo, cloth, 1s. net ; leather, 2s. 6d. net. Forming Vol. 70
in Home University Library ; for list, *see* p. 38.
CHEYNE (Rev. T. K., D.Litt., D.D.). Bible Problems and
the New Material for their Solution. A Plea for Thoroughness
of Investigation, addressed to Churchmen and Scholars. Crown
8vo. 4s. 6d. net. *See* Crown Theological Library, p. 34.

CHILD AND RELIGION, THE. Essays. By Prof. Henry Jones, M.A., LL.D., University of Glasgow; C. F. G. Masterman, M.A.; Prof. George T. Ladd, D.D., LL.D.; Rev. F. R. Tennant, M.A., B.Sc.; Rev. J. Cynddylan Jones, D.D.; Rev. Canon Hensley Henson, M.A.; Rev. Robert F. Horton, M.A., D.D.; Rev. G. Hill, M.A., D.D.; Rev. J. J. Thornton; Rev. Rabbi A. A. Green; Prof. Joseph Agar Beet, D.D. Edited by Thomas Stephens, B.A. Crown 8vo. 5s. net. *See* Crown Theological Library, p. 34.

COIT (STANTON, Ph.D.). National Idealism and a State Church. Demy 8vo, cloth. 7s. 6d. net.
—— **National Idealism and the Book of Common Prayer.** An Essay in Re-Interpretation and Revision. Demy 8vo, cloth. 10s. 6d. net.

COLBY (ALBERT LADD). Reinforced Concrete in Europe. Demy 8vo, cloth. 14s. 6d. net.

COLE (FRANK J.), and JAMES JOHNSTONE. Pleuro-nectes. With 11 Plates. 7s. net. *See* Liverpool Marine Biology Memoirs, p. 39.

COLLINS (F. H.). An Epitome of Synthetic Philosophy. With a Preface by Herbert Spencer. 5th Edition. The Synthetic Philosophy Completed. 8vo, cloth. Reduced to 5s. net.

CONYBEARE (F. C., M.A.). The Ring of Pope Xystus: a collection of Aphorisms and Short Sayings in use among Christian Communities in the Second Century. Beautifully printed on hand-made paper. 4s. 6d. net.

CORNILL (Prof. CARL). The Introduction to the Canonical Books of the Old Testament. Demy 8vo, cloth. 10s. 6d. net. *See* Theological Translation Library, p. 41.

CRANE (WALTER), contributor to "Character and Life," *see* p. 4.

CREIGHTON (Mrs). Missions: their Rise and Development. F'cap. 8vo, cloth, 1s. net; leather, 2s. 6d. net. Forming Volume 60 in the Home University Library; for list, *see* p. 38.

CREIGHTON (CHAS., M.D.). Cancer and other Tumours of the Breast. Researches showing their true seat and cause. The Author was sometime Demonstrator of Anatomy, Cambridge Medical School, and is the author of "Bovine Tuberculosis in Man," etc. With 24 Lithographic Plates containing 138 figures from the Author's drawings. Royal 8vo, cloth. 12s. 6d. net.
—— **Contributions to the Physiological Theory of Tuberculosis.** Royal 8vo, cloth. 12s. 6d. net.

CUSSANS (MARGARET, B.Sc.). Gammarus. With 4 Plates. 2s. net. *See* Liverpool Marine Biology Memoirs, p. 39.

DAKIN (W. J., M.Sc.). Pecton. With 9 Plates. 4s. 6d. net. *See* Liverpool Marine Biology Memoirs, p. 39.

DARBISHIRE (OTTO V.). Chondrus. With 7 Plates. 2s. 6d. net. *See* Liverpool Marine Biology Memoirs, p. 39.

DAUDET (A.). Contes Militaires. 2s. 6d. *See* Army Series, p. 33.

DAVENPORT (CHARLES BENEDICT). Heredity in re-
lation to Eugenics. The Author is Director, Department of Experi-
mental Evolution, Cold Spring Harbour, Long Island, N.Y.;
Secretary of the Eugenics Section American Breeders' Association.
With Diagrams and Coloured Plate. Demy 8vo, cloth. 8s. 6d. net.

DAVIDS (Mrs RHYS, M.A.). Buddhism. F'cap. 8vo, cloth,
1s. net; leather, 2s. 6d. net. Forming Vol. 47 in the Home
University Library; for list, *see* p. 38.

DAVIDS (T. W. RHYS). Lectures on Some Points in the His-
tory of Indian Buddhism. The Hibbert Lectures, 1881. 2nd Edition.
Demy 8vo, cloth. Library Edition, 10s. 6d. Cheap Edition, 3s. 6d.

DAVIS (H. W. C., M.A.). Mediæval Europe. (With Maps.)
F'cap. 8vo, cloth, 1s. net; leather, 2s. 6d. net. Forming Vol. 13
in the Home University Library; for list, *see* p. 37.

DELBOS (L.). Nautical Terms in English and French and
French and English. With Notes and Tables. For the use of
Naval Officers and Naval Cadets. By Leon Delbos, M.A., of
H.M.S. *Britannia*, Dartmouth. 4th Edition, thoroughly revised
and considerably enlarged, with additional Plates. Crown 8vo,
cloth. 7s. 6d. net.

—— **The Student's Graduated French Reader.** Remodelled and
rewritten. Edited, with Notes and a Complete Vocabulary. First
Year—Part I. Anecdotes, Tales, and Exercises. Part II. Tales,
Historical Pieces, and Exercises. 1s. 6d. each. Second Year—
Parts I. and II. in the Press.

DELITZSCH (Dr FRIEDRICH). Babel and Bible. Authorised
Translation. Edited, with an Introduction, by Rev. C. H. W.
Johns. Crown 8vo, with 77 illustrations, cloth. 4s. 6d. net.
See Crown Theological Library, p. 34.

DEWALL (JOHANNES V.). Auf Verlornem Posten and
Nazzarena Danti. 3s. *See* Army Series, p. 33.

DIBBLEE (G. BINNEY). The Newspaper. F'cap. 8vo, cloth
1s. net; leather, 2s. 6d. net. Forming Vol. 69 in Home University Library; for list, *see* p. 38.

DICKSON (H. N., D.Sc.). Climate and Weather. F'cap. 8vo,
cloth, 1s. net; leather, 2s. 6d. net. Forming Vol. 36 in the
Home University Library; for list, *see* p. 37.

DILLMANN (A.). Ethiopic Grammar. Translated from C.
Bezold's Second German Edition. By Rev. J. A. Crichton, D.D.
With Index of Passages, Philological Tables, etc. 1 vol., royal
8vo. 25s. net.

DÍPAVAMSA (THE): A Buddhist Historical Record in the
Pali Language. Edited, with an English Translation, by Dr
H. Oldenberg. 8vo, cloth. 21s.

DOBSCHÜTZ (ERNST VON, D.D.). Christian Life in the Primitive Church. The Author is Professor of New Testament Theology in the University of Strassburg. Translated by Rev. G. Bremner, and edited by the Rev. W. D. Morrison, LL.D. Demy 8vo, cloth. 10s. 6d. *See* Theological Translation Library, New Series, p. 41.

DOLE (CHARLES F.). The Ethics of Progress, or the Theory and the Practice by which Civilisation proceeds. Small demy 8vo, cloth. 6s. net.

DRUMMOND (Dr JAMES, LL.D.). Philo Judæus ; or, The Jewish Alexandrian Philosophy in its Development and Completion. 2 vols. 8vo, cloth. 21s.

—— **Via, Veritas, Vita.** Lectures on Christianity in its most Simple and Intelligible Form. Hibbert Lectures, 1894. Demy 8vo. Library Edition, 10s. 6d. Cheap Edition, 3s. 6d.

DUNCAN (DAVID, LL.D.). The Life and Letters of Herbert Spencer. With 17 Illustrations. Cheap Reissue. 6s. net.

EMERY (F. B., M.A.). Elementary Chemistry. With numerous Illustrations. 8s. 6d. net.

ENGELHARDT (V.). The Electrolysis of Water. 8vo. Pages x + 140. 90 Illustrations. 5s. net.

ENGLAND AND GERMANY. By Leaders of Public Opinion in both Empires, among whom may be mentioned :—Rt. Hon. Arthur J. Balfour, Viscount Haldane of Cloan, Rt. Hon. A. Bonar Law, Baron Alfred von Rothschild, Rt. Hon. Herbert Samuel, Sir Rufus Isaacs, Norman Angell, J. Ramsay MacDonald, M.P., J. A. Spender, Excell. Karl Galster, Ernst Basserman, Professor Dr Riesser, Baron Wilhelm von Pechmann, Professor Wilhelm Wundt, Dr Walther Rathenau, August Thyssen, sen., His Excellency Dr Adolf Wermuth, Excell. von Holleben, etc. With Portraits. Stiff wrapper. 1s. net.

ERMAN'S EGYPTIAN GRAMMAR. Translated, under Professor Erman's supervision, by J. H. Breasted, Professor of Egyptology in the University of Chicago. Crown 8vo, cloth. 18s.

ERSKINE (Prof. J.) and Prof. W. P. TRENT. Great Writers of America. F'cap. 8vo, cloth, 1s. net; leather, 2s. 6d. net. Forming Vol. 52 in the Home University Library ; for list, *see* p. 38.

EUCKEN (Dr RUDOLF, Jena). The Life of the Spirit. An Introduction to Philosophy. Second Edition. Third Impression. 8vo, cloth. 4s. 6d. net. *See* Crown Theological Library, p. 35.

—— **The Truth of Religion.** Translated from the latest revised German edition by Rev. W. Tudor Jones, Ph.D., with a special preface by the Author. Demy 8vo, cloth. 12s. 6d. net. *See* Theological Translation Library, New Series, p. 41.

EUGÈNE-FASNACHT (G.). Eugène's Student's Comparative Grammar of the French Language, with an Historical Sketch of the Formation of French. The Author was for many years French Master, Westminster School. For the use of Public Schools. With Exercises. 23rd Edition, thoroughly revised. Square crown 8vo, cloth, 5s. ; or separately, Grammar, 3s. ; Exercises, 2s.6d.

—— **French Method.** Elementary French Lessons preparatory to the same Author's Grammar. 18th Edition. Cloth. 1s. 6d.

EVANS (GEORGE). An Essay on Assyriology. With 4to Tables of Assyrian Inscriptions. 8vo, cloth. 5s.

EWALD'S (Dr H.) Commentary on the Prophets of the Old Testament. Translated by the Rev. J. F. Smith. [Vol. I. General Introduction, Yoel, Amos, Hosea, and Zakharya 9-11. Vol. II. Yesaya, Obadya, and Mikah. Vol. III. Nahûm, Ssephanya, Habaqqûq, Zakhârya, Yéremya. Vol. IV. Hezekiel, Yesaya xl.-lxvi. Vol. V. Haggai, Zakharya, Malaki, Jona, Baruc, Daniel, Appendix and Index.] 5 vols. 8vo, cloth. 30s. *See* Theological Translation Library, Old Series, p. 42.

—— **Commentary on the Psalms.** Translated by the Rev. E. Johnson, M.A. 2 vols. 8vo, cloth. 12s.

—— **Commentary on the Book of Job,** with Translation. Translated from the German by the Rev. J. Frederick Smith. 8vo, cloth. 6s.

FAGUET (Prof. EMILE, of the French Academy). Initiation into Philosophy. Translated by Sir Home Gordon, Bart. Crown 8vo, cloth. 2s. 6d. net.

FARMER (Prof. J. B.). Plant Life. (Illustrated.) F'cap. 8vo, cloth, 1s. net ; leather, 2s. 6d. net. Forming Vol. 72 in Home University Library ; for list, *see* p. 39.

FARNELL (L. R., D.Litt.). The Evolution of Religion : an Anthropological Study. Crown 8vo, cloth. 4s. 6d. net. *See* Crown Theological Library, p. 34.

—— **The Higher Aspects of Greek Religion.** Lectures delivered in Oxford and London. Being Vol. 1 of New Series of Hibbert Lectures. Demy 8vo, cloth. 6s. net. *See* Hibbert Lectures, p. 36.

FARQUHARSON (Rt. Hon. ROBERT, LL.D.) The House of Commons from Within, and other Reminiscences. Med. 8vo. With portrait by J. S. Sargent, R.A., never before published. 7s. 6d. net.

—— **In and Out of Parliament.** With a number of portraits and caricatures. Medium 8vo, cloth. 12s. 6d. net.

FARRIE (HUGH). Highways and Byways in Literature. A volume of original Studies. Demy 8vo, cloth. 5s. net.

FINDLAY (Prof. J. J., M.A., Ph.D.). The School. An Introduction to the Study of Education. F'cap. 8vo, cloth, 1s. net ; leather, 2s. 6d. net. Forming Vol. 38 in the Home University Library ; for list, *see* p. 38.

FISCHER (Prof. EMIL, of Berlin University). Introduction to the Preparation of Organic Compounds. Translated with the Author's sanction from the new German edition by R. V. Stanford, B.Sc., Ph.D. With figures in the text. Crown 8vo, cloth. 4s. net.

**FISHER (HERBERT, M.A., F.B.A., LL.D.), Editor, Home University Library; for list, see p. 37.
—— Napoleon.** (With Maps.) F'cap. 8vo, cloth, 1s. net; leather, 2s. 6d. net. Forming Vol. 61 in Home University Library; for list, see p. 38.

FOUR GOSPELS (THE) AS HISTORICAL RECORDS. 8vo, cloth. 15s.

FOWLER (W. WARDE, M.A.). Rome. F'cap. 8vo, cloth, 1s. net; leather, 2s. 6d. net. Forming Vol. 42 in the Home University Library; for list, see p. 38.

FOX (FRANK), Author of "Ramparts of Empire," etc. **Problems of the Pacific.** Demy 8vo, cloth. With Map. 7s. 6d. net.

FRY (The Rt. Hon. Sir EDWARD, G.C.B., etc.). Some Intimations of Immortality. From the Physical and Psychical Nature of Man. Royal 8vo, sewed. 1s. net.

GAMBLE (Prof. F. W., D.Sc., F.R.S.). The Animal World. With Introduction by Sir Oliver Lodge. Many Illustrations. F'cap. 8vo, cloth, 1s. net; leather, 2s. 6d. net. Forming Vol. 19 in the Home University Library; for list, see p. 37.

GARDNER (Prof. PERCY, D.Litt., F.B.A., Oxford). Modernity and the Churches. 4s. 6d. net. See Crown Theological Library, p. 35.
—— **The Religious Experience of St Paul.** Crown 8vo, cloth. 5s. net. See Crown Theological Library, p. 35.

GELDART (W. M., M.A., B.C.L.). Elements of English Law. F'cap. 8vo, cloth, 1s. net; leather, 2s. 6d. net. Forming Vol. 30 in the Home University Library; for list, see p. 37.

GIBBS (PHILIP). The Eighth Year. The Dangerous Year of Marriage. Crown 8vo, cloth. 2s. net.

GIBSON (R. J. H.) and HELEN P. AULD, B.Sc. Codium. With 3 Plates. Price 1s. 6d. net. See Liverpool Marine Biology Memoirs, p. 39.

GILES (H. A., LL.D.). The Civilisation of China. By the well-known Professor of Chinese in the University of Cambridge. F'cap. 8vo, cloth, 1s. net; leather, 2s. 6d. net. Forming Vol. 25 in the Home University Library; for list, see p. 37.

GILL (CHARLES). The Book of Enoch the Prophet. Translated from an Ethiopic MS. in the Bodleian Library, by the late Richard Laurence, LL.D., Archbishop of Cashel. The Text corrected from his latest Notes by Charles Gill. Re-issue, 8vo, cloth. 5s.

GIVEN (JOHN L.). Making a Newspaper. Cloth, above 300 pages. 6s. net.

GOLDAMMER (H.). The Kindergarten. A Guide to Fröbel's Method of Education. 2 vols. in 1. 120 pp. of Illustrations. 8vo, cloth. 10s. 6d.

GOOCH (G. P., M.A.). The History of our Time, 1885-1911. F'cap. 8vo, cloth, 1s. net; leather, 2s. 6d. net. Forming Vol. 23 in the Home University Library; for list, see p. 37.

GOULD (F. J.). Noble Pages from German History. Crown
8vo, cloth. Illustrated. 1s. 6d. net.

GRAVELY (F. H., M.Sc.). Polychaet Larvae. With 4 plates.
2s. 6d. net. *See* Liverpool Marine Biology Committee Memoirs, p. 39.

GRAY (Rev. H. B., D.D.). The Public Schools and the Empire.
A plea for higher education in citizenship. Cloth. 6s. net.

GREEN (Rt. Rev. A. V., D.D., Bishop of Ballarat). The Ephesian
Canonical Writings : Being the Moorhouse Lectures for 1910.
Crown 8vo, cloth. 5s. net.

GREEN (Mrs J. R.). Irish Nationality. F'cap. 8vo, cloth, 1s.
net; leather, 2s. 6d. net. Forming Vol. 6 in the Home University
Library ; for list, *see* p. 37.

GREGORY (Prof. J. W., F.R.S.). The Making of the Earth.
(With 38 Maps and Figures.) F'cap. 8vo, cloth, 1s. net ; leather,
2s. 6d. net. Forming Vol. 53 in the Home University Library ;
for list, *see* p. 38.

GRIEBEN'S ENGLISH GUIDES. Practical and handy ; size,
suitable for the pocket, 6¼ + 4¼, and bound in cloth.

    Switzerland. A practical guide with seven Maps. Cloth. 3s. net.
    Norway and Copenhagen. With six Maps. Cloth. 3s. net.
    Ostend and other Belgium Watering Places. With two
Maps. Cloth. 1s. 6d. net.
    Lakes of Northern Italy. With Maps. Cloth. 3s. net.
    The Rhine. With Maps. Cloth. 3s. net.
    North Sea Watering Places. Cloth. 3s. net.
    Belgium. With Maps. Cloth. 3s. net.
    Brussels and Antwerp. With Maps. Cloth. 1s. 6d. net.
    Holland. With Maps. Cloth. 3s. net.
    The Riviera. With Maps. Cloth. 3s. net.
    Winter Sports in Switzerland. A practical guide for those
visiting Switzerland in the winter. With Map. Cloth. 3s. net.
    Dresden and Environs. With Maps. Cloth. 1s. 6d. net.
    Munich and Environs. With Maps. Cloth. 1s. 6d. net.
    Nuremburg and Rothenburg on the Tauber. With 2 Maps.
1s. 6d. net.
    The Dolomites. With 3 Maps. 3s. net.
    Naples and Capri. With seven Maps and three Ground
Plans. 1s. 6d. net.

GUPPY (H. B., M.B., F.R.S.E.). Studies in Seeds and Fruits.
An Investigation with the Balance. Demy 8vo, cloth, nearly
600 pp. 15s. net.

HAERING (Prof. THEODOR). Ethics of the Christian Life.
Translated by Rev. J. S. Hill, B.D., and edited by Rev. W. D.
Morrison. Demy 8vo, cloth. 10s. 6d. net. *See* Theological
Translation Library, New Series. p. 41.

HALLIGAN (JAMES EDWARD), Chemist in charge Louisiana
State Experiment Station. Soil Fertility and Fertilisers. With
Illustrations and Tables. Demy 8vo, cloth. 14s. 6d. net.

HANNAY (DAVID). The Navy and Sea Power. F'cap. 8vo, cloth, 1s. net; leather, 2s. 6d. net. Forming Vol. 66 in Home University Library; for list, *see* p. 38.

HANTZSCH (A.). Elements of Stereochemistry. Translated by Wolf. 12mo. Pages viii + 206. 26 Figures. 6s. 6d. net.

HARDY. Elements of Analytical Geometry. 8vo. Pages iv + 365. 163 Figures. 8s. 6d. net.

—— Infinitesimals and Limits. Sm. 12mo, paper. 22 pp. 6 Figures. 1s. net.

HARNACK (ADOLF, D.D.). The Acts of the Apostles. Being Vol. III. of Dr Harnack's New Testament Studies. Crown 8vo, cloth. 5s. net. Vol. 26 in the Crown Theological Library; for list, *see* p. 35.

—— Bible Reading in the Early Church. Forming Vol. V. of New Testament Studies. 5s. net. *See* Crown Theological Library, p. 35.

—— The Constitution and Law of the Church in the First Two Centuries. Crown 8vo, cloth. 5s. net. Vol. 31 in the Crown Theological Library, p. 35.

—— The Date of the Acts and of the Synoptic Gospels. Crown 8vo, cloth. 5s. net. Forming Vol. IV. in Dr Harnack's New Testament Studies, and Vol. 33 in the Crown Theological Library, p. 35.

—— History of Dogma. Translated from the Third German Edition. Edited by the late Rev. Prof. A. B. Bruce, D.D. 7 vols. 8vo, cloth, each 10s. 6d. ; half-leather, suitable for presentation, 12s. 6d. *See* Theological Translation Library, New Series, p. 40.

—— Letter to the "Preussische Jahrbücher" on the German Emperor's Criticism of Prof. Delitzsch's Lectures on "Babel and Bible." Translated into English by Thomas Bailey Saunders. 6d. net.

—— Luke, the Physician. Translated by the Rev. J. R. Wilkinson, M.A. Being Vol. I. of Dr Harnack's New Testament Studies. Crown 8vo, cloth. 5s. net. *See* Crown Theological Library, p. 34.

—— The Mission and Expansion of Christianity in the First Three Centuries. Second, revised and much enlarged Edition. 25s. net. Forming Vols. 19 and 20 in Theological Translation Library, New Series; *see* p. 41.

—— Monasticism: Its Ideals and History; and The Confessions of St Augustine. Two Lectures. Translated into English by E. E. Kellet, M.A., and F. H. Marseille, Ph.D. Crown 8vo, cloth. 3s. 6d. net. Forming Vol. 28 in the Crown Theological Library, p. 35.

—— The Sayings of Jesus. Being Vol. II. of Dr Harnack's New Testament Studies. Crown 8vo, cloth. 5s. net. Forming Vol. 23 in the Crown Theological Library, p. 35.

—— What is Christianity? Translated by Thomas Bailey Saunders. Third and Revised Edition. Crown 8vo. 4s. 6d. net. Forming Vol. 5 in the Crown Theological Library, p. 34.

—— and Prof. W. HERRMANN, of Marburg. Essays on the Social Gospel. Crown 8vo, cloth. 4s. net. Forming Vol. 18 in the Crown Theological Library, p. 34.

HARNACK (AXEL). Introduction to the Elements of the Differential and Integral Calculus. From the German. Royal 8vo, cloth. 10s. 6d.

HARRISON (JANE, LL.D., D.Litt.). Ancient Art and Ritual. F'cap. 8vo, cloth, 1s. net; leather, 2s. 6d. net. Forming Vol. 75 in Home University Library; for list, *see* p. 39.

HART (EDWARD, Ph.D.**).** Chemistry for Beginners. Sm. 12mo.
    Vol. I. Inorganic. Pages viii + 188. 55 Illustrations and 2 Plates. 4th Edition. 4s. 6d. net.
    Vol. II. Organic. Pages iv + 98. 11 Illustrations. 2s. net.
    Vol. III. Experiments. Separately. 60 pages. 1s. net.
—— Second Year Chemistry. Small 12mo. 165 pages. 31 Illustrations. 5s. net.

HATCH (Rev. Dr). Lectures on the Influence of Greek Ideas and Usages upon the Christian Church. Edited by Dr Fairbairn. Hibbert Lectures, 1888. 3rd Edition. 8vo, cloth. 10s. 6d. Cheap Edition, 3s. 6d.

HAUSRATH (Prof. A.). History of the New Testament Times. The Time of the Apostles. Translated by Leonard Huxley. With a Preface by Mrs Humphry Ward. 4 vols. 8vo, cloth. 42s. (Uniform with the Theological Translation Library, Old Series.)
—— History of the New Testament Times. The Time of Jesus. Trans. by the Revs. C. T. Poynting and P. Quenzer. 2 vols. 8vo, cloth. 12s. *See* Theological Translation Library, Old Series, p. 42.

HAWORTH (PAUL LELAND). Reconstruction and Union, 1865–1912. F'cap. 8vo, cloth. 2s. 6d. net.

HEATH (FRANCIS GEORGE). Nervation of Plants. By the well-known Author of "Our Woodland Trees," "The Fern World," etc. Well Illustrated. Crown 8vo. 3s. 6d. net.

HEBREW TEXTS, in large type for Classes:
Genesis. 2nd Edition. 16mo, cloth. 1s. 6d. Psalms. 16mo, cloth. 1s. Isaiah. 16mo, cloth. 1s. Job. 16mo, cloth. 1s.

HENSLOW (Rev. G.). The Vulgate; The Source of False Doctrine. Crown 8vo, cloth. 2s. 6d. net.

HERDMAN (W. A.). Ascidia. With 5 Plates. 2s. net. *See* Liverpool Marine Biology Committee Memoirs, p. 39.

HERFORD (Rev. R. TRAVERS). Christianity in Talmud and Midrash. Demy 8vo, cloth. 18s. net.
—— Pharisaism: Its Aims and its Methods: Crown 8vo, cloth. 5s. net. Forming Vol. 35 in the Crown Theological Library, p. 35.

HERRMANN (Prof. WILHELM). The Communion of the Christian with God. Translated from the new German Edition by Rev. J. S. Stanyon, M.A., and Rev. R. W. Stewart, B.D., B.Sc. Crown 8vo, cloth. 4s. 6d. net. Forming Vol. 15 in the Crown Theological Library, p. 34.
—— Faith and Morals. New Edition. Crown 8vo, cloth. 4s. 6d. net. Forming Vol. 6 in the Crown Theological Library, p. 34.

HEWITT (C. GORDON, B.Sc.**).** Ligia. With 4 Plates. 2s. net. *See* Liverpool Marine Biology Memoirs, p. 39.

HIBBERT JOURNAL: A Quarterly Review of Religion, Theology, and Philosophy. Edited by L. P. Jacks and G. Dawes Hicks. In quarterly issues, 2s. 6d. net ; or yearly volumes bound in cloth. 12s. 6d. net. Annual Subscription, 10s. post free.

HIBBERT JOURNAL SUPPLEMENT, 1909, **entitled JESUS OR CHRIST?** Containing 18 Essays by leading Theologians and Thinkers. Super royal 8vo, cloth. 5s. net.

HICKSON (SYDNEY J., D.Sc., F.R.S.). **Alcyonium.** With 3 Plates. Price 1s. 6d. net. *See* Liverpool Marine Biology Committee Memoirs, p. 39.

HINKS (A. R., M.A.). Astronomy. F'cap. 8vo, cloth, 1s. net ; leather, 2s. 6d. net. Forming Vol. 31 in the Home University Library ; for list, *see* p. 37.

HIRST (F. W., M.A.). The Stock Exchange. F'cap. 8vo, cloth, 1s. net ; leather, 2s. 6d. net. Forming Vol. 5 in the Home University Library ; for list, *see* page 37.

HOBHOUSE (Prof. L. T., M.A.). Liberalism. F'cap. 8vo, cloth, 1s. net ; leather, 2s. 6d. net. Forming Vol. 21 in the Home University Library ; for list, *see* p. 37.

HOBSON (J. A., M.A.). The Science of Wealth. F'cap. 8vo, cloth, 1s. net; leather, 2s. 6d. net. Forming Vol. 16 in the Home University Library ; for list, *see* p. 37.
—— **Character and Life.** *See* p. 4.

HÖFER (E.). Erzählungen. 3s. *See* Army Series of French and German Novels, p. 33.

HOFF (J. H. VAN'T). Studies in Chemical Dynamics. Revised and enlarged by Dr Ernst Cohen, Assistant in the Chemical Laboratory of the University of Amsterdam. Translated by Thomas Ewan, M.Sc., Ph.D., Demonstrator of Chemistry in the Yorkshire College, Leeds. Royal 8vo, cloth. 10s. 6d.

HOLDERNESS (Sir T. W., K.C.S.I.). Peoples and Problems of India. The Author is Secretary of the Revenue, Statistics, and Commerce Department of the India Office. F'cap. 8vo, cloth, 1s. net; leather, 2s. 6d. net. Forming Vol. 37 in the Home University Library ; *see* p. 38.

HOLLINS (DOROTHEA). The Quest. A Romance of Deliverance. Demy 8vo, cloth. 4s. 6d. net.

HOME UNIVERSITY LIBRARY OF MODERN KNOWLEDGE. Every volume is specially written for this Library by a recognised authority of high standing. Each volume is complete and independent, but the series has been planned as a whole to form a comprehensive library of modern knowledge. The Library is published under the direction of Professor Gilbert Murray and Mr Herbert Fisher of Oxford, Professor J. Arthur Thomson of Aberdeen, and Professor William T. Brewster of New York. Each volume consists of 256 pages and is issued bound in cloth at 1s. net, or in leather, 2s. 6d. net. For list of volumes, *see* p. 37.

HORNELL (JAMES, F.L.S.). **Report to the Government of** Baroda on the Marine Zoology of Okhamandal in Kattiawar. With Supplementary Reports on Special Groups by other Zoologists. Demy 4to, cloth, with full-page Plates. Part I. 15s. net.

HOWE (J. L., Washington and Lee University). **Inorganic** Chemistry for Schools and Colleges. Being a Second Edition of "Inorganic Chemistry according to the Periodic Law." By F. P. Venable and J. L. Howe. Demy 8vo, cloth. 12s. 6d. net.

HUGO (VICTOR). Les Misérables : Les Principaux Episodes. Edited, with Life and Notes, by the late J. Boïelle. 2 vols. 6th Edition. Crown 8vo, cloth. Each 3s.

—— **Notre Dame de ¡Paris.** Adapted for the use of Schools and Colleges. By the late J. Boïelle. 2 vols. 2nd Edition. Crown 8vo, cloth. Each 3s.

HUNTER (Rev. J., D.D.). **De Profundis Clamavi, and Other** Sermons. Large crown 8vo, cloth. 5s. net.

—— **God and Life.** A Series of Discourses. Uniform with "De Profundis Clamavi." Cloth. 5s. net.

—— **The Coming Church.** A Plea for a Church simply Christian. Cloth. 1s. 6d. net.

ILBERT (Sir C. P., K.C.B.). **Parliament.** Its History, Constitution, and Practice. F'cap. 8vo, cloth, 1s. net; leather, 2s. 6d. net. Forming Vol. 1 in the Home University Library; for list, *see* p. 37.

IMMS (A. D., B.Sc. (Lond.). **Anurida.** With 7 Plates. 4s. net. *See* Liverpool Marine Biology Memoirs, p. 39.

ISGROVE (ANNIE, M.Sc.). **Eledone.** With 10 Plates. 4s. 6d. net. *See* Liverpool Marine Biology Memoirs, p. 39.

JACKS (L. P.), Editor of the Hibbert Journal. **Mad Shepherds, and** Other Human Studies. With a frontispiece drawing by Leslie Brooke. Crown 8vo, cloth. 4s. 6d. net.

—— **Among the Idolmakers.** Crown 8vo, cloth. 5s. net.

—— **The Alchemy of Thought and Other Essays.** Demy 8vo, cloth. 10s. 6d. net.

JEREMIAS (Prof. ALFRED). The Old Testament in the Light of the Ancient East. The translation is edited by Professor C. H. W. Johns of Cambridge. With a large number of Illustrations. In two volumes, demy 8vo, at 25s. net. *See* Theological Translation Library, New Series, p. 41.

JOHNSTON (Sir H. H., K.C.B., D.Sc.). **The Opening-up of** Africa. (With Maps.) F'cap. 8vo, cloth, 1s. net ; leather, 2s. 6d. net. Forming Vol. 12 in the Home University Library ; for list, *see* p. 37.

—— **Views and Reviews.** Essays on Racial, Political, and Colonial Questions. Crown 8vo, cloth. 3s. 6d. net.

JOHNSTONE (J.). British Fisheries : Their Administration and their Problems. A short account of the Origin and Growth of British Sea Fishery Authorities and Regulations. 10s. 6d. net.

JOHNSTONE (J.).   Cardium. With 7 Plates. Price 2s. 6d. net.
See Liverpool Marine Biology Memoirs, p. 38.

**JONES.   The Freezing Point, Boiling Point, and Conductivity
Methods.** 12mo. Pages vii+64. 14 Illustrations. 3s. net.

JONES (J. T. SHARE-).   Surgical Anatomy of the Horse. To be
completed in 4 Parts. With above 100 Illustrations, a number
being in colour. Part I. Head and Neck. Part II. Fore Limb.
Part III. Hind Limb. Price per part, 15s. net, sewed; cloth,
16s. 6d. net.

—— **Life-Size Models, Illustrating the Superficial Anatomy of the
Limbs of the Horse.** Price per set of four models, £21; or
separately—Fore Limb, Inner and Outer Aspects, £6, 16s. 6d.
each; Hind Limb, Inner and Outer Aspects, £6, 6s. each.

JONES (Rev. R. CROMPTON).   Hymns of Duty and Faith.
Selected and Arranged. 247 pp. F'cap. 8vo, cloth. 2nd
Edition. 3s. 6d.

—— **Chants, Psalms, and Canticles.** Selected and Pointed for
Chanting. 18mo, cloth. 1s. 6d.

—— **Anthems.** With Indexes and References to the Music. 18mo,
cloth. 1s. 3d.

—— **The Chants and Anthems.** Together in 1 vol. Cloth. 2s.

—— **A Book of Prayer.** In Thirty Orders of Worship, with Additional
Prayers and Thanksgivings. 18mo, cloth. 2s. 6d. With Chants,
in 1 vol. 18mo, cloth. 3s.

**JONES (Rev. W. TUDOR, Ph.D.).   An Interpretation of Rudolf
Eucken's Philosophy.** Crown 8vo. 5s. net.

JORDAN (HUMFREY, R.), B.A.   Blaise Pascal. A Study in
Religious Psychology. Crown 8vo, cloth. 4s. 6d. net.

JOURNAL OF THE LINNEAN SOCIETY.   Botany. At
various prices. Index to Journal (Botany), 20s. Zoology. At
various prices. General Index to the first 20 vols. of the Journal
(Zoology) and the Zoological portion of the Proceedings, 20s.

**JOURNAL OF THE QUEKETT MICROSCOPICAL
CLUB.** Nos. 1–26, 1s. net; Nos. 27–31, 2s. 6d. net. 1893,
No. 32, and following Nos., half-yearly 3s. 6d. net.

JOURNAL OF THE ROYAL MICROSCOPICAL SOCIETY,
containing its Transactions and Proceedings, with other Microscopical Information. Bi-monthly. Previous to 1893 at various prices;
after that date bi-monthly, each 6s. net.

KAPP (GISBERT, D.Eng., M.I.E.E., M.I.C.E.).   Electricity. The
Author is Professor of Electrical Engineering in the University of
Birmingham. (Illustrated.) F'cap. 8vo, cloth. 1s. net; leather, 2s. 6d.
net. Forming Vol. 58 in the Home University Library; *see* p. 38.

KAUFFMAN (RUTH and R. W.).   The Latter Day Saints: A
Study of the Mormons in the Light of Economic Conditions.
Medium 8vo, cloth. 10s. 6d. net.

KAUTZSCH (E., Professor at Halle). **An Outline of the History** of the Literature of the Old Testament. With Chronological Tables for the History of the Israelites, and other Aids to the Explanation of the Old Testament. Reprinted from the "Supplement to the Translation of the Old Testament." Edited by the Author. Translated by John Taylor, D. Litt., M.A., etc. Demy 8vo, cloth. 6s. 6d.

KEIM'S History of Jesus of Nazara: Considered in its connection with the National Life of Israel, and related in detail. Translated from the German by Arthur Ransom and the Rev. E. M. Geldart. In 6 vols. Demy 8vo, cloth. 6s. each. *See* Theological Translation Fund Library, p. 42.

KEITH (A., M.D., LL.D.). **The Human Body.** The Author is Conservator of Museum and Hunterian Professor, Royal College of Surgeons. (Illustrated.) F'cap. 8vo, cloth, 1s. net; leather, 2s. 6d. net. Forming Vol. 57, Home University Library; for list, *see* p. 38.

KENNEDY (Rev. JAS.). **Introduction to Biblical Hebrew,** presenting Graduated Instruction in the Language of the Old Testament. 8vo, cloth. 12s.

—— **Studies in Hebrew Synonyms.** Demy 8vo, cloth. 5s.

KER (Prof. W. P., M.A.). **English Literature: Mediæval.** F'cap. 8vo, cloth, 1s. net; leather, 2s. 6d. net. Forming Vol. 43 in the Home University Library; for list, *see* p. 38.

KIEPERT'S Wall Maps of the Ancient World—
Wall-Map of Ancient Italy. Italia antiqua. For the study of Livy, Sallust, Cicero, Dionysius, etc. Scale 1 : 800,000. Mounted on rollers, varnished. 20s.

General Wall-Map of the Old World. Tabula orbis terrarum antiqui ad illustrandum potissimum antiquissimi ævi usque ad Alexandrum M. historiam. For the study of ancient history, especially the history of the Oriental peoples: the Indians, Medes, Persians, Babylonians, Assyrians, Egyptians, Phœnicians, etc. Scale 1 : 5,400,000. Mounted on rollers, varnished. 20s.

General Wall-Map of the Roman Empire. Imperii Romani tabula geographica. For the study of the development of the Roman Empire. Scale 1 : 300,000. Mounted on rollers, varnished. 24s.

Wall-Map of Ancient Latium. Latii Veteris et finitimarum regionum tabula. For the study of Livy, Dionysius, etc. Scale 1 : 125,000. With supplement: Environs of Rome. Scale 1 : 25,000. Mounted on rollers, varnished. 18s.

Wall-Map of Ancient Greece. Græciæ Antiquæ tabula. For the study of Herodotus, Thucydides, Xenophon, Strabo, Cornelius Nepos, etc. Scale 1 : 500,000. Mounted on rollers, varnished. 24s.

Wall-Map of the Empires of the Persians and of Alexander the Great. Imperia Persarum et Macedonum. For the study of Herodotus, Xenophon, Justinian, Arian, Curtius. Scale 1 : 300,000. Mounted on rollers and varnished. 20s.

KIEPERT'S Wall-Maps of the Ancient World —*continued.*
    Wall-Map of Gaul, with Portions of Ancient Britain and Ancient Germany. Galliæ Cisalpinæ et Transalpinæ cum partibus Britanniæ et Germaniæ tabula. For the study of Cæsar, Justinian, Livy, Tacitus, etc. Scale 1 : 1,000,000. Mounted on rollers and varnished 24s.
    Wall-Map of Ancient Asia Minor. Asiæ Minoris Antiquæ tabula. For the study of Herodotus, Xenophon, Justinian, Arian, Curtius, etc. Scale 1 : 800,000. Mounted on rollers and varnished. 20s.

—— **New Atlas Antiquus.** Twelve Maps of the Ancient World, for Schools and Colleges. Third hundred thousand. 12th Edition, with a complete Geographical Index. Folio, boards. 6s. Strongly bound in cloth. 7s. 6d.

KING, THE, TO HIS PEOPLE. Being the Speeches and Messages of His Majesty George V. as Prince and Sovereign. Published by permission. Square 8vo, art canvas. 5s. net.

KITTEL (Dr RUDOLF, of Breslau). **A History of the Hebrews.** In 2 vols. 8vo, cloth. Each volume, 10s. 6d. Forming Vols. 3 and 6 of the Theological Translation Library, New Series ; for list, see p. 41.

—— **The Scientific Study of the Old Testament :** Its Principal Results, and their Bearing upon Religious Instruction. Illustrated. 5s. net. Forming Vol. 32 in the Crown Theological Library ; for list, see p. 35.

KUENEN (Dr A., of Leiden). **The Religion of Israel to the Fall** of the Jewish State. Translated from the Dutch by A. H. May. 3 vols. 8vo, cloth. 18s. *See* Theological Translation Fund Library, p. 35.

KYRIAKIDES (A.). **Modern Greek-English Dictionary.** With a Cypriote Vocabulary. 2nd Edition, revised throughout. Medium 8vo. 920 pages. Cloth. 15s. net.

—— **A Modern Greek-English and English-Modern Greek Pocket** Dictionary. In 2 vols., about 650 pages each. 7s. net each volume.

LAKE (KIRSOPP). **The Historical Evidence for the Resurrec-**tion of Jesus Christ. The Author is Professor of New Testament Exegesis in the University of Leiden, Holland. Crown 8vo, cloth. 4s. 6d. net. Forming Vol. 21 in the Crown Theological Library ; see p. 34.

LANDOLT (Dr HANS). **The Optical Rotating Power of** Organic Substances and its Practical Applications. 8vo. Pages xxi + 751. 83 Illustrations. 31s. 6d. net.

LAURIE (Prof. SIMON). **Ethica : or, the Ethics of Reason.** By Scotus Novanticus. 2nd Edition. 8vo, cloth. 6s.

—— **Metaphysica Nova et Vetusta : A Return to Dualism.** 2nd Edition. Crown 8vo, cloth. 6s.

LEA (HENRY CHARLES, LL.D.). **History of Sacerdotal** Celibacy in the Christian Church. 3rd Edition. Thoroughly Revised and Reset. 2 vols. Medium 8vo, cloth. 21s. net.

LEAVENWORTH (Prof. W. S., M.Sc.). **Inorganic Qualitative** Chemical Analysis for Advanced Schools and Colleges. 8vo. Pages vi + 154. 6s. 6d. net.

LEBLANC (Dr MAX). The Production of Chromium and its Compounds by the Aid of the Electric Current. Demy 8vo, cloth. 5s. net.

LEIPOLDT (C. LOUIS, F.R.C.S. Eng.). **Common-sense Diet-**etics. Strongly bound in cloth. Crown 8vo. 2s. 6d. net.

LE ROY (Edouard). A New Philosophy : Henri Bergson. Translated by Vincent Benson, M.A. Crown 8vo, cloth, 5s. net.

LETHABY (Prof. W. R.). Architecture. Over 40 Illustrations. F'cap. 8vo, cloth, 1s. net; leather, 2s. 6d. net. Forming Vol. 39 in the Home University Library; for list, *see* page 38.

LEWIS (AGNES SMITH), Edited by. **Old Syriac Gospels, or** Evangelion Da-Mepharreshe. This is the Text of the Sinai Palimpsest, including the latest additions and emendations, with the variants of the Curetonian Text, corroborations from many other MSS., and a list of quotations from ancient authors. With 4 facsimiles. Quarto, bound half-leather. 25s. net.

LLURIA (Dr ENRIQUE). Super-Organic Evolution. Nature and the Social Problem. With a Preface by Dr D. Santiago Ramon y Cajal. Large Crown 8vo. Illustrated. 7s. 6d. net.

LOBSTEIN (PAUL). The Virgin Birth of Christ: An Historical and Critical Essay. The Author is Professor of Dogmatics in the University of Strassburg. Translated by Victor Leuliette, A.K.C., B.-ès-L., Paris. Edited, with an Introduction, by Rev. W. D. Morrison, LL.D. Crown 8vo. 2s. 6d. net. Forming Vol. 2 in the Crown Theological Library ; for list, *see* p. 34.

LODGE (Sir O.). Life and Matter : An Exposition of Part of the Philosophy of Science, with Special References to the Influence of Professor Haeckel. Second Edition, with an Appendix of Definitions and Explanations. Crown 8vo, cloth. 2s. 6d. net. Popular Edition. Paper Cover. 6d. net.

—— **School Teaching and School Reform.** A Course of Four Lectures on School Curricula and Methods, delivered to Secondary Teachers and Teachers in Training at Birmingham. 3s.

LONDON LIBRARY (St James's Square), **Catalogue of.** xiv + 1626 pages. 4to, bound in buckram. 42s. net. Supplements I.–VIII., bound in buckram, 5s. each.

—— **Subject Index.** 4to, bound in buckram. xxxviii + 1256 pages. 31s. 6d. net.

LONG (J. H.). A Text-book of Urine Analysis. Small 8vo. Pages v + 249. 31 Illustrations. 6s. 6d. net.

LORIA (ACHILLE). Les Bases Economiques de la Justice Internationale. 4to, 3s. 6d. net. Forming Vol. 2 of Publications de l'Institut Nobel Norvégien.

LYALL (Sir C. J., M.A., K.C.I.E.). **Ancient Arabian Poetry,** chiefly Præ-Islamic. Translations, with an Introduction and Notes. F'cap. 4to, cloth. 10s. 6d.

MACAN (R. W.). **The Resurrection of Jesus Christ.** An Essay in Three Chapters. 8vo, cloth. 5s.

MACAULAY (THOMAS BABINGTON). **The Lays of Ancient Rome.** With 8 Illustrations faithfully reproduced in colours, and a number in black-and-white, from original drawings by Norman Ault. Small 4to, cloth. 6s. net.

MACCOLL (HUGH). **Man's Origin, Destiny, and Duty.** Crown 8vo, cloth. 4s. 6d. net.

MACDONALD (J. RAMSAY, M.P.). **The Socialist Movement.** F'cap. 8vo, cloth, 1s. net; leather, 2s. 6d. net. Vol. 10 in the Home University Library; for list, see p. 37.

McDOUGALL (Prof. W., F.R.S., M.B.). **Psychology: the Study of Behaviour.** F'cap. 8vo, cloth, 1s. net; leather, 2s. 6d. net. Vol. 49 in the Home University Library; for list, see p. 38.

MACFIE (RONALD C., M.A., M.B.). **Science, Matter, and Immortality.** Crown 8vo, cloth. 5s. net.

MACGREGOR (Prof. D. H., M.A.). **The Evolution of Industry.** F'cap. 8vo, cloth, 1s. net; leather, 2s. 6d. net. Vol. 24 in the Home University Library; for list, see p. 37.

McKENDRICK (Prof. J. G., M.D.). **The Principles of Physiology.** F'cap. 8vo, cloth, 1s. net; leather, 2s. 6d. net. Vol. 44 in the Home University Library; for list, see p. 38.

MACKENZIE (W. LESLIE, M.D.). **Health and Disease.** F'cap. 8vo, cloth, 1s. net; leather, 2s. 6d. net. Forming Vol. 17 in the Home University Library; for list, see p. 37.

MAIR (G. H., M.A.). **English Literature: Modern.** F'cap. 8vo, cloth, 1s. net; leather, 2s. 6d. net. Forming Vol. 27 in the Home University Library; for list, see p. 37.

MARETT (R. R., M.A., of Oxford). **Anthropology.** F'cap. 8vo, cloth, 1s. net; leather, 2s. 6d. net. Forming Vol. 41 in the Home University Library; for list, see p. 38.

MARGOLIOUTH (Prof. D. S., M.A., D.Litt.). **Mohammedanism.** F'cap. 8vo, cloth, 1s. net; leather, 2s. 6d. net. Forming Vol. 15 in the Home University Library; for list, see p. 37.

MARKHAM (Sir CLEMENTS, K.C.B.). **Vocabularies of the General Language of the Incas of Peru.** Crown 8vo, cloth. 7s. 6d. net.

MARRINER (GEORGE R., F.R.M.S.). **The Kea: A New Zealand Problem.** With Illustrations. Demy 8vo, cloth. 7s. 6d. net.

MARTI (KARL, Professor of Old Testament Exegesis, Bern). **The Religion of the Old Testament: Its Place among the Religions of the Nearer East.** Crown 8vo, cloth, 4s. net. Forming Vol. 19 in the Crown Theological Library; for list, see p. 34.

MARTINEAU (Mrs ALICE). The Herbaceous Border.
Gives full particulars how to make and arrange hardy borders,
and containing an alphabetical index of the most suitable plants.
With a large number of illustrations and a frontispiece in colour.
Demy 8vo, cloth. 7s. 6d. net.

MARTINEAU (Rev. Dr JAMES). The Relation between
Ethics and Religion. An Address. 8vo, sewed. 1s.
—— Modern Materialism: Its Attitude towards Theology. A
Critique and Defence. 8vo, sewed. 2s. 6d.

MASEFIELD (JOHN). Shakespeare. F'cap. 8vo, cloth, 1s. net;
leather, 2s. 6d. net. Forming Vol. 2 in the Home University
Library; for list, *see* p. 37.

MASON (W. P.). Notes on Qualitative Analysis. Sm. 12mo.
56 pp. 3s. 6d. net.

MEADE (RICHARD K., B.Sc.). Chemist's Pocket Manual.
16mo. Leather. Pocket Edition. Second Edition. 12s. 6d. net.
—— Portland Cement: Its Composition, Raw Materials, Manufacture, Testing, and Analysis. Second Edition. With 170 Illustrations. 20s. net.

MELDOLA (Prof. RAPHAEL, D.Sc., LL.D.). Chemistry.
F'cap. 8vo, cloth, 1s. net; leather, 2s. 6d. Forming Vol. 67 in
Home University Library; for list, see p. 38.

MELVILLE (HELEN and LEWIS). The Seasons. An
Anthology in Prose and Verse. Forming an attractive volume,
bound in art linen. 3s. 6d. net.

**MERCER (Rt. Rev. J. EDWARD, D.D.). The Soul of Pro-
gress.** Being the Moorhouse Lectures for 1907. Cr. 8vo, cloth. 6s.

MERCIER (Dr C. A., F.R.C.P.). Crime and Insanity. F'cap.
8vo, cloth, 1s. net; leather, 2s. 6d. net. Forming Vol. 22 in
the Home University Library; for list, *see* p. 37.

MEREDITH (LEWIS B.). Rock Gardens. How to Make and
Maintain them. With an Introduction by F. W. Moore, A.L.S.,
and an Alphabetical List of Plants suitable for the Rock Garden,
with Notes on the aspect and soil they require. Demy 8vo, with
Plates. 7s. 6d. net.

MERIMÉE (PROSPER). Le Coup de Pistolet, etc. 2s. 6d.
See Army Series of French and German Novels, p. 33.

MILINDAPAÑHO, THE. Being Dialogues between King
Milinda and the Buddhist Sage Nāgasena. The Pali Text, edited
by V. Trenckner. Crown 8vo, sewed. 21s.

MITCHELL (Rev. A. F.). How to Teach the Bible. 2nd
Edition, thoroughly revised and reset. Cr. 8vo, cloth. 2s. 6d. net.

MITCHELL (Rev. C. W.). The Refutation of Mani, Marcion,
and Bardaisan of St. Ephraim. 21s. net. *See* Text and Translation
Society, p. 40.

MOISSON (HENRI). The Electric Furnace. 8vo. Pages x + 305.
41 Illustrations. 10s. 6d. net.

MONTEFIORE (C. G.). Origin and Growth of Religion as Illustrated by the Religion of the Ancient Hebrews. The Hibbert Lectures, 1892. 2nd Edition. 8vo, cloth. 10s. 6d. Cheap Edition, 3s. 6d.

MOORE (Prof. BENJAMIN). The Origin and Nature of Life. F'cap. 8vo, cloth, 1s. net; leather, 2s. 6d. net. Forming Vol. 62 in Home University Library; for list, *see* p. 38.

MOORE (G. E., M.A.). Ethics. The Author is Lecturer in Moral Science in Cambridge University. F'cap. 8vo, cloth, 1s. net; leather, 2s. 6d. net. Forming Vol. 54 in the Home University Library; for list, *see* p. 38.

MÜNSTERBERG (Prof. HUGO, of Harvard). The Americans. Translated by Edwin B. Holt, Ph.D., Instructor at Harvard University. Royal 8vo, cloth. 12s. 6d. net.

MURRAY (Prof. GILBERT, D.Litt., LL.D., F.B.A.)., Editor of the Home University Library. For list, *see* p. 37.

MYRES (J. L., M.A., F.S.A.). The Dawn of History. The Author is Wykeham Professor of Ancient History, Oxford. F'cap. 8vo, cloth, 1s. net; leather, 2s. 6d. net. Forming Vol. 29 in the Home University Library; for list, *see* p. 37.

NAVILLE (EDOUARD, Ph.D., Litt.D.). The Old Egyptian Faith. Translated by Colin Campbell, M.A., D.D. Illustrated. 4s. 6d. net. Vol. 30 in Crown Theological Library; for list, *see* p. 35.

NESTLE (Prof. EBERHARD, of Maulbronn). An Introduction to the Textual Criticism of the Greek New Testament. Translated from the Second Edition, with Corrections and Additions by the Author, by William Edie, B.D., and edited, with a Preface, by Allan Menzies, D.D., Professor of Divinity and Biblical Criticism in the University of St Andrews. With eleven reproductions of Texts. Demy 8vo, 10s. 6d.; half-leather, 12s. 6d. Forming Vol. 13 in the Theological Translation Library, New Series, p. 41.

NEWBIGIN (Dr MARION). Modern Geography. Illustrated. F'cap. 8vo, cloth, 1s. net.; leather, 2s. 6d. net. Forming Vol. 7 in the Home University Library; for list, *see* p. 37.

NEW HEBREW SCHOOL OF POETS OF THE SPANISH-ARABIAN EPOCH. Selected Texts with Introduction, Notes, and Dictionary. Edited by H. Brodey, Ph.D., Rabbi in Lachod (Bohemia), and K. Albrecht, Ph.D., Professor in Oldenburg (Grand Duchy). English Translation of the Introduction, etc., by Mrs Karl Albrecht. Cloth. 7s. 6d. net.

NIBELUNGENLIED. "The Fall of the Nibelungens," otherwise "The Book of Kriemhild." An English Translation by W. N. Lettsom. 5th Edition. 8vo, cloth. 5s.

NIKAIDO (Y., B.Sc., M.A.). Beet-Sugar Making and its Chemical Control. With a number of valuable Tables and Illustrations. Demy 8vo, cloth. 12s. 6d. net.

NISSENSON. The Arrangements of Electrolytic Laboratories. Demy 8vo. 52 Illustrations. 5s. net.

NOLDEKE (Prof. THEODOR). Compendious Syriac Grammar. With a Table of Characters by Julius Euting. Translated (with the sanction of the Author) from the Second and Improved German Edition by Rev. James A. Crichton, D.D. Royal 8vo. 18s. net.

—— Delectus Veterum Carminum Arabicorum Glossarium Confecit A. Muller. Crown 8vo, cloth. 7s. 6d.

NOYES (ARTHUR A., Ph.D.). Organic Chemistry for the Laboratory. Small 12mo. Pp. xii + 257. 22 Illus. 6s. 6d. net.

—— and **SAMUEL P. MULLIKEN,** Ph.D. Laboratory Experiments on Class Reactions and Identification of Organic Substances. 8vo. 81 pp. 2s. net.

O'GRADY (STANDISH H.). Silva Gadelica (I.–XXXI.). A Collection of Tales in Irish, with Extracts illustrating Persons and Places. Edited from MSS. and translated. 2 vols. royal 8vo, cloth. 42s. Or separately, Vol. 1, Irish Text; and Vol. 2, Translation and Notes. Each Vol. 21s.

OORDT (J. F. VAN, B.A.). Cape Dutch. Phrases and Dialogues, with Translations, preceded by short Grammatical Notes. Crown 8vo, cloth. 2s. 6d. net.

ORTH (SAMUEL P., Ph.D.). Socialism and Democracy in Europe. Demy 8vo. 360 pages. Cloth. 6s. net.

OSTWALD (WILHELM). Natural Philosophy. Translated by Thomas Seltzer. Crown 8vo, cloth. 4s. net.

OTTO (Prof. RUDOLF). Naturalism and Religion. Translated by J. Arthur Thomson, Professor of Natural History in the University of Aberdeen, and Margaret R. Thomson. Edited with an Introduction by Rev. W. D. Morrison, LL.D. Crown 8vo. 5s. net. Forming Vol. 17 in the Crown Theological Library; *see* p. 34.

PARKER (PERCY. L.), Editor of "Public Opinion." Character and Life. A Symposium. Containing contributions by Dr Alfred Russel Wallace, John A. Hobson, Walter Crane, Harold Begbie, and the late Dr Emil Reich. Crown 8vo, cloth. 3s. 6d. net.

PAXSON (Prof. F. L.). The American Civil War. With Maps. F'cap. 8vo, cloth, 1s. net; leather, 2s. 6d. net. Forming Vol. 48 in the Home University Library; for list, *see* p. 38.

PEARSON (JOSEPH, M.Sc.). Cancer. With 13 Plates. 6s. 6d. net. *See* Liverpool Marine Biology Memoirs, p. 39.

PEDDIE (R. A.). Printing at Brescia in the Fifteenth Century. A List of the Issues. 5s. net.

PERCIVAL (G. H.). The Incarnate Purpose. Essays on the Spiritual Unity of Life. Crown 8vo, cloth. 2s. 6d. net.

PEROWNE (J. T. W., M.A.)., Editor of the Army Series of French and German Novels For list, *see* p. 33.

PERRIS (G. H.). A Short History of War and Peace. F'cap. 8vo, cloth, 1s. net; leather, 2s. 6d. net. Forming Vol. 4 in the Home University Library; for list, *see* p. 37.

PETERS (JOHN P., D.D.). Early Hebrew Story. A Study of the Origin, the Value, and the Historical Background of the Legends of Israel. Crown 8vo, cloth. 4s. 6d. net. Forming Vol. 7 in the Crown Theological Library ; for list, *see* p. 34.

PETIT (ROBERT). How to Build an Aeroplane. Translated from the French, with some additional matter, by Messrs T. O'B. Hubbard and J. H. Ledeboer. With nearly 100 Illustrations. Demy 8vo, cloth. 2s. 6d. net.

PFANHAUSER (Dr W.). Production of Metallic Objects Electrolytically. 5s. net.

PFLEIDERER (Dr O.). Lectures on the Influence of the Apostle Paul on the Development of Christianity. Translated by Rev. J. Frederick Smith. Being the Hibbert Lectures for 1885. Library Edition. Demy 8vo, cloth. 10s. 6d. Cheap Edition, cloth. 3s. 6d. *See* The Hibbert Lectures, p. 36.

—— **Paulinism : A Contribution to the History of Primitive** Christianity. 2 vols. Demy 8vo, cloth. 12s. *See* Theological Translation Library, Old Series, p. 42.

—— **Philosophy of Religion on the Basis of its History.** In 4 vols. Demy 8vo, cloth. 24s. *See* Theological Translation Library, Old Series, p. 42. [Vol. 2 quite out of print.]

—— **Primitive Christianity : Its Writings and Teachings in their** Historical Connections. 4 vols. 10s. 6d. net each. *See* Theological Translation Library, New Series, p. 41.

—— **The Early Christian Conception of Christ : Its Significance** and Value in the History of Religion. 3s. net. *See* Crown Theological Library, p. 34.

PHILLIPPS (V., B.A.). A Short Sketch of German Literature, for Schools. 2nd Edition, revised. Pott 8vo, cloth. 1s.

PHILLIPS (FRANCIS C.). Methods for the Analysis of Ores, Pig Iron, and Steel. 2nd Edition. 8vo. Pages viii + 170. 3 Illustrations. 4s. 6d. net.

PICTON (J. ALLANSON, M.A. Lond.). Man and the Bible. A Review of the Place of the Bible in Human History. Demy 8vo, cloth. 6s. net.

PIDDINGTON (HENRY). The Sailors' Horn-Book for the Law of Storms. Being a Practical Exposition ot the Theory of the Law of Storms, and its uses to Mariners of all Classes in all Parts of the World. Shown by transparent Storm Cards and useful Lessons. 7th Edition. Demy 8vo, cloth. 10s. 6d.

PLATTS (J. T.), Hon. M.A. (Oxon.)). A Grammar of the Persian Language. Part I. Accidence. Broad crown 8vo. 10s. 6d.

POLLARD (Prof. A. F., M.A.). The History of England : A Study in Political Evolution. With a Chronological Table. F'cap. 8vo, cloth, 1s. net ; leather, 2s. 6d. net. Forming Vol. 33 in the Home University Library ; for list, *see* p. 37.

PRAY (Dr). **Astigmatic Letters.** Printed on Millboard, size 22 by 14 inches. 1s.

PROCEEDINGS OF INTERNATIONAL CONFERENCE under the Auspices of the American Society for Judicial Settlement of International Disputes, held at Washington, Dec. 1910. In 1 vol., sewed. 4s. net.

PROCEEDINGS OF THE ARISTOTELIAN SOCIETY FOR THE SYSTEMATIC STUDY OF PHILOSOPHY. Old Series—Odd Numbers at various prices. New Series (yearly volumes bound in buckram)—Vols. I.-XI. ready, 10s. 6d. each net.

PROCEEDINGS OF THE OPTICAL CONVENTION, No. 1, 1905. Crown 4to, cloth. 10s. net.

PROCEEDINGS AND PAPERS OF THE FIFTH INTERNATIONAL CONGRESS OF FREE CHRISTIANITY. Held at Berlin, 1910. Edited by C. W. Wendte, D.D., and V. D. Davis, B.A. Medium 8vo, cloth. 9s. 6d. net. Sewed, 8s. 6d. net.

PUNNETT (R. C., B.A.). **Lineus.** With 4 Plates. 2s. net. *See* Liverpool Marine Biology Memoirs, p. 39.

RÆDER (A.). **L'Arbitrage International chez les Hellènes.** 4to, sewed. 10s. net. Being Vol. I. of Publications de l'Institut Nobel Norvégien.

RAY (Prof. P. C.). **A History of Hindu Chemistry from the Earliest Times to the Middle of the Sixteenth Century A.D.** With Sanskrit Texts, Variants, Translation, and Illustrations. Vol. I. 2nd Edition. Revised and Enlarged. Crown 8vo, 10s. 6d. net. Vol. II. Cloth. 10s. 6d. net.

REICH (Dr EMIL), Contributor to "Character and Life." *See* p. 4.

RENAN (E.). **On the Influence of the Institutions, Thought,** and Culture of Rome on Christianity and the Development of the Catholic Church. Translated by the Rev. Charles Beard. Being the Hibbert Lectures, 1880. 8vo, cloth. 10s. 6d. Cheap Edition (3rd Edition), 3s. 6d.

RENOUF (P. LE PAGE). **On the Religion of Ancient Egypt.** Hibbert Lectures, 1879. 3rd Edition. 8vo, cloth. 10s. 6d. Cheap Edition, 3s. 6d.

RÉVILLE (Dr A.). **On the Native Religions of Mexico and** Peru. Translated by the Rev. P. H. Wicksteed. Hibbert Lectures, 1884. 8vo, cloth. 10s. 6d. Cheap Edition, 3s. 6d.
—— **Prolegomena of the History of Religions.** With an Introduction by Prof. F. Max Müller. 8vo, cloth. 6s. See Theological Translation Library, Old Series, p. 42.

RÉVILLE (Prof. JEAN). **Liberal Christianity: Its Origin,** Nature, and Mission. Translated and edited by Victor Leuliette, A.K.C., B.-ès-L. Crown 8vo, cloth. 3s. 6d. net. Forming Vol. 4 in the Crown Theological Library; for list, *see* p. 34.

RHYS (Prof. J.). On the Origin and Growth of Religion as Illustrated by Celtic Heathendom. Hibbert Lectures, 1886. 8vo, cloth. 10s. 6d. Cheap Edition, 3s. 6d.

RIEDEL (Prof. W.) and W. E. CRUM. The Canons of Athanasius of Alexandria, in Arabic, Ethiopic, and Coptic. 21s. net. *See* Text and Translation Society, p. 40.

RIX (HERBERT). Tent and Testament. A Camping Tour in Palestine, with some Notes on Scripture Sites. With 61 Illustrations, Frontispiece, and Maps. Demy 8vo, cloth. 8s. 6d. net.

ROBERTSON (Prof. J. G., M.A.). The Literature of Germany. F'cap. 8vo, cloth, 1s. net; leather, 2s. 6d. net. Forming Vol. 65 in Home University Library; for list, *see* p. 38.

ROGET (F. F.). An Introduction to Old French. History, Grammar, Chrestomathy, and Glossary. 2nd Edition. Crown 8vo, cloth. 6s.

—— First Steps in French History, Literature, and Philology. For Candidates for the Scotch Leaving Certificate Examinations, the various Universities Local Examinations, and the Army Examinations. 4th Edition. Crown 8vo, cloth. 5s.

RUFFINI (FRANCESCO). Religious Liberty. The Author is Ordinary Professor at the Royal University of Turin. With an Introduction by Prof. J. B. Bury of Cambridge. Demy 8vo. 12s. 6d. net. Forming Vol. 32 in the Theological Translation Library; *see* p. 41.

RUSSELL (Hon. BERTRAND, F.R.S.). The Problems of Philosophy. F'cap. 8vo, cloth, 1s. net; leather, 2s. 6d. net. Forming Vol. 40 in Home University Library; for list, *see* p. 38.

SABATIER (Late AUGUSTE). The Doctrine of the Atonement and its Historical Evolution; and Religion and Modern Culture. Translated by Victor Leuliette, A.K.C., B.-ès-L. Crown 8vo. 4s. net. Forming Vol. 9 in the Crown Theological Library; *see* p. 34.

—— The Religions of Authority and the Religion of the Spirit. New impression. Demy 8vo, cloth. 10s. 6d. *See* Theological Translation Library, New Series, p. 41.

SADI. The Gulistan (Rose Garden) of Shaik Sadi of Shiraz. A new Edition of the Persian Text, with a Vocabulary, by F. Johnson. Square royal 8vo, cloth. 15s.

SADLER (Rev. Dr). Prayers for Christian Worship. Crown 8vo, cloth. 3s. 6d.

—— Closet Prayers, Original and Compiled. 18mo, cloth. 1s. 6d.

SADLER (GILBERT, M.A., LL.B.). A Short Introduction to the Bible. Crown 8vo, cloth. 2s. 6d. net.

SAGAS OF OLAF TRYGGVASON AND OF HAROLD THE TYRANT. A new translation, well illustrated with drawings by Erik Werenskiold, Christian Krogh, and others of the best Norwegian artists. In small 4to, printed on specially mould-made paper, comprising above 200 pages, bound with linen back and paper sides, done up in box. 12s. 6d. net.

SALEEBY (C. W., M.D., F.R.S.).   Individualism and Collectivism. Crown 8vo, cloth. 2s.

SAUNDERS (T. BAILEY).   Professor Harnack and his Oxford Critics. Crown 8vo, cloth. 1s. 6d. net.

SAYCE (Prof. A. H.).   On the Origin and Growth of Religion as illustrated by the Religion of the Ancient Babylonians. 5th Edition. Hibbert Lectures, 1887. 8vo, cloth. 10s. 6d. Cheap Edition, 3s. 6d.

SCHLOSS (DAVID F.).   Methods of Industrial Remuneration. 3rd Edition, revised and enlarged. Crown 8vo, cloth. 7s. 6d. Popular Edition. 3s. 6d.

SCHRADER (Prof. E.).   The Cuneiform Inscriptions and the Old Testament. Translated from the Second Enlarged Edition, with Additions by the Author, and an Introduction by the Rev. Owen C. Whitehouse, M.A. 2 vols. With a Map. 8vo, cloth. 12s. *See* Theological Translation Library, Old Series, p. 42.

SCHREBER (D. G. M.).   Medical Indoor Gymnastics, or a System of Hygienic Exercises for Home Use, to be practised anywhere, without apparatus or assistance, by young and old of either sex, for the preservation of health and general activity. Revised and Supplemented by Rudolf Graefe, M.D. With a large plate and 45 illustrations in the text. Royal 8vo, cloth. 2s. 6d. net.

SCHROEN (L.).   Seven-Figure Logarithms of Numbers from 1 to 108,000, and of Sines, Cosines, Tangents, Cotangents to every 10 Seconds of the Quadrant. With a Table of Proportional Parts. By Dr Ludwig Schroen, Director of the Observatory of Jena, etc., etc. 5th Edition, corrected and stereotyped. With a description of the Tables by A. De Morgan, Professor of Mathematics in University College, London. Imp. 8vo, cloth, printed on light green paper. 9s.

SCHUBERT (HANS VON).   History of the Church. Translated from the Second German Edition. By arrangement with the Author, an Additional Chapter has been added on "Religious Movements in England in the Nineteenth Century," by Miss Alice Gardner, Lecturer and Associate of Newnham College, Cambridge. Demy 8vo, cloth. 10s. 6d. *See* Theological Translation Library, New Series, p. 41.

SCHURMAN (J. GOULD).   Kantian Ethics and the Ethics of Evolution. 8vo, cloth. 5s.
—— **The Ethical Import of Darwinism.** Crown 8vo, cloth. 5s.

SCHUSTER (ERNEST J.).   The Wife in Ancient and Modern Times. Crown 8vo, cloth. 4s. 6d. net.

SCOTT (ANDREW).   Lepeophtheirus and Lernea. With 5 Plates. 2s. net. *See* Liverpool Marine Biology Committee Memoirs on Typical British Marine Plants and Animals, p. 39.

SCOTT (Dr D. H., M.A., F.R.S.).   The Evolution of Plants. Fully illustrated. F'cap. 8vo, cloth, 1s. net; leather, 2s. 6d. net. Forming Vol. 9 in the Home University Library; for list, *see* p. 37.

SCOTT (E. F., M.A.). The Apologetic of the New Testament. Cr. 8vo, cloth. 4s. 6d. net. *See* Crown Theological Library, p. 35.

SEEBERG (Prof. R., of Berlin). The Fundamental Truths of the Christian Religion. Sixteen Lectures delivered before the Students of all Faculties in the University of Berlin. Crown 8vo. 350 pp. 4s. 6d. net. *See* Crown Theological Library, p. 35.

SEGER (HERMAN AUGUST), Collected Writings of. Papers on Manufacture of Pottery. 2 vols. Large 8vo. £3, 3s. net per set.

SELBIE (Principal W. B., M.A.). Nonconformity : Its Origin and Progress. F'cap. 8vo, cloth, 1s. net ; leather, 2s. 6d. net. Forming Vol. 50 in the Home University Library ; for list, *see* p. 38.

SEVERUS (Patriarch of Antioch). The Sixth Book of the Select Letters of Severus, Patriarch of Antioch, in the Syriac Version of Athanasius of Nisibis. Edited and Translated by E. W. Brooks. Vol. I. (Text), Part 1, and Vol. II. (Translation), Part 1. 2 vols. 8vo, cloth. 42s. net. Vol. I. (Text), Part 2, and Vol. II. (Translation), Part 2. 2 vols. 8vo, cloth. 42s. net. *See* Text and Translation Society, p. 40.

SHARPE (HENRY). Britain B.C. : As Described in Classical Writings. With an Inquiry into the positions of the Cassiterides and Thule, and an attempt to ascertain the ancient coast-line of Kent and East Sussex. With Maps. Crown 8vo, cloth. 5s. net.

SHEARMAN (A. T., M.A.). The Development of Symbolic Logic. A Critical Historical Study of the Logical Calculus. Crown 8vo, cloth. 5s. net.

SMITH (The Rt. Hon. F.E., K.C., M.P.). Unionist Policy and other Essays. Large 8vo, cloth. 5s. net.

SMITH (L. PEARSALL, M.A.). The English Language. F'cap. 8vo, cloth, 1s. net ; leather, 2s. 6d. net. Forming Vol. 45 in the Home University Library ; for list, *see* p. 38.

SNELLEN'S OPHTHALMIC TEST TYPES. Best Types. for the Determination of the Acuteness of Vision. 14th Edition, considerably augmented and improved. 8vo, sewed. 4s. Single Sheets : E T B, M O V, B D E, ШШШ, and Large Clock Sheet. 8d. each. Small Clock Sheet and R T V Z. 4d. each.

SNYDER (HARRY, B.Sc.). Soils and Fertilisers. 2nd Edition. 8vo. Pages x + 294. 1 Plate, 40 Illustrations. 6s. 6d. net.

SODDY (F., M.A., F.R.S.). Matter and Energy. F'cap. 8vo, cloth, 1s. net ; leather, 2s. 6d. net. Forming Vol. 46 in the Home University Library ; for list, *see* p. 38.

SODEN (Prof. H. VON, D.D.). The Books of the New Testament. Translated by the Rev. J. R. Wilkinson, and edited by Rev. W. D. Morrison, LL.D. Crown 8vo, cloth. 4s. 6d. net. *See* Crown Theological Library, p. 34.

SOLILOQUIES OF ST AUGUSTINE, THE. Translated into English by Rose Elizabeth Cleveland. With Notes and Introduction by the Translator. Small demy 8vo, cloth. 6s. net.

SOMERVILLE (Prof. W., D.Sc.). Agriculture. F'cap. 8vo, cloth, 1s. net; leather, 2s. 6d. net. Forming Vol. 26 in the Home University Library; for list, *see* p. 37.

SONNTAG (C. O.) A Pocket Flora of Edinburgh and the Surrounding District. A Collection and full Description of all Phanerogamic and the principal Cryptogamic Plants, classified after the Natural System, with an artificial Key and a Glossary of Botanical Terms. By the late C. O. Sonntag. F'cap. 8vo, limp cloth. 3s. 6d. net.

SORENSEN (S., Ph.D.), Compiled by. An Index to the Names in the Mahabharata. With short explanations. Royal 4to, in twelve parts, which are not sold separately, at 7s. 6d. per part net. Parts I. to VI. now ready.

SPEARS (J. R.). Master Mariners. F'cap. 8vo, cloth, 1s. net; leather, 2s. 6d. net. Forming Vol. 55 in the Home University Library; for list, *see* p. 38.

SPENCER (HERBERT). A System of Synthetic Philosophy—

Vol. I. First Principles. With an Appendix and a Portrait. Finally revised. New Edition, large crown 8vo, cloth. 7s. 6d. Specially printed cheap edition, bound in cloth. 2 vols. of 240 pages each. 1s. net per volume. Complete in one volume. 2s. net.

Vols. II. and III. The Principles of Biology. 6th Thousand 8vo, cloth. Revised and greatly enlarged. 2 vols. 18s. each.

Vols. IV. and V. The Principles of Psychology. 5th Thousand. 2 vols. 8vo, cloth. 36s.

Vol. VI. The Principles of Sociology. Vol. I. Part 1, The Data of Sociology; Part 2, The Inductions of Sociology; Part 3, Domestic Institutions. 4th Thousand, revised and enlarged. 8vo, cloth. 21s.

Vol. VII. The Principles of Sociology. Vol. II. Part 4, Ceremonial Institutions; Part 5, Political Institutions. 3rd Thousand. 8vo, cloth. 18s.

Vol. VIII. The Principles of Sociology. Vol. III. Part 6, Ecclesiastical Institutions; Part 7, Professional Institutions; Part 8, Industrial Institutions. 2nd Thousand. 8vo, cloth. 16s.

Vol. IX. The Principles of Ethics. Vol. I. Part 1, The Data of Ethics; Part 2, The Inductions of Ethics; Part 3, The Ethics of Individual Life. 8vo, cloth. 15s.

Vol. X. The Principles of Ethics. Vol. II. Part 4, Justice; Part 5, Negative Beneficence; Part 6, Positive Beneficence; Appendices. Demy 8vo. cloth. 12s. 6d.

—— A Rejoinder to Professor Weismann. Sewed. 6d.

—— Data of Ethics. Reset uniform with popular edition of "First Principles." Sewed, 2s. 6d. net; cloth, 3s. net.

SPENCER (HERBERT). Descriptive Sociology ; or, Groups of Sociological Facts. Compiled and abstracted by Professor D. Duncan of Madras, Dr Richard Scheppig, and James Collier. Folio, boards.

No. 1. **English.** 18s.
No. 2. **Ancient American Races.** 16s.
No. 3. **Lowest Races, Negritto Races, Polynesians.** 18s.
No. 4. **African Races.** 16s.
No. 5. **Asiatic Races.** 18s.
No. 6. **American Races.** 18s.
No. 7. **Hebrews and Phœnicians.** 21s.
No. 8. **The French Civilisation.** 30s.
No. 9. **Chinese.** Compiled and abstracted by E. T. C. Werner, H.M.'s Consular Service, China. 63s.
No. 10. **Greeks : Hellenic Era.** By Rev. Dr J. P. Mahaffy, and Professor W. A. Goligher, Trinity College, Dublin. 21s.

—— **Education : Intellectual, Moral, and Physical.** Popular Edition. Entirely reset. Crown 8vo, cloth. 2s. 6d. Cheap Edition, cloth, 1s. net.

—— **Essays : Scientific, Political, and Speculative.** A new Edition, rearranged, with additional Essays. 3 vols. 8vo, cloth. (Each 10s.) 30s.

—— **Facts and Comments.** Demy 8vo, cloth. 6s.

—— **Justice.** Being Part 4 of the Principles of Ethics. 2nd Thousand. 8vo, cloth. 6s.

—— **Reasons for Dissenting from the Philosophy of M. Comte.** Sewed. 6d.

—— **Social Statics.** Abridged and revised, together with "The Man v. The State." 8vo, cloth. 10s.

—— **The Man versus The State.** 14th Thousand. Sewed. 1s.

—— **The Study of Sociology.** Library Edition (21st Thousand), with a Postscript. 8vo, cloth. 10s. 6d.

—— **Various Fragments.** Uniform in Library binding. Demy 8vo, cloth. Enlarged Edition. 6s.

STATUTES, THE, OF THE APOSTLES. The hitherto unedited Ethiopic and Arabic Texts, with Translations of Ethiopic, Arabic, and Coptic Texts, by G. Horner, M.A.

STEPHEN (Rev. Canon REGINALD, M.A.). Democracy and Character. Being the Moorhouse Lectures for 1908. Crown 8vo, cloth. 5s.

STERNE (LAURENCE). A Sentimental Journey through France and Italy. With 12 Illustrations faithfully reproduced from water-colour drawings by Everard Hopkins. Ordinary Edition in crown 4to, 10s. 6d. net. Edition de Luxe, limited to 500 copies, in demy 4to, 21s. net.

STILLMAN (THOS. B., M.Sc., Ph.D.**). Engineering Chemistry.** 4th Edition. The 4th edition has been mostly rewritten and altered to incorporate the latest approved methods of chemical testing. Medium 8vo. With 147 Figures in the text. 21s. net.

STOCKER (R. DIMSDALE). Social Idealism. Crown 8vo, cloth. 3s. net.

STRACHEY (G. L.). Landmarks in French Literature. F'cap. 8vo, cloth, 1s. net; leather, 2s. 6d. net. Forming Vol. 35 in the Home University Library; for list, *see* p. 37.

TAYLOR (A. CAMERON). General Sir Alexander Taylor. A Memoir by his Daughter. 2 vols. Demy 8vo, cloth.

TAYLOR (Rev. Dr J.). The Massoretic Text and the Ancient Versions of the Book of Micah. Crown 8vo, cloth. 5s.

TEN SERVICES OF PUBLIC PRAYER, with Special Collects. 8vo, cloth, 3s.; or 32mo, cloth, 1s. 6d.

—— **PSALMS AND CANTICLES.** 8vo, cloth. 1s. 6d.

—— **PSALMS AND CANTICLES, with Anthems.** 8vo, cloth. 2s.

—— **SERVICES OF PUBLIC PRAYER, taken in Substance** from the Common Prayer for Christian Worship, with a few additional Prayers for particular Days. 8vo, cloth, 2s. 6d.; or 32mo, cloth, 1s.

TENNYSON (ALFRED, LORD). The Princess: A Medley. With Six Illustrations beautifully reproduced in colours, and a number in black-and-white, from Original Drawings by Everard Hopkins. Small 4to. 7s. 6d. net.

THOMAS (Rev. J. M. LLOYD). A Free Catholic Church. Crown 8vo, cloth. 1s. 6d. net.

THOMSON (J. ARTHUR, M.A., LL.D.**). Introduction to Science.** F'cap. 8vo, cloth, 1s. net; leather, 2s. 6d. net. Forming Vol. 32 in the Home University Library; for list, *see* p. 37.

—— **and Prof. PATRICK GEDDES. Evolution.** F'cap. 8vo, cloth, 1s. net; leather, 2s. 6d. net. Forming Vol. 20 in the Home University Library; for list, *see* p. 37.

—— Editor of the Home University Library; for list, *see* p. 37.

THURSTON (E. TEMPLE). The "Flower of Gloster." By the well-known Author of "City of Beautiful Nonsense," "Sally Bishop," etc. With six Illustrations faithfully reproduced in colours, and other Illustrations in black-and-white, from drawings by W. R. Dakin. Small 4to, cloth. 7s. 6d. net.

TISCHENDORF (C.). The New Testament. Novum Testamentum Græce. 3 vols. 8vo. 70s. net.

TOWER (CHARLES). Germany of To-day. F'cap. 8vo, cloth, 1s. net; leather, 2s. 6d. net. Forming Vol. 71 in Home University Library; for list, *see* p. 39.

TOWER (O. F., Ph.D.**). The Conductivity of Liquids.** 8vo Pages iv + 190. 20 Illustrations. 6s. 6d. net.

TRANSACTIONS OF THE ROYAL DUBLIN SOCIETY. Issued in parts at various prices.

TRANSACTIONS OF THE ROYAL IRISH ACADEMY, DUBLIN. Vols. I.-XX. 4to. £22, 5s. 6d. Vols. XXI.-XXXI. Various prices.

TRANSACTIONS OF THE ROYAL SOCIETY OF EDINBURGH. Issued in parts at various prices. General Index to First Thirty-four Volumes (1783-1888), with History of the Institution. 4to, cloth. 21s.

TRENCKNER (V.). Pali Miscellany. Part·I. The Introductory Part of the Milanda Panho, with an English Translation and Notes. 8vo, sewed. 4s.

TRENT (Prof. W. P.) and ERSKINE (Prof. J.). Great Writers of America. F'cap. 8vo, cloth, 1s. net; leather, 2s. 6d. net. Forming Vol. 52, Home University Library; for list, see p. 38.

TROELTSCH (Prof. ERNEST, of Jena). Protestantism and Progress: The Significance of Protestantism in the Rise of the Modern World. Translated into English by Rev. W. Montgomery, B.D. See Crown Theological Library, p. 35.

UPTON (Rev. C. B.). On the Bases of Religious Belief. Hibbert Lectures, 1893. Demy 8vo, cloth. 10s. 6d. Cheap Edition, 3s. 6d.

VEGA. Logarithmic Tables of Numbers and Trigonometrical Functions. Translated from the 40th, or Dr Bremiker's Edition, thoroughly revised and enlarged, by W. L. Fischer, M.A., F.R.S., Fellow of Clare College, Cambridge; Professor of Natural Philosophy in the University of St Andrews. 75th Stereotyped Edition. Royal 8vo, cloth. 7s.

VEILED FIGURE, THE, and other Poems. Large post 8vo, buckram, gilt, cover designed by Mr T. Blake Wirgman. 2s. 6d.

VELASQUEZ. Large Spanish Dictionary. Composed from the Dictionaries of the Spanish Academy, Terreros and Salva. Spanish-English and English-Spanish. 1279 pp., triple columns. 2 vols. in 1. Imp. 8vo, cloth. 24s.

VENABLE (T. C., Ph.D.). The Development of the Periodic Law. Small 12mo. Pages viii + 321. Illustrated. 10s. 6d. net.
—— **The Study of the Atom.** 12mo. Pages vi + 290. 8s. 6d. net.
—— and **HOWE. Inorganic Chemistry according to the Periodic Law.** 2nd Edition. See under Howe, p. 14.

VINCENT (JACQUES). Vaillante. 2s. 6d. See Army Series of French and German Novels, p. 33.

WALFORD (Mrs L. B.). Recollections of a Scottish Novelist. With Portraits and other Illustrations. Demy 8vo, cloth. 10s. 6d. net.

WALLACE (Dr ALFRED RUSSEL). See Character and Life, p. 4.

WEDMORE (Sir FREDERICK). Painters and Painting. Illustrated. F'cap 8vo, cloth, 1s. net; leather, 2s. 6d. net. Forming Vol. 63 in Home University Library; for list, see p. 38.

WEINEL (Prof. H., of the University of Jena). St Paul: The Man and his Work. Translated by Rev. G. A. Bienemann, M.A. Edited by Rev. W. D. Morrison, M.A., LL.D. Demy 8vo, cloth. 10s. 6d. *See* Theological Translation Library, New Series, p. 41.

WEIR (T. H., B.D.). A Short History of the Hebrew Text of the Old Testament. By Thomas H. Weir, Assistant to the Professor of Oriental Languages in the University of Glasgow. 2nd Edition, with Additions. Crown 8vo, cloth. 6s.

WEISSE (T. H.). A Short Guide to German Idioms : being a Collection of the Idioms most in use. With Examination Papers. 3rd Edition. Cloth. 2s.

—— Elements of German. With a Course of Exercises instructing in Simpler Composition. Crown 8vo, cloth. 3s.

WEIZSÄCKER (Prof. CARL VON). The Apostolic Age. Trans. by James Millar, B.D. Demy 8vo, 2 vols., cloth. Each 10s. 6d. *See* Theological Translation Library, New Series, p. 40.

WELD (A. G.). Glimpses of Tennyson and of Some of his Friends. With an Appendix by the late Bertram Tennyson. Illustrated with Portraits in photogravure and colour, and with a facsimile of a MS. poem. F'cap 8vo, art linen. 4s. 6d. net.

WERNER (A.) and G. HUNT. Elementary Lessons in Cape Dutch (Afrikander Taal). 16mo, cloth. 1s. 6d.

WERNLE (PAUL). The Beginnings of Christianity. The Author is Professor Extraordinary of Modern Church History at the University of Basel. Revised by the Author, and translated by the Rev. G. A. Bienemann, M.A., and edited, with an Introduction, by the Rev. W. D. Morrison, LL.D. Demy 8vo. 10s. 6d. per volume. *See* Theological Translation Library, New Series, p. 41.

WHITEHEAD (A. N., Sc.D., F.R.S.). Introduction to Mathematics. With Diagrams. F'cap. 8vo, cloth, 1s. net ; leather, 2s. 6d. net. Forming Vol. 18 in the Home University Library ; for list, *see* p. 37.

WILEY (HARVEY W., A.M., Ph.D.). Principles and Practice of Agricultural Chemical Analysis. 3 vols. 8vo. New Edition in preparation. Vol. I. Soils. Ready. 18s. net. Vol. II. Fertilisers. 20s. net. Vol. III. in active preparation.

WILLIAMS (The Right Rev. W. L., D.C.L.). A Dictionary of the New Zealand Language. 4th Edition. Edited by the Right Rev. Bishop W. L. Williams, with numerous additions and corrections. Demy 8vo, cloth. 12s. 6d.

—— Lessons in Maori. 3rd Edition. F'cap. 8vo, cloth. 3s.

WIMMER (R., Pastor of Weisweil-am-Rhein in Baden). My Struggle for Light : Confessions of a Preacher. Crown 8vo, cloth. 3s. net. *See* Crown Theological Library, p. 34.

WINSTEDT (E. O.), Edited by. Coptic Texts on St Theodore the General, St Theodore the Eastern, Chamoul and Justus. 21s. net. *See* Text and Translation Society, p. 37.

WOODS (C. E.). **The Gospel of Rightness.** A Study in Pauline Philosophy. 300 pages, cloth. 5s. net.

WRIGHT (Rev. C. H. H.). **Light from Egyptian Papyri on** Jewish History before Christ. Crown 8vo, cloth. 3s. net.

WRIGHT (G. H. BATESON, D.D.). **The Book of Job.** A new critically revised Translation, with Essays on Scansion, Date, etc. 8vo, cloth. 6s.

—— **Was Israel ever in Egypt?** or, A Lost Tradition. 8vo, art linen. 7s. 6d.

WRIGHT (W. ALDIS, LL.D.), Edited by. A Rabbinic Commentary on the Book of Job, contained in a unique MS. at Cambridge. With Translation and Commentary. 21s. net. *See* Text and Translation Society, p. 40.

WUNDT (WILHELM). **Outlines of Psychology.** Translated, with the co-operation of the Author, by Charles Hubbard Judd, Ph.D., Instructor in the Wesleyan University. 3rd Enlarged Edition. Demy 8vo, cloth. 8s. net.

WYSOR (HENRY, B.S., Assistant Professor of Analytical Chemistry, Lafayette College). **Metallurgy.** A Condensed Treatise. Demy 8vo, cloth. 12s. 6d. net.

YOUNGHUSBAND (Col. Sir FRANCIS E.), K.C.I.E. Within : Thoughts during Convalescence. 3s. 6d. net.

COMPLETE LIST OF LIBRARIES & SERIES ARRANGED IN ALPHABETICAL ORDER.

ARMY SERIES OF FRENCH AND GERMAN NOVELS.

Edited, with short Notes, by J. T. W. Perowne, M.A.

This series is equally well adapted for general reading, and for those preparing for the Army, Oxford and Cambridge Certificates, and other Examinations—in fact, for all who wish to keep up or improve their French and German. The notes are as concise as possible, with an occasional etymology or illustration to assist the memory. The books selected being by recent or living authors, are adapted for the study of most modern French and German.

Le Coup de Pistolet, etc. Prosper Merimée. 2s. 6d.

Vaillante. Jacques Vincent. 2s. 6d.

Auf Verlornem Posten and Nazzarena Danti. Johannes v. Dewall. 3s.

Contes Militaires. A. Daudet. 2s. 6d.

Erzählungen. E. Höfer. 3s.

CROWN THEOLOGICAL LIBRARY.

The only undertaking of its kind in the English language; each writer is at liberty to express his deepest convictions with absolute freedom—a freedom which is the only ultimate security of truth.

Vol. I.—**Babel and Bible.** By Dr Friedrich Delitzsch. 4s. 6d. net.

Vol. II.—**The Virgin Birth of Christ.** An Historical and Critical Essay. By Paul Lobstein. 2s. 6d. net.

Vol. III.—**My Struggle for Light.** Confessions of a Preacher. By R. Wimmer. 3s. net.

Vol. IV.—**Liberal Christianity.** Its Origin, Nature, and Mission. By Jean Réville. 3s. 6d. net.

Vol. V.—**What is Christianity?** By Adolf Harnack. 4s. 6d. net.

Vol. VI.—**Faith and Morals.** By W. Herrmann. 4s. 6d. net.

Vol. VII.—**Early Hebrew Story.** A Study of the Origin, the Value, and the Historical Background of the Legends of Israel. By John P. Peters, D.D. 4s. 6d. net.

Vol. VIII.—**Bible Problems and the New Material for their Solution.** By Prof. T. K. Cheyne, D.Litt., D.D. 4s. 6d. net.

Vol. IX.—**The Doctrine of the Atonement and its Historical Evolution, and Religion and Modern Culture.** By the late Auguste Sabatier. 4s. net.

Vol. X.—**The Early Christian Conception of Christ.** Its Significance and Value in the History of Religion. By Otto Pfleiderer. 3s net.

Vol. XI.—**The Child and Religion.** Eleven Essays by Various Writers. 5s. net.

Vol. XII.—**The Evolution of Religion.** An Anthropological Study. By L. R. Farnell, M.A., D.Litt. 4s. 6d. net.

Vol. XIII.—**The Books of the New Testament.** By Baron Hermann von Soden, D.D. 4s. 6d. net.

Vol. XIV.—**Jesus.** By W. Bousset. 3s. 6d. net.

Vol. XV.—**The Communion of the Christian with God.** By W. Herrmann. Revised and much enlarged edition. 4s. 6d. net.

Vol. XVI.—**Hebrew Religion.** To the Establishment of Judaism under Ezra. By W. E. Addis, M.A. 4s. 6d. net.

Vol. XVII.—**Naturalism and Religion.** By Rudolf Otto. 5s. net.

Vol. XVIII.—**Essays on the Social Gospel.** By Dr Adolf Harnack and Dr Herrmann. 4s. net.

Vol. XIX.—**The Religion of the Old Testament.** By Karl Marti. 4s. net.

Vol. XX.—**Luke the Physician.** Being Volume One of Dr Adolf Harnack's New Testament Studies. 5s. net.

Vol. XXI.—**The Historical Evidence for the Resurrection of Jesus Christ.** By Prof. Kirsopp Lake. 4s. 6d. net.

14 Henrietta Street, Covent Garden, London, W.C.

Crown Theological Library—*continued.*

Vol. XXII.—**The Apologetic of the New Testament.** By E. F. Scott. 4s. 6d. net.

Vol. XXIII.—**The Sayings of Jesus.** Being Volume Two of Dr Adolf Harnack's New Testament Studies. 5s. net.

Vol. XXIV.—**Anglican Liberalism.** By Twelve Churchmen. 4s. 6d. net.

Vol. XXV.—**The Fundamental Truths of the Christian Religion.** By Dr R. Seeberg. 4s. 6d. net.

Vol. XXVI.—**The Life of the Spirit.** An Introduction to Philosophy. By Dr Rudolf Eucken. 4s. 6d. net.

Vol. XXVII.—**The Acts of the Apostles.** Being Volume Three of Dr Adolf Harnack's New Testament Studies. 5s. net.

Vol. XXVIII.—**Monasticism and the Confessions of St Augustine.** By Dr Adolf Harnack. 3s. 6d. net.

Vol. XXIX.—**Modernity and the Churches.** By Prof. Percy Gardner. 4s. 6d. net.

Vol. XXX.—**The Old Egyptian Faith.** By Prof. Edouard Naville. Illustrated. 4s. 6d. net.

Vol. XXXI.—**The Constitution and Law of the Church in the First Two Centuries.** By Dr Adolf Harnack. 5s. net.

Vol. XXXII.—**The Scientific Study of the Old Testament.** Illustrated. By Dr Rudolf Kittel. 5s. net.

Vol. XXXIII.—**The Date of the Acts and of the Synoptic Gospels.** Being Volume Four of Dr Adolf Harnack's New Testament Studies. Cloth. 5s. net.

Vol. XXXIV.—**The Religious Experience of St Paul.** By Prof. Percy Gardner. 5s. net.

Vol. XXXV.—**Pharisaism : Its Aims and its Methods.** By R. Travers Herford, B.A. Cloth. 5s. net.

Vol. XXXVI.—**Bible Reading in the Early Church.** Being Volume Five of Dr Adolf Harnack's New Testament Studies. Cloth. 5s. net.

Vol. XXXVII.—**Protestantism and Progress.** By Prof. Ernest Troeltsch of Jena. Cloth. 3s. 6d. net.

Descriptive Prospectus on Application.

THE HIBBERT LECTURES.

Library Edition, demy 8vo. 10s. 6d. per volume.
Cheap Popular Edition, 3s. 6d. per volume.

Alviella (Count Goblet D'). Lectures on the Origin and the Growth of the Conception of God, as illustrated by Anthropology and History. Translated by the Rev. P. H. Wicksteed. (Hibbert Lectures, 1891.) Cloth. 10s. 6d. Cheap Edition, 3s. 6d.

Beard (Rev. Dr C.). Lectures on the Reformation of the Sixteenth Century in its Relation to Modern Thought and Knowledge. (Hibbert Lectures, 1883.) 8vo, cloth. 10s. 6d. Cheap Edition, 3s. 6d.

The Hibbert Lectures—*continued.*

Davids (T. W. Rhys). Lectures on Some Points in the History of Indian Buddhism. (Hibbert Lectures, 1881.) 2nd Edition. 8vo, cloth. 10s. 6d. Cheap Edition, 3s. 6d.

Drummond (Dr). Via, Veritas, Vita Lectures on Christianity in its most Simple and Intelligible Form. (The Hibbert Lectures, 1894.) 10s. 6d. Cheap Edition, 3s. 6d.

Hatch (Rev. Dr). Lectures on the Influence of Greek Ideas and Usages upon the Christian Church. Ed. by Dr Fairbairn. (Hibbert Lectures, 1888.) 3rd Ed. 8vo, cloth. 10s. 6d. Cheap Edition, 3s. 6d.

Kuenen (Dr A.). Lectures on National Religions and Universal Religion. (The Hibbert Lectures, 1882.) 8vo, cloth. 10s. 6d. Cheap Edition, 3s. 6d.

Montefiore (C. G.). Origin and Growth of Religion as Illustrated by the Religion of the Ancient Hebrews. (The Hibbert Lectures, 1892.) 2nd Edition. 8vo, cloth. 10s. 6d. Cheap Edition, 3s. 6d.

Pfleiderer (Dr O.). Lectures on the Influence of the Apostle Paul on the Development of Christianity. Translated by the Rev. J. Frederick Smith. (Hibbert Lectures, 1885.) 2nd Edition. 8vo, cloth. 10s. 6d. Cheap Edition, 3s. 6d.

Renan (E.). On the Influence of the Institutions, Thoughts and Culture of Rome on Christianity, and the Development of the Catholic Church. Translated by the Rev. Charles Beard. (Hibbert Lectures, 1880.) 8vo, cloth. 10s. 6d. Cheap Edition, 3rd Edition, 3s. 6d.

Renouf (P. Le Page). On the Religion of Ancient Egypt. (Hibbert Lectures, 1879.) 3rd Edition. 8vo, cloth. 10s. 6d. Cheap Edition, 3s. 6d.

Rhys (Prof. J.). On the Origin and Growth of Religion as Illustrated by Celtic Heathendom. (Hibbert Lectures, 1886.) 8vo, cloth. 10s. 6d. Cheap Edition, 3s. 6d.

Réville (Dr A.). On the Native Religions of Mexico and Peru. Translated by the Rev. P. H. Wicksteed. (Hibbert Lectures, 1884.) 8vo, cloth. 10s. 6d. Cheap Edition, 3s. 6d.

Sayce (Prof. A. H.). On the Religion of Ancient Assyria and Babylonia. 4th Edition. (Hibbert Lectures, 1887.) 8vo, cloth. 10s. 6d. Cheap Edition, 3s. 6d.

Upton (Rev. C. B.). On the Bases of Religious Belief. (Hibbert Lectures, 1893.) Demy 8vo, cloth. 10s. 6d. Cheap Edition, 3s. 6d.

Second Series.

Farnell (L. R., D.Litt., Wilde Lecturer in the University of Oxford). The Higher Aspects of Greek Religion. Lectures delivered in Oxford and London in 1911. Demy 8vo, cloth. 6s. net.

HOME UNIVERSITY LIBRARY OF MODERN KNOWLEDGE.

Editors: Prof. Gilbert Murray, D.Litt., LL.D., F.B.A., Herbert Fisher, M.A., F.B.A., LL.D., Professor J. Arthur Thomson, LL.D., and Professor Wm. T. Brewster. Each volume is written by an expert of the very first rank, and consists of 256 pages. Issued bound in cloth at 1s. net, or beautifully bound in leather, levant morocco grain, 2s. 6d. net.

Sixty Volumes Now Ready.

1. **Parliament.** Sir C. P. Ilbert, K.C.B.
2. **Shakespeare.** John Masefield.
3. **French Revolution.** (With Maps.) Hilaire Belloc, M.A.
4. **History of War and Peace.** G. H. Perris.
5. **Stock Exchange.** F. W. Hirst, M.A.
6. **Irish Nationality.** Mrs J. R. Green.
7. **Modern Geography.** (Illustrated.) Dr M. Newbigin.
8. **Polar Exploration.** (With Maps.) Dr W. S. Bruce.
9. **Evolution of Plants.** (Fully Illustrated.) Dr D. H. Scott, F.R.S.
10. **Socialist Movement.** J. Ramsay MacDonald, M.P.
11. **Conservatism.** Lord Hugh Cecil, M.A., M.P.
12. **Opening Up of Africa.** (With Maps.) Sir H. H. Johnston, G.C.M.G.
13. **Mediæval Europe.** (With Maps.) H. W. C. Davis, M.A.
14. **The Papacy and Modern Times.** Rev. Dr W. Barry.
15. **Mohammedanism.** Prof. D. S. Margoliouth.
16. **The Science of Wealth.** J. A. Hobson, M.A.
17. **Health and Disease.** Dr W. L. Mackenzie.
18. **Introduction to Mathematics.** (With Diagrams.) A. N. Whitehead, Sc.D., F.R.S.   [F. W. Gamble.
19. **The Animal World.** (With many Illustrations.) Prof.
20. **Evolution.** Prof. J. A. Thomson and Prof. P. Geddes.
21. **Liberalism.** Prof. L. T. Hobhouse.
22. **Crime and Insanity.** Dr C. A. Mercier.
23. **History of our Time, 1885-1911.** G. P. Gooch, M.A.
24. **The Evolution of Industry.** Prof. D. H. MacGregor.
25. **The Civilisation of China.** Prof. H. A. Giles, LL.D.
26. **Agriculture.** Prof. W. Somerville, D.Sc.
27. **English Literature: Modern.** George Mair, M.A.
28. **Psychical Research.** Sir W. F. Barrett, F.R.S.
29. **The Dawn of History.** Prof. J. L. Myres.
30. **Elements of English Law.** Prof. W. M. Geldart, B.C.L.
31. **Astronomy.** A. R. Hinks, M.A.   [M.A.
32. **The Introduction to Science.** Prof. J. Arthur Thomson,
33. **The History of England:** A Study in Political Evolution. Prof. A. F. Pollard.
34. **Canada.** A. G. Bradley.
35. **Landmarks in French Literature.** G. L. Strachey.
36. **Climate and Weather.** (With Diagrams.) Prof. H. N. Dickson, D.Sc.

Home University Library of Modern Knowledge—*continued.*

37. **Peoples and Problems of India.** Sir T. W. Holderness, K.C.S.I.   [Prof. J. J. Findlay.
38. **The School.**   An Introduction to the Study of Education.
39. **Architecture.** (Over 40 Illustrations.) Prof. W. R. Lethaby.
40. **Problems of Philosophy.**   The Hon. Bertrand Russell
41. **Anthropology.**   R. R. Marett, M.A.   [F.R.S.
42. **Rome.**   W. Warde-Fowler, M.A.
43. **English Literature : Mediæval.**   Prof. W. P. Ker.
44. **Principles of Physiology.**   Prof. J. G. M'Kendrick.
45. **The English Language.**   J. Pearsall Smith, M.A.
46. **Matter and Energy.**   F. Soddy, F.R.S.
47. **Buddhism.**   Mrs Rhys Davids.
48. **The American Civil War.**   (Maps.)   Prof. F. L. Paxson.
49. **Psychology.**   The Study of Behaviour.   Prof. W. McDougall.   [W. B. Selbie.
50. **Nonconformity,** Its Origin and Progress.   Principal
51. **Warfare in England.** (With Maps.) Hilaire Belloc, M.A.
52. **Great Writers of America.**   Profs. W. P. Trent and J. Erskine.   [Prof. J. W. Gregory, F.R.S.
53. **The Making of the Earth.**   (With 38 Maps and Figures.)
54. **Ethics.**   G. E. Moore, M.A.
55. **Master Mariners.**   J. R. Spears.   [LL.D., D.D.
56. **Making of the New Testament.**   Prof. B. W. Bacon,
57. **The Human Body** (Illustrated).   Prof. Arthur Keith, M.D., F.R.C.S.   [M.I.E.E.
58. **Electricity** (Illustrated).   Dr Gisbert Kapp, D.Eng.,
59. **Political Economy.**   Prof. S. J. Chapman, M.A.
60. **Missions :** Their Rise and Development   Mrs Creighton.
61. **Napoleon.**   (Maps.)   Herbert Fisher, M.A., F.B.A.
62. **The Origin and Nature of Life.**   Prof. Benjamin Moore.
63 **Painters and Painting.**   (Illustrated.)   Sir Frederick Wedmore.
64. **Dr Johnson and his Circle.**   John Bailey, M.A.
65. **The Literature of Germany.**   Prof. J. G. Robertson, M.A., Ph.D.
66. **The Navy and Sea Power.**   David Hannay.
67. **Chemistry.**   Prof. Raphael Meldola, D.Sc., LL.D.
68. **Comparative Religion.**   Prof. J. Estlin Carpenter, LL.D.
69. **The Newspaper.**   (Illustrated.)   G. Binney Dibblee.
70. **The Victorian Age in Literature.**   G. K. Chesterton.
71. **Germany of To-day.**   By Charles Tower.
72. **Plant Life** (Illustrated).   By Prof. J. B. Farmer, F.R.S.
73 **The Writing of English.**   By Prof. W. T. Brewster.
74. **A History of Freedom of Thought.**   By Prof. J. B. Bury, Litt.D.
75. **Ancient Art and Ritual.**   By Jane Harrison, LL.D., D.Litt.

A Detailed List, containing Particulars of more than One Hundred Volumes, to be had upon application.

14 Henrietta Street, Covent Garden, London, W.C.

LIVERPOOL MARINE BIOLOGY COMMITTEE. MEMOIRS ON TYPICAL BRITISH MARINE PLANTS AND ANIMALS.

Edited by W. A. Herdman, D.Sc., F.R.S. All demy 8vo, stiff boards.

1. **Ascidia.** By W. A. Herdman. With 5 Plates. 2s. net.
2. **Cardium.** By J. Johnstone, Fisheries Assistant, University College, Liverpool. With 7 Plates. 2s. 6d. net.
3. **Echinus.** By Herbert Clifton Chadwick, Curator of the Port Erin Biological Station. With 5 Plates. 2s. net.
4. **Codium.** By R. J. Harvey Gibson, M.A., F.L.S., Professor of Botany in University College, Liverpool, and Helen P. Auld, B.Sc. With 3 Plates. 1s. 6d. net.
5. **Alcyonium.** By Sydney J. Hickson, M.A., D.Sc., F.R.S., Beyer Professor of Zoology in Owens College, Manchester. With 3 Plates. 1s. 6d. net.
6. **Lepeophtheirus and Lernea.** By Andrew Scott, Resident Fisheries Assistant at the Peel Hatchery. With 5 Plates. 2s. net.
7. **Lineus.** By R. C. Punnett, B.A. With 4 Plates. 2s. net.
8. **Pleuronectes.** By Frank J. Cole, Jesus College, Oxford Lecturer in the Victoria University, Demonstrator of Zoology, University, Liverpool, and James Johnstone, B.Sc. Lond., Fisheries Assistant, University, Liverpool. With 11 Plates. 7s. net.
9. **Chondrus.** By Otto V. Darbishire, Owens College, Manchester. With 7 Plates. 2s. 6d. net.
10. **Patella (the Common Limpet).** By J. R. Ainsworth Davis, M.A., Professor of Zoology in the University College of Wales, Aberystwyth, and H. J. Fleure, B.Sc., Fellow of the University of Wales. With 4 Plates. 2s 6d. net.
11. **Arenicola (the Lug-Worm).** By J. H. Ashworth, D.Sc., Lecturer in Invertebrate Zoology in the University of Edinburgh. With 8 Plates. 4s. 6d. net.
12. **Gammarus.** By Margaret Cussans, B.Sc., Zoological Department, University of Liverpool. With 4 Plates. 2s. net.
13. **Anurida.** By A. D. Imms, B.Sc.(Lond.). With 7 Plates. 4s. net.
14. **Ligia.** By C. Gordon Hewitt, B.Sc., Demonstrator in Zoology, University of Manchester. With 4 Plates. 2s. net.
15. **Antedon.** By Herbert Clifton Chadwick. With 7 Plates. 2s. 6d. net.
16. **Cancer.** By Joseph Pearson, M.Sc., Demonstrator in Zoology, University of Liverpool. With 13 Plates. 6s. 6d. net.
17. **Pecton.** By W. J. Dakin, M.Sc. With 9 Plates. 4s. 6d. net.
18. **Eledone.** By Annie Isgrove, M.Sc. With 10 Plates. 4s. 6d. net.
19. **Polychaet Larvae.** By F. H. Gravely, M.Sc. With 4 Plates. 2s. 6d. net.

14 Henrietta Street, Covent Garden, London, W.C.

TEXT AND TRANSLATION SOCIETY. Established for the purpose of editing and translating Oriental Texts chiefly preserved in the British Museum.

The Sixth Book of the Select Letters of Severus, Patriarch of Antioch, in the Syriac Version of Athanasius of Nisibis. Edited and translated by E. W. Brooks, M.A. Vol. I. Text, Parts I. and II. Vol. II. Translation, Parts I. and II. 84s. net.

The Canons of Athanasius of Alexandria, in Arabic, Ethiopic, and Coptic. Edited and translated by Prof. W. Riedel (Griefswald) and W. E. Crum. 21s. net.

A Rabbinic Commentary on the Book of Job, contained in a unique MS. at Cambridge. Edited, with Translation and Commentary, by W. Aldis Wright, LL.D. 21s. net.

An Ancient Armenian Version of the Apocalypse of St John; also **The Armenian Texts of Cyril of Alexandria, Scholia de Incarnatione and Epistle to Theodosius upon Easter,** the former incompletely preserved in Greek, the latter unknown in Greek or Latin. All edited, with English versions, etc., by F. C. Conybeare, formerly Fellow of University College, Oxford.

Remnants of the Later Syriac Versions of the Bible. Part I. (Sixth Century). The Four Minor Catholic Epistles. Reconstructed Text, with Apparatus Criticus. Part II. (Seventh Century). Extracts, hitherto unedited, from the Syro-Hexaplar Text of Chronicles, Nehemiah, etc. All edited, with Greek versions, etc., by John Gwynn, D.D., Regius Professor of Divinity, Dublin. 21s. net.

Coptic Texts on St Theodore the General, St Theodore the Eastern, Chamoul and Justus. Edited and Translated by E. O. Winstedt, late Senior Demy of Magdalen College, Oxford. 21s. net.

The Refutation of Mani, Marcion, and Bardaisan of St Ephraim. Edited by the Rev. C. W. Mitchell. 21s. net.

Euphemia and the Goth. With the Acts of Martyrdom of the Confessors of Edessa. Edited and examined by Prof. F. C. Burkitt. 21s. net.

THEOLOGICAL TRANSLATION LIBRARY.

New Series. A Series of Translations by which the best results of recent Theological Investigations on the Continent, conducted without reference to doctrinal considerations, and with the sole purpose of arriving at the truth, are placed within reach of English readers.

Vols. I. and V.—**The Apostolic Age.** By Prof. Carl von Weizsäcker. Translated by James Millar, B.D. 2 vols. 10s. 6d. each.

Vols. II., VII., VIII., IX., X., XI., XII.—**A History of Dogma.** By Adolf Harnack, Berlin. Translated from the Third German Edition. Edited by the late Rev. Prof. A. B. Bruce, D.D. 7 vols. 10s. 6d. each.

Theological Translation Library—*continued.*

Vols. III. and VI.—**A History of the Hebrews.** By R. Kittel, Ordinary Professor of Theology in the University of Breslau. 10s. 6d. per volume.

Vol. IV.—**The Communion of the Christian with God:** A Discussion in Agreement with the View of Luther. By W. Herrmann, Dr Theol., Professor of Dogmatic Theology in the University of Marburg. 10s. 6d. net.

Vol. XIII.—**An Introduction to the Textual Criticism of the Greek New Testament.** By Prof. Eberhard Nestle, of Maulbronn. Cloth, 10s. 6d. ; half-leather, 12s. 6d.

Vols. XV. and XVII.—**The Beginnings of Christianity.** By Paul Wernle, Professor Extraordinary of Modern Church History at the University of Basel. Vol. I. The Rise of the Religion. Vol. II. The Development of the Church. 10s. 6d. per volume.

Vol. XVI.—**The Religions of Authority and the Religion of the Spirit.** By the late Auguste Sabatier. 10s. 6d.

Vol. XVIII.—**Christian Life in the Primitive Church.** By Ernst von Dobschütz, D.D., Professor of New Testament Theology in the University of Strassburg. 10s. 6d.

Vols. XIX. and XX.—**The Mission and Expansion of Christianity in the First Three Centuries.** By Adolf Harnack, Berlin. Second, revised and much enlarged edition, 25s. net. Vols. not sold separately.

Vol. XXI.—**St Paul:** The Man and his Work. By Prof. H. Weinel, of the University of Jena. 10s. 6d.

Vols. XXII., XXVI., XXVII., and XXXI.—**Primitive Christianity:** Its Writings and Teachings in their Historical Connections. By Otto Pfleiderer, Professor of Practical Theology in the University of Berlin. 4 vols. 10s. 6d. each net.

Vol. XXIII.—**The Introduction to the Canonical Books of the Old Testament.** By Carl Cornill, Professor of Old Testament Theology at the University of Breslau. 10s. 6d. net.

Vol. XXIV.—**History of the Church.** By Hans von Schubert, Professor of Church History at Kiel. 10s. 6d. net.

Vol. XXV.—**Ethics of the Christian Life.** By Theodor von Haering, Professor of New Testament Dogmatics and Ethics at Tübingen. 10s. 6d. net.

Vols. XXVIII. and XXIX.—**The Old Testament in the Light of the Ancient East.** By Alfred Jeremias, Pastor of the Lutherkirche, and Lecturer at the University of Leipzig. With numerous illustrations and maps, 25s. net. Vols. not sold separately.

Vol. XXX.—**The Truth of Religion.** By Dr Rudolf Eucken, Senior Professor of Philosophy in the University of Jena. 12s. 6d. net.

Vol. XXXII.—**Religious Liberty.** By Prof. Francesco Ruffini. With a Preface to the English Edition by Prof. J. B. Bury of Cambridge. Demy 8vo, cloth. 12s. 6d. net.

THEOLOGICAL TRANSLATION FUND LIBRARY.

Old Series. Uniform Price per Volume, 6s.

Baur (F. C.). Church History of the First Three Centuries. Translated from the Third German Edition. Edited by Rev. Allan Menzies. 2 vols. 8vo, cloth. 12s.

—— Paul, the Apostle of Jesus Christ, His Life and Work, His Epistles and Doctrine. A Contribution to a Critical History of Primitive Christianity. Edited by Rev. Allan Menzies. 2nd Edition. 2 vols. 8vo, cloth. 12s.

Ewald's (Dr H.) Commentary on the Prophets of the Old Testament. Translated by the Rev. J. F. Smith. 5 vols. 8vo, cloth. 30s.

—— Commentary on the Psalms. Translated by the Rev. E. Johnson, M.A. 2 vols. 8vo, cloth. 12s.

—— Commentary on the Book of Job, with Translation. Translated from the German by the Rev. J. Frederick Smith. 8vo, cloth. 6s.

Hausrath (Prof. A.). History of the New Testament Times. The Time of Jesus. Translated by the Revs. C. T. Poynting and P. Quenzer. 2 vols. 8vo, cloth. 12s.

Keim's History of Jesus of Nazara : Considered in its connection with the National Life of Israel, and related in detail. Translated from the German by Arthur Ransom and the Rev. E. M. Geldart. Complete in 6 vols. 8vo. 36s. (Vol. I. only to be had when a complete set of the work is ordered.)

Kuenen (Dr A.). The Religion of Israel to the Fall of the Jewish State. Translated from the Dutch by A. H. May. 3 vols. 8vo, cloth. 18s.

Pfleiderer (O.). Paulinism: A Contribution to the History of Primitive Christian Theology. Translated by E. Peters. 2nd Edition. 2 vols. 8vo, cloth. 12s.

—— Philosophy of Religion on the Basis of its History. Translated by Prof. Allan Menzies and the Rev. Alex. Stewart. 4 vols. 8vo, cloth. 24s. (Vol. I. out of print).

Réville (Dr A.). Prolegomena of the History of Religions. With an Introduction by Prof. F. Max Müller. 8vo, cloth. 6s.

Schrader (Prof. E.). The Cuneiform Inscriptions and the Old Testament. Translated from the Second Enlarged Edition, with Additions by the Author, and an Introduction by the Rev. Owen C. Whitehouse, M.A. 2 vols. With a Map. 8vo, cloth. 12s.

LIST OF PERIODICALS, REVIEWS, AND TRANS-ACTIONS AND PROCEEDINGS OF LEARNED SOCIETIES published by Williams & Norgate.

The British Review. With which is incorporated the Oxford and Cambridge Review. Monthly, 1s. net. Postage inland, 3d. ; abroad, 4d.

The Hibbert Journal : A Quarterly Review of Religion, Theology, and Philosophy. Single numbers, 2s. 6d. net. Subscription, 10s. per annum, post free.

List of Periodicals, Reviews, etc.—*continued*.

Journal of the Federated Malay States Museums. Issued quarterly. Single numbers, 1s. 6d. net. Subscription, 5s. per annum.

Journal of the Royal Microscopical Society, containing its Transactions and Proceedings, with other Microscopical Information. Bi-monthly. 6s. net. Yearly subscriptions, 37s. 6d., post free.

Journal of the Quekett Microscopical Club. Issued half-yearly, April and November. Price 3s. 6d. net. 7s. 6d. per annum, post free.

Linnean Society of London. Journal of Botany and Journal of Zoology. Published irregularly at various prices. Also Transactions, published irregularly.

Royal Society of Edinburgh. Transactions. Issued irregularly at various prices.

Liverpool Marine Biology Committee. Memoirs. I.–XIX. already published at various prices. Fauna of Liverpool Bay. Fifth Report, written by Members of the Committee and other Naturalists. Cloth. 8s. 6d. net. *See* p. 39.

Publications de l'Institut Nobel Norvégien. Vol. I. L'Arbitrage International chez les Hellènes. Par A. Raedar. 4to. 10s. net. Vol. II. Les Bases Economiques de la Justice Internationale. By Achille Loria. 3s. 6d. net.

Royal Irish Academy. Transactions and Proceedings issued irregularly; prices vary. Cunningham Memoirs. Vols. I.–XI. already issued at various prices. *See* p. 31.

Royal Dublin Society. Transactions and Proceedings. Issued irregularly at various prices.

INDEX OF TITLES.

Canada. A. G. Bradley, 3.

Cancer. *Vide* L.M.B.C. Memoirs, 37.

Cancer and other Tumours. Chas. Creighton, 5.

Canonical Books of the Old Testament. Cornill, 5.

Cape Dutch. J. F. Van Oordt, 22.

Cape Dutch, Werner's Elementary Lessons in, 32.

Capri and Naples, Guide to, 10.

Captain Cartwright and his Labrador Journal, 4.

Cardium. *Vide* L.M.B.C. Memoirs, 39.

Catalogue of the London Library, 17.

Celtic Heathendom. Prof. J. Rhys, 25.

Channing's Complete Works, 4.

Chants and Anthems, 15; Chants, Psalms, and Canticles. Crompton Jones, 15.

Character and Life, 4.

Chemical Dynamics, Studies in. J. H. Van't Hoff, 13.

Chemistry. Prof. Meldola, 20.

Chemistry, Elementary. Emery, 7.

Chemistry for Beginners. Edward Hart, 11.

Chemist's Pocket Manual, 20.

Child and Religion, The, 5.

China, The Civilisation of. Prof. H.A. Giles, 9.

Chinese. Descriptive Sociology. Werner, 27.

Chondrus. *Vide* L.M.B.C. Memoirs, 39.

Christian Life, Ethics of the. Chas. F. Dole, 10.

Christian Life in the Primitive Church. Dobschütz, 7.

Christian Religion, Fundamental Truths of the. R. Seeberg, 25.

Christianity, Beginnings of. Paul Wernle, 32.

Christianity in Talmud and Midrash. R. Travers Herford, 12.

Christianity? What is. Adolf Harnack, 11.

Chromium, Production of. Max Leblanc, 18.

Church History. Baur, 2; Schubert, 24.

Civilisation of China. H. A. Giles, 9.

Climate and Weather. H. N. Dickson, 6.

Closet Prayers. Dr. Sadler, 23.

Codium. *Vide* L.M.B.C. Memoirs, 39.

Collected Writings of Seger, 27.

Colonial Period, The. C. M. Andrews, 1.

Coming Church. Dr John Hunter, 14.

Commentary on the Book of Job, Ewald, 7; Wright and Hirsch, 30; Commentary on the Old Testament. Ewald, 7; Commentary on the Psalms. Ewald, 7.

Common-Sense Dietetics. C. Louis Leipoldt, 18.

Communion with God. Wilhelm Herrmann, 12.

Comparative Religion. Princ. J. E. Carpenter, 4.

Conception of God. Alviella, 1.

Concrete, Reinforced. Colby, 5.

Conductivity of Liquids. Tower, 30.

Confessions of St Augustine. Adolf Harnack, 11.

Conservatism. Lord Hugh Cecil, 4.

Constitution and Law of the Church, Adolf Harnack, 11.

Contes Militaires. A. Daudet, 33.

Copenhagen and Norway, Guide to, 10.

Coptic Texts on St. Theodore. E. O. Winstedt, 32.

Crime and Insanity. Dr. C. A. Mercier, 20.

Crown Theological Library, 34.

Cuneiform Inscriptions, The. Prof. E. Schrader, 26.

Date, The, of the Acts and of the Synoptic Gospels. Harnack, 11.

Dawn of History, The. Prof. J. L. Myres, 21.

Delectus Veterum. Theodor Nöldeke, 20.

Democracy and Character. Canon Stephen, 29.

Democracy, Socialism and, in Europe. Samuel P. Orth, 22.

De Profundis Clamavi. Dr John Hunter, 14.

Descriptive Sociology. Herbert Spencer, 26.

Development of the Periodic Law. Venable, 31.

Differential and Integral Calculus, The. Axel Harnack, 11.

Dipavamsa, The. Edited by Oldenberg, 6.

Doctrine of the Atonement. A. Sabatier, 25.

Dogma, History of. Adolf Harnack, 11.

Dolomites, The, Practical Guide to, 10.

Dresden and Environs, Guide to, 10.

Early Hebrew Story. John P. Peters, 23.

Early Christian Conception. Otto Pfleiderer, 23.

Echinus. *Vide* L.M.B.C. Memoirs, 36.

Education. Herbert Spencer, 28.

Education and Ethics. Emile Boutroux, 3.

Egyptian Faith, The Old. Edouard Naville, 21.

Egyptian Grammar, Erman's, 7.

Eighth Year, The. Philip Gibbs, 9.

Electric Furnace. H. Moisson, 20.

Electricity. Prof. Gisbert Kapp, 15.

Electrolysis of Water. V. Engelhardt, 7.

Electrolytic Laboratories. Nissenson, 22.

Eledone. *Vide* L.M.B.C. Memoirs, 39.

Elementary Chemistry. Emery, 6.

46 WILLIAMS & NORGATE'S

Elementary Organic Analysis. F. E. Benedict, 2.
Elements of English Law. W. M. Geldart, 9.
Engineering Chemistry. T. B. Stillman, 30.
England and Germany, 6.
English Language. L. P. Smith, 27.
English Literature, Mediæval. W. P. Ker, 16.
English Literature, Modern. G. H. Mair, 19.
Enoch, Book of, C. Gill, 9.
Ephesian Canonical Writings. Rt. Rev. A. V. Green, 9.
Epitome of Synthetic Philosophy. F. H. Collins, 4.
Erzählungen. Höfer, 33.
Essays on the Social Gospel. Harnack and Herrmann, 11.
Essays. Herbert Spencer, 29.
Ethica. Prof. Simon Laurie, 17.
Ethics, Data of. Herbert Spencer, 28.
Ethics, Education and. Emile Boutroux, 3.
Ethics. G. E. Moore, 21.
Ethics, Principles of. Herbert Spencer, 28.
Ethics of the Christian Life. Prof. T. Haering, 10.
Ethics of Progress, The. Chas. F. Dole, 6.
Ethiopic Grammar. A. Dillmann, 6.
Eucken's Philosophy, An Interpretation of. W. Tudor Jones, 15.
Euphemia and the Goth. Prof. F. C. Burkitt, 4, 40.
Europe, Mediæval. H. W. C. Davis, 6.
Evolution. Thomson and Geddes, 30.
Evolution of Industry. Prof. D. H. Macgregor, 19.
Evolution of Plants. Dr. D. H. Scott, 26.
Evolution of Religion, The. L. R. Farnell, 7.
Exploration, Polar. Dr W. S. Bruce, 4.

Facts and Comments. Herbert Spencer, 29.
Faith and Morals. W. Herrmann, 11.
Fertilisers, Soil Fertility and. Halligan, 10.
First Principles. Herbert Spencer, 28.
First Three Gospels in Greek. Rev. Canon Colin Campbell, 3.
Flower of Gloster, The. E. Temple Thurston, 30.
Four Gospels as Historical Records, 9.
Free Catholic Church. Rev. J. M. Thomas, 30.
Freedom of Thought. Bury, 4.
Freezing Point, The. Jones, 13.
French Composition. Jas. Boïelle, 3.

French History, First Steps in. F. F. Roget, 23.
French Language, Grammar of. Eugène, 7.
French Literature, Landmarks in. G. L. Strachey, 30.
French Reader. Leon Delbos, 6.
French Revolution, The. Hilaire Belloc, 2.
Fundamental Truths of the Christian Religion. R. Seeberg, 27.

Gammarus. Vide L.M.B.C. Memoirs, 37.
Gaul, Wall Map of, 16.
General Language of the Incas of Peru. Sir Clements Markham, 19.
Genesis, Book of, in Hebrew Text. Rev. C. H. H. Wright, 28.
Genesis and Evolution of the Soul. J. O. Bevan, 2.
Genesis, Hebrew Text, 11.
Geography, Modern. Dr M. Newbigin, 21.
Geometry, Analytical, Elements of. Hardy, 11.
German History, Noble Pages from. F. J. Gould, 10.
German Idioms, Short Guide to. T. H. Weisse, 30.
German Literature, A Short Sketch of. V. Phillipps, B.A., 23.
Germany, England and, 6.
Germany of To-day. Tower, 30.
Germany, The Literature of. Prof. J. G. Robertson, 25.
Glimpses of Tennyson. A. G. Weld, 32.
God and Life. Dr John Hunter, 14.
Gospel of Rightness. C. E. Woods, 33.
Gospels in Greek, First Three. Rev. Colin Campbell, 4.
Grammar, Egyptian. Erman, 7.
Grammar, Ethiopic. A. Dillman, 6.
Greek-English Dictionary, Modern, 17.
Greek Ideas, Lectures on. Rev. Dr. Hatch, 11.
Greek, New Testament. Prof. Edouard Nestle, 19.
Greek Religion, Higher Aspects of. L. R. Farnell, 8.
Greeks: Hellenic Era, 27.
Grieben's English Guides, 9.
Gulistan, The (Rose Garden), of Shaik Sadi of Shiraz, 23.
Gymnastics, Medical Indoor. Dr Schreber, 24.

14 Henrietta Street, Covent Garden, London, W.C.

Journal of the Linnean Society. Botany and Zoology, 15.
Journal of the Quekett Microscopical Club, 15.
Journal of the Royal Microscopical Society, 15.
Justice. Herbert Spencer, 29.

Kantian Ethics. J. G. Schurman, 26.
Kea, The. George R. Marriner, 19.
Kiepert's New Atlas Antiquus, 15.
Kiepert's Wall-Maps of the Ancient World, 15.
Kindergarten, The. H. Goldammer, 9.
King, The, to His People, 17.
Kingdom, The Mineral. Dr Reinhard Brauns, 3.

Laboratory Experiments. Noyes and Mulliken, 20.
Lakes of Northern Italy, Guide to, 10.
Landmarks in French Literature. G. L. Strachey, 30.
Latter Day Saints, The. Ruth and R. W. Kauffman, 15.
Law, English, Elements of. W. M. Geldart, 9.
Lays of Ancient Rome. Macaulay, 19.
Leabhar Na H-Uidbri, 41.
Le Coup de Pistolet. Merimée, 33.
Lepeophtheirus and Lernea. *Vide* L.M.B.C. Memoirs, 39.
Letter to the "Preussiche Jahrbucher." Adolf Harnack, 11.
Les Misérables. Victor Hugo, 14.
Liberal Christianity. Jean Réville, 24.
Liberalism. Prof. L. T. Hobhouse, 13.
Life and Matter. Sir O. Lodge, 18.
Life of the Spirit, The. Rudolf Eucken, 7.
Ligia. *Vide* L.M.B.C. Memoirs, 39.
Lineus. *Vide* L.M.B.C. Memoirs, 39.
Linnean Society of London, Journals of, 15.
Literature, English Mediæval. Prof. W. P. Ker, 16.
Literature, Highways and Byways in. Hugh Farrie, 8.
Literature of Germany. Prof. J. G. Robertson, 25.
Literature of the Old Testament. Kautzsch, 16.
Literature, The Victorian Age in. G. K. Chesterton, 4.
Liverpool Marine Biology Committee Memoirs, 39.
Liverpool Marine Biology Committee Memoirs; I.—XVII., 36, 37.

Logarithmic Tables. Schroen, 26.
London Library, Catalogue of, 18.
London Library Subject Index, 18.
Luke the Physician. Adolf Harnack, 11.

Mad Shepherds, and other Studies. Prof. L. P. Jacks, 14.
Mahabharata, Index to. S. Sorensen, 28.
Making a Newspaper. John L. Given, 9.
Making of the Earth. Prof. J. W. Gregory, 10.
Making of the New Testament. Prof. B. W. Bacon, 1.
Man and the Bible. J. A. Picton, 23.
Man *versus* the State. Herbert Spencer, 29.
Man's Origin, Destiny, and Duty. Hugh M'Coll, 19.
Maori, Lessons in. Right Rev. W. L. Williams, 30.
Maori, New and Complete Manual of. Williams, 30.
Marine Zoology of Okhamandal. Hornell, 14.
Massoretic Text. Rev. Dr J. Taylor, 30.
Master Mariners. J. R. Spears, 28.
Mathematics, Introduction to. A. N. Whitehead, 32.
Matter and Energy. F. Soddy, 27.
Mediæval Europe. H. W. C. Davis, 6.
Metallic Objects, Production of. Dr. W. Pfanhauser, 23.
Metallurgy. Wysor, 31.
Metaphysica Nova et Vetusta. Prof. Simon Laurie, 17.
Midrash, Christianity in. Travers Herford, 12.
Milando Panho, The. Edited by V. Trenckner, 20.
Mineral Kingdom, The. Dr R. Brauns, 3.
Mission and Expansion of Christianity. Adolf Harnack, 11.
Missions. Mrs Creighton, 5.
Modern Greek-English Dictionary. A. Kyriakides, 16.
Modern Materialism. Rev. Dr James Martineau, 18.
Modernity and the Churches. Percy Gardner, 9.
Mohammedanism. Prof. D. S. Margoliouth, 19.
Molecular Weights. Methods of Determining. Henry Biltz, 27.
Monasticism. Adolf Harnack, 11.
Moorhouse Lectures. *Vide* Mercer's Soul of Progress, 18; Stephen, Democracy and Character, 27.

Seeds and Fruits, Studies in. H. B. Guppy, 10.

Seger. Collected Writings, 27.

Sentimental Journey. Laurence Sterne, 29.

Seven-Figure Logarithms. L. Schroen, 26.

Severus, Patriarch of Antioch, Letters of, 27.

Short History of the Hebrew Text. T. H. Weir, 32.

Silva Gadelica. Standish H. O'Grady, 22.

Social Gospel, Essays on the, 11.

Social Idealism. R. Dimsdale Stocker, 30.

Social Statics. Herbert Spencer, 29.

Socialism and Democracy in Europe. Samuel P. Orth, 22.

Socialist Movement, The. J. R. MacDonald, 19.

Sociology, Descriptive. Herbert Spencer, 29.

Sociology, Principles of. Herbert Spencer, 28.

Sociology, Study of. Herbert Spencer, 29.

Soil, Fertility, and Fertilisers. Halligan, 10.

Soils. Vide Wiley's Agricultural Analysis, 32.

Soils and Fertilisers. Snyder, 27.

Soliloquies of St Augustine. Cleveland, 27.

Soul of Progress. Bishop Mercer, 20.

Spencer, Herbert, Life and Letters of. D. Duncan, 7.

Spinal Cord, Topographical Atlas of. Alex. Bruce, M.A., etc., 4.

Spirit, The Life of. Rudolf Eucken, 7.

St. Paul, The Religious Experience of. Prof. P. Gardner, 9.

Statuette, The, and the Background. H. B. Brewster, 3.

Statutes, The, of the Apostles. G. Horner, 29.

Stereochemistry, Elements of. Hantzsch, 11.

Stock Exchange, The. F. W. Hirst, 13.

Storms. H. Piddington, 23.

Studies from the Yale Psychological Laboratory. Edward W. Scripture, Ph.D., 31.

Studies in Seeds and Fruits. H. B. Guppy, 10.

Studies on Northern Mythology. Geo. Stephens, 56.

Study of the Atom. Venable, 31.

Study of the Saviour. Alex. Robinson, 24.

Subject-Index to London Library Catalogue, 54.

Super-Organic Evolution. Dr Enrique Lluria, 18.

Surgical Anatomy of the Horse. J. T. Share Jones, 46.

Switzerland, Practical Guide to, 10; Winter Sports in, 10.

Symbolic Logic. A. T. Shearman, 27.

Symbolism, Lost Language of. Harold Bayley, 2.

Synoptic Gospels, The Date of the. Adolf Harnack, 11.

Synthetic Philosophy, Epitome of. F. H. Collins, 5.

Syriac Grammar. Theodor Nöldeke, 22.

System of Synthetic Philosophy. Herbert Spencer, 31.

Talmud and Midrash, Christianity in. . R. Travers Herford, 12.

Taylor, General Sir Alexander. A Memoir by his Daughter, 30.

Ten Services and Psalms and Canticles, 27.

Ten Services of Public Prayer, 27.

Tent and Testament. Herbert Rix, 25.

Testament, Old. Canonical Books of, 5; Religions of, 19; Cuneiform Inscriptions, 26; Hebrew Text, Weir, 32; Literature, 16.

Testament, The New, Critical Notes on. C. Tischendorf, 30.

Testament Times, New, 12; Acts of the Apostles, 11; Apologetic of, 26; Books of the, 27; Commentary, Protestant, 8; Luke the Physician, 11; Textual Criticism, 21.

Test Types. Pray, 24; Snellen, 27.

Text and Translation Society, Works by, 40.

Theological Translation Library, 40.

Theories of Anarchy and of Law. H. B. Brewster, 3.

Thermometer, History of the. Bolton, 3.

Tourist Guides. Grieben's, 10.

Transactions of the Royal Dublin Society, 30.

Transactions of the Royal Irish Academy, 31.

Transactions of the Royal Society of Edinburgh, 31.

Truth, The, of Religion. Eucken, 7.

Unionist Policy. Rt. Hon. F. E. Smith, 27.

Universal Christ. Rev. Dr. C. Beard, 2.

Universalism Asserted. Rev. Thos. Allin, 1.

Urine Analysis, A Text-Book of. Long, 18.

Vaillante, Vincent, 33.

Various Fragments. Herbert Spencer, 29.

Veiled Figure, The, 31.

Via, Veritas, Vita. Dr. Drummond, 7.

PRINTED BY NEILL AND CO., LTD., EDINBURGH.

FOURTEEN DAY USE
RETURN TO DESK FROM WHICH BORROWED

This book is due on the last date stamped below, or
on the date to which renewed.
Renewed books are subject to immediate recall.

9 Feb '56 VH

MAY 7 - 1956 LU

MAR 2 1 2000

2 Nov '58 MH

NOV 18 1958 L U

1 Apr '59 ES
REC'D LD

MAR 18 1959

DEC 5 1969 5 ?

REC'D LD DEC 5 '69 -2PM

REC. CIR. AUG 3 1 78

NOV 1 1977

R. C. CIR. 1 77

CPSIA information can be obtained
at www.ICGtesting.com
Printed in the USA
BVHW040940070619

550448BV00010B/178/P

9 781342 522610